Lecture Notes in Computer Science 12703

More information about this subseries at http://www.springer.com/series/7410

Nils Gruschka · Luís Filipe Coelho Antunes ·
Kai Rannenberg · Prokopios Drogkaris (Eds.)

Privacy Technologies and Policy

9th Annual Privacy Forum, APF 2021
Oslo, Norway, June 17–18, 2021
Proceedings

Springer

Editors
Nils Gruschka ⓘ
University of Oslo
Oslo, Norway

Kai Rannenberg
Goethe University Frankfurt
Frankfurt, Germany

Luís Filipe Coelho Antunes ⓘ
Department of Computer Science
University of Porto
Porto, Portugal

Prokopios Drogkaris ⓘ
ENISA
Athens, Greece

ISSN 0302-9743   ISSN 1611-3349   (electronic)
Lecture Notes in Computer Science
ISBN 978-3-030-76662-7   ISBN 978-3-030-76663-4   (eBook)
https://doi.org/10.1007/978-3-030-76663-4

LNCS Sublibrary: SL4 – Security and Cryptology

This Springer imprint is published by the registered company Springer Nature Switzerland AG
The registered company address is: Gewerbestrasse 11, 6330 Cham, Switzerland

Preface

With this volume we introduce the proceedings of the 2021 edition of the Annual Privacy Forum (APF). APF 2021 was organized by the European Union Agency for Cybersecurity (ENISA), DG Connect of the European Commission, and the Department of Informatics at the University of Oslo, Norway. The conference was planned to be hosted in Oslo, Norway. Unfortunately, as it coincided with the second year of the COVID-19 pandemic, it had to be conducted as virtual event.

This conference, already in its 9th edition, was established as an opportunity to bring together key communities, namely policy, academia, and industry, in the broader area of privacy and data protection while focusing on privacy-related application areas. Like in the previous edition, a large focus of the 2021 conference was on the General Data Protection Regulation (GDPR), which came into effect in the year before.

There were 43 submissions in response to the APF call for papers. Each paper was peer-reviewed by three members of the international Program Committee (PC). On the basis of significance, novelty, and scientific quality, 9 papers were selected (a 21% acceptance rate) and these are compiled in this volume. The papers are organized across three thematic areas:

- Implementing Personal Data Processing Principles ("The Right to Customization: Conceptualizing the Right to Repair for Informational Privacy", "A case study on the implementation of the right of access in privacy dashboards", "Consent Management Platforms under the GDPR: processors and/or controllers?", "Improving the Transparency of Privacy Terms Updates")
- Privacy Enhancing Technologies ("User-generated pseudonyms through Merkle trees", "Towards Improving Privacy of Synthetic DataSets")
- Promoting Compliance with the GDPR ("Protection of Personal Data in High Performance Computing Platform for Scientific Research Purposes", "Representing Data Protection Aspects in Process Models by Coloring", "Trackers in Your Inbox: Criticizing Current Email Tracking Practices")

We wish to thank the members of the PC, for devoting their time to reviewing the submitted papers and providing constructive feedback, the authors, whose papers make up the bulk of the content of this conference, and the attendees, whose interest in the conference is the main driver for its organization.

June 2021

Nils Gruschka
Luís Antunes
Kai Rannenberg
Prokopios Drogkaris

Organization

General Co-chairs

Nils Gruschka   University of Oslo, Norway
Luís Filipe Coelho Antunes   University of Porto, Portugal
Kai Rannenberg   Goethe University Frankfurt, Germany
Prokopios Drogkaris   ENISA, Greece

Program Committee

Monika Adamczyk   ENISA, Greece
Florian Adamsky   Hof University of Applied Sciences, Germany
Pedro Adão   Universidade de Lisboa, Portugal
Paolo Balboni   Maastricht University, Netherlands
Harsha Banavara   Signify North America Corporation, USA
Bettina Berendt   Katholieke Universiteit Leuven, Belgium
Athena Bourka   ENISA, Greece
Claude Castelluccia   Inria, France
Giuseppe D'Acquisto   Garante per la protezione dei dati personali, Italy
José M. Del Álamo   Universidad Politécnica de Madrid, Spain
Matteo Dell'Amico   Eurecom, France
Katerina Demetzou   Radboud University, Netherlands
Diana Dimitrova   FIZ Karlsruhe, Germany
Petros Efstathopoulos   NortonLifeLock, USA
Michael Friedewald   Fraunhofer, Germany
Lothar Fritsch   Oslo Metropolitan University, Norway
Christian Geminn   Universität Kassel, Germany
Marko Hölbl   University of Maribor, Slovenia
Sotiris Ioannidis   Technical University of Crete, Greece
Kristina Irion   University of Amsterdam, Netherlands
Meiko Jensen   Kiel University of Applied Sciences, Germany
Christos Kalloniatis   University of the Aegean, Greece
Irene Kamara   VUB and TILT, Netherlands
Sokratis Katsikas   Open University of Cyprus, Greece
Cedric Lauradoux   Inria, France
Daniel Le Métayer   Inria, France
Herbert Leitold   A-SIT, Austria
Alessandro Mantelero   Politecnico di Torino, Italy
Lilian Mitrou   University of the Aegean, Greece
Konstantinos Moulinos   ENISA, Greece
Panos Papadimitratos   KTH Royal Institute of Technology, Sweden
Cristiana Santos   Utrecht University, Netherlands

Stefan Schiffner   University of Luxembourg, Luxembourg
Fernando Silva   Banco de Portugal, Portugal

Additional Reviewers

Eftychia Lakka   Derya Sözen Esen
Emmanouil Michalodimitrakis   Frederic Tronnier
Ahad Niknia   Katerina Vgena
Argyri Pattakou   Dominik Ziegler
Nikolaos Petroulakis

Contents

Implementing Personal Data Processing Principles

The Right to Customization: Conceptualizing the Right to Repair
for Informational Privacy   3
    Aurelia Tamò-Larrieux, Zaira Zihlmann, Kimberly Garcia,
    and Simon Mayer

A Case Study on the Implementation of the Right of Access
in Privacy Dashboards   23
    Jan Tolsdorf, Michael Fischer, and Luigi Lo Iacono

Consent Management Platforms Under the GDPR: Processors
and/or Controllers?   47
    Cristiana Santos, Midas Nouwens, Michael Toth, Nataliia Bielova,
    and Vincent Roca

Improving the Transparency of Privacy Terms Updates   70
    Alexandr Railean and Delphine Reinhardt

Privacy Enhancing Technologies

User-Generated Pseudonyms Through Merkle Trees   89
    Georgios Kermezis, Konstantinos Limniotis, and Nicholas Kolokotronis

Towards Improving Privacy of Synthetic DataSets   106
    Aditya Kuppa, Lamine Aouad, and Nhien-An Le-Khac

Promoting Compliance with the GDPR

Protection of Personal Data in High Performance Computing Platform
for Scientific Research Purposes   123
    Ludovica Paseri, Sébastien Varrette, and Pascal Bouvry

Representing Data Protection Aspects in Process Models by Coloring   143
    Melanie Windrich, Andreas Speck, and Nils Gruschka

Trackers in Your Inbox: Criticizing Current Email Tracking Practices   156
    Shirin Kalantari, Andreas Put, and Bart De Decker

Author Index   169

Implementing Personal Data Processing Principles

The Right to Customization: Conceptualizing the Right to Repair for Informational Privacy

Aurelia Tamò-Larrieux[1]([envelope]) [ID], Zaira Zihlmann[2] [ID], Kimberly Garcia[1] [ID],
and Simon Mayer[1] [ID]

[1] University of St. Gallen, St. Gallen, Switzerland
aurelia.tamo@unisg.ch
[2] University of Lucerne, Lucerne, Switzerland

Abstract. Terms of use of a digital service are often framed in a binary way: Either one agrees to the service provider's data processing practices, and is granted access to the service, or one does not, and is denied the service. Many scholars have lamented these 'take-it-or-leave-it' situations, as this goes against the ideals of data protection law. To address this inadequacy, computer scientists and legal scholars have tried to come up with approaches to enable more privacy-friendly products and services. In this article, we call for a right to customize the processing of user data. Our arguments build upon technology-driven approaches as well as on the ideals of privacy by design and the now codified data protection by design and default norm within the General Data Protection Regulation. In addition, we draw upon the right to repair that is propagated to empower consumers and enable a more circular economy. We propose two technologically-oriented approaches, termed 'variants' and 'alternatives' that could enable the technical implementation of a right to customization. We posit that these approaches cannot be demanded without limitation, and that restrictions will depend on how reasonable a customization demand is.

Keywords: Right to customization · Right to repair · Consent · GDPR · Informational privacy

1 Introduction

When WhatsApp announced a change to its privacy policy in January 2021, the world reacted by downloading Signal instead [39]. This shift could be seen as the market working, yet hardly any privacy scholar would argue that the market for privacy-friendly technologies works. In fact, we have seen the many limitations of consent in the digital economy. While still a central cornerstone of data privacy regulations, multiple studies have poked holes in the concept, showing that individuals are unlikely to make rational and informed decisions about their disclosure of personal information [6, 45, 70, 79]. One major challenge is the binary option of agreeing or not agreeing to certain data processing practices that consent provides. This is inadequate to foster the ideals of data protection law and data protection authorities (DPA) seem to be aware of the failures

N. Gruschka et al. (Eds.): APF 2021, LNCS 12703, pp. 3–22, 2021.
https://doi.org/10.1007/978-3-030-76663-4_1

of 'take-it-or-leave-it' approaches: For instance, the Norwegian DPA has issued a hefty fine to Grindr for not providing a real choice to its users [22].

In this article we call for a right to customize the data processing in a more privacy-friendly manner when reasonable to do so. We start by elaborating on the limitations of consent and how the codified principle of Privacy by Design (PbD), which is referred to as Data Protection by Design and Default (DPbDD) within the General Data Protection Regulation (GDPR), could be used as a stepping stone to enable the customization or negotiation of more fine-grained data processing operations. DPbDD demands that data controllers adhere to the data protection principles throughout the whole life cycle of data (i.e., the collection of personal data, its analysis, the use of the data for specific decisions, and its erasure). These principles include the principles concerning individual rights such as the principle of individual participation and control. Third, "Article 25 prevent[s], on its face, controllers from using technologies that collect more personal data than are strictly necessary for technological functionality or that 'leak' personal data to outsiders" [14 p. 578].

We continue by elaborating on past technologically-grounded attempts by individuals, activist groups, standardization bodies, and even industry consortia to give users more fine-grained control about aspects of their digital online privacy. This analysis shows that engineering-based regulation has failed so far, but that there is a new hope for regulation-based engineering approaches. Upon this basis, we elaborate on the right to repair, as a source of inspiration for the proposed right to customization. The right to repair has so far always related to equipment or hardware. More recently, software has been included in the bigger picture: A newly issued European Commission Report 'Circular Economy Action Plan' (2020) [30] states that the Information and Communications Technology (ICT) sector should implement a sector-wide right to repair "including a right to update obsolete software" (p. 10). This inclusion would considerably change the landscape of a right to repair and provides inspiration for the right to customization.

We elaborate on two approaches that would technically enable the right to customization: The first one focuses on deciding the type of processing at the data controllers ('variants'), while the second one focuses on deciding what data reaches which data controller ('alternatives'). However, these technical customizations must be 'reasonable'. The term reasonable is consciously broad, since different contexts will require different thresholds. While our analysis on the subject matter is not exhaustive, we elaborate on three aspects to determine the scope of reasonable customization. We end with a discussion that includes the limitations of our approach and points to further research needs.

2   Limitations of Consent in the Digital Environment

Consent is a crucial instrument for achieving informational self-determination [29, 70]. Consent has been a key legal ground since the very beginning of data protection and privacy law [47]. The importance of consent in the EU data protection regime has been anchored by Article 8 of the Charter of Fundamental Rights, where consent is identified as a basis for lawful processing of personal data [15]. Individual consent as lawful ground was also enshrined through Articles 6 and 7 of the Data Protection Directive 45/96 [23]. Its successor, the GDPR, has tightened up the requirements for establishing valid consent

[18, 49]. This may seem rather paradoxical in light of the fact that consent is a contested concept in European data protection legislation [79]. Given the transformative nature of consent [28] along with its connection to the idea that the data subject should have control over the use of his or her data [4], it can be very well argued that consent should (continue to) be treated as a pivotal part of the data protection regime [9]. However, many authors have pointed to its flaws, challenging the legitimacy of consent in the digital economy altogether [6, 45, 70].

There are multiple reasons for the limitations of consent in the digital economy. A central issue is the fact that individuals tend to accept privacy policies without reading them [18, 19], thus seriously challenging the notion of 'rational and informed' decision-making. Multiple reasons contribute to this challenge: The terminologies in which privacy policies are written are difficult to understand, the time needed to do so would be exorbitant, and on top of that, there are too many of them [20, 52, 67]. As a consequence, users of digital services tend to provide personal data even though they indicate that they are aware of the privacy issues and concerned about data processing practices. This phenomenon is also called the 'privacy paradox' [56]. The possible reasons for this phenomenon are manifold [55], and many authors are trying to explain it by means of concepts such as privacy fatigue [17] or privacy cynicism [50]. However, there are also authors who doubt that there is evidence for such a paradox to exist [44] or challenge the concept insofar as they argue that the paradox is not so paradoxical after all [71, 80]. In fact, considering that setting privacy preferences is context-dependent and users tend to be uncertain about their privacy preferences, thus they are susceptible to biases [2], which in consequence also limits the capacity to translate the received information into evidence-based privacy choices [81]. Interrelated with the user's uncertainty and the context dependence of privacy preference is the malleability, i.e., the notion that several and sometimes subtle factors can be deployed to trigger or suppress privacy concerns, which in turn influences behavior [2]. This may extend to manipulative uses of designs to frame processing practices in a certain light and manipulate users to share more personal information [35, 38, 80]. For instance, choices that are less privacy friendly may be presented only in a positive light (be it through wording, settings, or situations), whereas possible negative consequences for the user are intentionally omitted [57]. This is referred to as 'dark patterns' and is highly topical within various research fields [35, 51, 58] as well as for policymakers. Policymakers in California are even taking measures to outlaw such practices [69].

Moreover, consent is often constructed as a binary option, as in a 'take-it-or-leave-it' decision by a user [8, 77]. This is especially problematic in areas where data subjects are dependent on the service of a small number of dominant online platforms, thus creating a significant power imbalance between data controllers and data subjects [18]. Individual control over personal data seems illusory in such environments, because there is no room for negotiation of the terms of use of personal data [67]. This problem is potentially exacerbated by the lack of other (privacy-friendlier) providers for the desired service [45] as well as the potential significant social costs of not using platforms that have become the default mode of interaction [59].

In light of the above findings, the question on how this problem can be addressed arises. The legislator has not only tightened the requirements for valid consent under the GDPR, but also introduced additional provisions to strengthen the data protection rights of individuals. Among these is the principle of PbD, which could help redress the failure of consent. This can, for instance, be done by encouraging the development of systems where the consent request is designed to allow separate consent for different purposes and types of processing [19], as well as providing multi-layered and granular information to provide both accurate and understandable information to the data subject [66, 68]. However, as we will show below, PbD might be an improvement, yet it is merely a stepping stone towards what we call the right to customization.

3   Privacy by Design as a Stepping Stone for a Right to Customization?

3.1   Codifying Privacy by Design

Article 25 of the GDPR codifies the principle of PbD into law. With it, overarching design principles for better privacy and security of products and services which had been around since 2009 [16] developed some legal teeth. Of course, the notion that privacy-enhancing technologies (PETs) could enable restoring the balance between data processing entities and data subjects had been around for many decades. But, as described below (see Sect. 4), these technologies have not become widely popular [12, 13]. Nonetheless, a rich literature emerged within the field of privacy engineering [21, 37, 48], upon which newer proposals within the field of encoding data protection law have emerged [26].

While DPbDD under the GDPR is "less 'free'" than the original PbD principles, its inherent connection with the fundamental principles of European data protection law make it simultaneously more "ambitious and wide ranging" than PbD [12 p. 761]. In fact, Article 25 of the GDPR has been called a hollow norm [73] since the article refers back to the implementing all fundamental principles of data protection law through technical and organizational measures. The DPbDD norm distinguishes itself from other articles within the GDPR and its predecessor (the Directive 95/46/EC) by mandating the implementation of technical and organizational measures throughout the whole life cycle of data and focusing not only on security issues but the overall adherence to the principles of processing [14, 73]. Moreover, Article 25 focuses "more strongly on the data subjects and their rights to technical protection measures, rather than leaving the implementation to the discretion of the data controller. The latter are called upon to ensure that certain privacy protection features are used by default" [73 p. 86].

3.2   Operationalizing Data Protection by Design and Default

The norm addressees of Article 25 GDPR are clearly data controllers; they are the ones responsible for implementing measures by design and by default [14]. While this interpretation does not take into account that the design of technical infrastructures are often designed by a third party, it imposes the duty to comply with the norm to the data controller as soon as the controller actually determines the means and purposes of processing [14]. Even though the lack of broadening the norm addressee has been criticized, as it undermines "the goal of ensuring the privacy interest are fully integrated into information system architectures" [14 p. 578], the contextual dimensions of data flows and thus resulting informational privacy issues would likely make it very difficult to demand from software companies that all their products adhere to the fundamental principles of data protection by design and default. Such an interpretation would require breaking from the current approach and envisaging a more privacy engineering approach to DPbDD, which would mandate broader implementation of available privacy-enhancing technologies by developers [62]. Until now, it remains the data controllers' responsibility to mandate developers within their entity and contracted third parties to ensure that principles concerning the legality of the data processing (e.g., transparency, lawfulness, purpose limitation, information requirements), principles concerning the design of the data processing (e.g., data minimization and proportionality, disclosure and storage limitation, security, data quality), principles concerning individual rights (e.g., participation principle, accessibility, enabling erasure and object to the processing), as well as principles concerning the compliance and enforcement (e.g., accountability, documentation) are implemented by appropriate technical and organizational measures [73].

Yet, operalizing DPbDD has proven to be difficult [12, 33, 62, 65, 74]. This is due to multiple reasons, an important one being that overall European data protection law represents a compromise between different regimes which combines overarching principles with to-be-fulfilled (or justificatory) legal grounds; this duality requires data controllers to not only prove compliance with pre-determined grounds, but enables them - within boundaries - to determine how (strictly) to implement the rather vaguely defined principles that are designed to leave room for interpretation [33, 74]. In fact, the principles must be interpreted taking contextual factors into account, requiring data controllers among others (1) to conduct data protection impact assessments to determine risks of processing [14], (2) to make assumptions not only about the efficacy of their risk-management strategies but also about how to determine which legal ground is appropriate in a given context (e.g., setting ad hoc hierarchies), (3) to solve conflicts within the law or generalize legal terms (which they are not equipped to do), and (4) to determine how the balancing of different interests can be encoded [33, 74]. At best, encoding data protection law is thus an imperfect remedy [33, 74], and it is no surprise that academics have argued that the character of privacy norms renders its implementation into code impossible [46, 65].

Even if it is fair to criticize DPbDD and hardwiring data protection approaches, Article 25 has been called upon by data protection authorities—showing PbD fletching its (legal) teeth. To name just one example, in Germany a company unable to delete employee data was fined, because of non-adherence with Article 25 [5]. It remains to be seen how far Article 25 in conjunction with the fundamental principles will be called upon by data protection authorities. Potentially, the scope of Article 25 could be enlarged to lead to what below will be described as a 'right to customization'. However, as to date such an interpretation has not been seen in practice, the following builds upon DPbDD to call for a right to customization. Instead of having to rely on an interpretation of a contested article, such a right would take the ambiguity away and lead to more legal certainty for data subjects.

3.3 Building Upon Data Protection by Design

With respect to the below outlined right to customization it is key to highlight three aspects within the duty of data controllers to implement data protection by design and default: First, with respect to the timing it is key to adhere to the data protection principles throughout the entire life cycle of data (i.e., the collection of personal data, its analysis, the use of the data for specific decisions, and its erasure). In connection with this, there is also the obligation of controllers to take into account the state of the art. In the context of technology, 'state of the art' can be defined as "the procedures, equipment or operating methods available in the trade in goods and services for which the application thereof is most effective in achieving the respective legal protection objectives" [75 p. 11]. Yet, Article 25 is silent on the meaning of 'state of the art' in its context. This may lead to the conclusion that it is a rather vague concept [62]. However, it can also be viewed as a benchmark [42] that requires data controllers to have knowledge of, and stay up to date on technological advances, meaning that as soon as technical measures and safeguards for the effective implementation of the principles and rights of data subjects are available on the market, data controllers have to either use them or implement their own equivalent or better solutions, provided that this is feasible at a reasonable expense [31, 75]. Second, the principles concerning individual rights include the principle of individual participation and control. While, unlike the OECD Privacy Guidelines (1980, 2013), the GDPR does not contain one single provision ensuring participation, it is nonetheless a key ideal rooted in data protection law codified in different articles including the right to access and objection. Third, Article 25 wants to prohibit data controllers from employing technologies that collect a greater amount of data than necessary for the functionalities they offer [14]. According to Bygrave [14] Article 25 "might shape the market and technology foundations for information systems development in a privacy-friendly direction" (p. 578). However, this optimism must be contrasted with the often broad purposes that data controllers use in their privacy policies, thereby circumventing the ideal of the purpose limitation principle altogether.

Nonetheless, these requirements can be interpreted to create a stepping stone for a right to customization: The focus on the entire life cycle of data and not only the design phase and the related obligation to take into account the current technological advancements in order to ensure the effective protection of data subjects rights; the focus on individual rights and participation of data subjects; and the prohibition to collect more data than necessary sets the basis to better implement the ideals of data protection law through a right to customization.

Unlike other legal fields (e.g., copyright law and the discussion on Digital Rights Management Systems), privacy by design initiatives and the development of PETs endows a "high degree of normative and sociological legitimacy, in large part because of its close association with furtherance of citizens' autonomy, privacy, and related civil liberties" [12 p. 766]. This is an important leverage that researchers in this field have, yet should not take for granted. As Burkert [10 p. 135] postulates: "PET design itself must be open to participatory elements. This implies that designing PETs and implementing them in social systems must involve those whom these enhancements are supposed to serve."

4   Technology Solutions to Enhance Online Privacy

4.1   The Challenges of 'Engineering-Based Regulation'

We have in the past already seen technologically-grounded attempts by individuals, activist groups, standardization bodies, and even industry consortia to implement PETs that allow users more fine-grained control about aspects of their digital online privacy. A specifically well-researched area in this domain is the automatic management of what information a user agent (e.g., a Web browser) shares with a website. For example, the Platform for Privacy Preferences Project (P3P) created a standard format that allows websites to express their privacy practices in a way that can be interpreted by user agents to provide a notice and choice approach to users. The P3P 1.0 specification[1], which defines the syntax and semantics of such privacy policies, was officially turned into a recommendation by the World Wide Web Consortium (W3C) in April 2002, updated to version 1.1[2] following community feedback on limitations and shortcomings in November 2006, and was obsoleted and retired in August 2018 as the underlying working group discontinued working on the specification. P3P enables websites to specify in concrete terms the user data they collect and process. These specifications are then automatically mapped by user agents to concrete user preferences. For instance, if a website asks for the user's telephone number, the user agent might immediately accept this request with or without notifying the user, ask the user for consent to share this specific data item, or cancel the transaction altogether. P3P furthermore allows for information requests to be tied to specific purposes, permitting more fine-grained control by the user - e.g., allowing a website to collect a specific data item, but not to share it with third parties.

P3P is implemented by having origin servers hold a policy reference file in a well-known location, by returning HTML link tags in their HTML representation, or by including a P3P HTTP header with a referrer to a P3P policy reference of the requested resource, in their HTTP response. Individual P3P policies are then required to disclose data that is collected by forms as well as the activity by background scripts that track the behavior of the user (e.g., dwelling time or clickstreams), and disclose whenever (previously consented) data is transmitted to a third party. Furthermore, policies include the purpose of the collection and processing of data, e.g., 'Tailoring' of a website or 'Contact,' where it can be specified for each of these purposes whether the processing is required ('always' required/'opt-in'/'opt-out'), what retention policy applies to the data item, and also to differentiate between identifiable and non-identifiable data (i.e., data that is anonymized upon collection).

P3P is representative of a top-down view of creating vocabularies and specifications that are able to cover a significant part of the possible use cases but (necessarily) become very complex to implement and manage. Later, bottom-up approaches aimed to make it more amenable to websites to adhere to the user preferences they communicate. One popular mechanisms of this kind, the W3C Tracking Preference Expression[3] (known as Do Not Track; DNT), today takes the form of a HTTP header that would 'politely

---

[1] https://www.w3.org/TR/P3P/.

[2] https://www.w3.org/TR/P3P11/.

[3] https://www.w3.org/TR/tracking-dnt/.

ask' websites to not track a user[4]. Implementing DNT headers is simple and since they are merely a binary flag (0/1), it is trivial for users to activate them through a browser setting (e.g., DNT headers are activated in private browsing modes across browsers). However, the central problem with DNT is, again, enforcement: Neither is it defined what precisely a server should do differently when receiving the header, nor are there any sanctions in place if a server does not change its behavior in response to a DNT flag. Given the body's previous experience with P3P, it is thus no surprise that the DNT header was never standardized by the W3C but merely reached the candidate recommendation stage.

Both the DNT initiative as well as P3P represent forms of 'engineering-based regulation.' This is very visible in P3P and it is seen as the main reason for its downfall: P3P policies were regarded as being too bulky and complex. The P3P working group reacted by creating more compact policies as a performance optimization in P3P 1.1. This however did not do enough to remedy the (semantic) complexity involved when creating P3P policies (for data-collection organizations), implementing P3P user agents (for Web browser implementers), and configuring preferences (for users). In addition, P3P user agents would by default exclude websites that do not publish P3P policies, thereby punishing organizations that practice high privacy standards but do not publish these as P3P, and at the same time putting large corporations with the resources to implement P3P policies at an advantage versus smaller enterprises. The most important reason for the lack of adoption of P3P, DNT, and similar systems is, however, a lack of enforcement: There are no consequences if a website does not abide by its specified policy, which undermines the core goal of this approach and also implies that companies that indeed do publish policies and abide by them are left standing without tangible benefits other than (potentially) increased user trust.

4.2 New Hope for 'Regulation-Based Engineering'

More recently, the Global Privacy Control (GPC) header[5] was introduced as a form of 'regulation-based engineering' (instead of the other way around). Far from attempting to give users the ability to customize their online privacy, GPC is specific to enabling users to opt out of the sale of their data to third parties. However, the major difference between GPC on the one side and P3P and DNT on the other is that GPC has regulatory grounding in the California Customer Privacy Act (CCPA) and in GDPR. This means that the header itself is merely a simple way of enabling users to communicate that they want to exercise their (legally guaranteed) right to opt-out of the sale of their data. So, while DNT headers merely 'politely ask,' GPC directly refers to prevailing legislation and, similar to how some online services[6] enable users to access their data based on GDPR, enables users to efficiently act upon their pre-existing rights on this basis; although GPC will need to prove itself, we see such regulation-based engineering, i.e., that technical tools facilitate the exercise of already guaranteed rights by consumers, as the only possible way forward. It is, on the basis of simple and focused solutions such as GPC, furthermore entirely

---

[4] https://news.ycombinator.com/item?id=16110570.

[5] https://globalprivacycontrol.org/.

[6] E.g., the service https://bitsabout.me/ in Switzerland.

conceivable that these will be extended towards the breadth and scope of P3P, while remaining fully grounded in regulation.

5 Right to Customization

5.1 Inspired by the Right to Repair: Calling for a Right to Customization

Our call for a right to customization is inspired by the right to repair. As shown above, today's data protection is confronted with a multitude of malfunctions and implementation difficulties—be it on the legal or on the technical side. However, this situation is not unique to data protection law. Consumers who aim to repair their devices face the problem that many manufacturers have made this increasingly difficult [63]. For example, Apple restricts consumers' ability to repair their devices through requiring the use of specific tools or authorized parts [61]. Against this backdrop, individuals, activists, and academics have called for manufacturers to design their products in such a way as to facilitate their repair [40].

These calls have meanwhile been heard by policymakers and the right to repair has emerged in legislation on both sides of the Atlantic [36, 53, 72]. The goals of such legislation are twofold: On the one hand, consumers should be empowered to repair their purchased goods (such as cars and phones) and not have to re-purchase new ones whenever minor defects arise outside of the warranty period. On the other hand, the right to repair wants to enable a more circular economy that makes more efficient use of resources. For instance, the European Parliament has issued reports and resolutions[7] demanding more durable and repairable products. With the Green Deal[8], the right to repair will likely gain further momentum.

The focus of the right to repair has so far always been related to hardware. At the forefront of the discussion and activist claims are now electronic devices which are often cheaper to buy than to have repaired. In order to reach both goals, the empowerment of users and the promotion of a sustainable economy, in Europe, the Directive 2019/771[9] on contracts on sales of goods promotes the right to repair of goods. The term 'goods' includes 'goods with digital elements' which are defined in the Directive as "any tangible movable items that incorporate or are inter-connected with digital content or a digital

---

[7] E.g., European Parliament report on a longer lifetime for products ((2016/2272(INI)) <https://www.europarl.europa.eu/doceo/document/A-8-2017-0214_EN.html>; European Parliament resolution of 31 May 2018 on the implementation of the Ecodesign Directive (2009/125/EC) (2017/2087(INI)) <https://www.europarl.europa.eu/doceo/document/TA-8-2018-0241_EN.html>; European Parliament, towards a more sustainable single market for business and consumers (2020/2021(INI)) <https://www.europarl.europa.eu/doceo/document/TA-9-2020-0318_EN.pdf>.

[8] European Commission, Communication from the Commission, The European Green Deal (COM/2019/640 final) <https://eur-lex.europa.eu/legal-content/EN/TXT/HTML/?uri=CELEX:52019DC0640&from=EN>.

[9] Directive (EU) 2019/771 of the European Parliament and of the Council of 20 May 2019 on certain aspects concerning contracts for the sale of goods, amending Regulation (EU) 2017/2394 and Directive 2009/22/EC, and repealing Directive 1999/44/EC (Text with EEA relevance) OJ L 136, 22.5.2019, p. 28–50.

service in such a way that the absence of that digital content or digital service would prevent the goods from performing their functions" (Art. 2(5)). While the focus so far has rested on products (including electronic products including 'goods with digital elements'), software has only recently been included into the bigger picture. A newly issued European Commission Report 'Circular Economy Action Plan' (2020) [30] states that the Information and Communications Technology sector should implement a sector-wide right to repair, "including a right to update obsolete software" (p. 10). This inclusion would considerably change the landscape of a right to repair and provides inspiration for the right to customization.

While a right to repair might intuitively be understood as granting the individual to make repairs on a device, the right to repair for instance in the Directive 2019/771 states this as a responsibility of the seller to conduct the repair. This makes sense, when looking at the challenges posed by the right to repair from a perspective of the goods providers. In fact, a rich discussion on closed-access repairs (i.e., consumers cannot conduct the repair themselves) versus open-access repairs can be found in the literature [72]. From a goods provider perspective, closed-access repairs are clearly preferred, as issues such as reputational ones (e.g., relating to brand management) would thereby not be inflicted. It is thus not surprising that through contractual terms only closed-access repairs are enabled by goods providers [72]. Moreover, other legal terms, such as copyright law prohibiting unauthorized circumvention of DRM also sets legal barriers to open-access repairs [53]. These legal challenges as well as sometimes offsetting prices of repair prohibit consumers from choosing freely by whom, what, and for how much to repair their products [72].

Based on the ongoing discussion and progress on a right to repair for hardware and software products and coupling this debate with the fallacies of 'take-it-or-leave-it' consent, we propose a right to customization. This right should enable users to demand the modification of a software-based service offering to better align the service with their privacy requirements. In the following, we introduce two options to technically enable such a right to customization, and subsequently discuss what types of customizations customers might reasonably expect under this right.

5.2 Technological Approaches Enabling the Customization of Consent Variants

Consider the 'take-it-or-leave-it' approach that WhatsApp took when introducing its privacy policy changes in early 2021. Arguably, this communication approach made even unconcerned users look into instant messaging alternatives that could bring them a better sense of safety for their personal data. Although new statements[10] about the data that WhatsApp collects and processes have been issued after the initial in-app notifications, users are still wary and have migrated to other apps, enduring the social burden of agreeing with social circles on the new instant messaging app to use, the inconvenience of starting a new conversation history (e.g., losing or backing up pictures, documents, and relevant links), learning to interact with a new user interface, and hoping that the company that owns the newly-agreed application takes a more stable approach

---

[10] https://faq.whatsapp.com/general/security-and-privacy/answering-your-questions-about-whatsapps-privacy-policy (last access 29.01.2021).

to data privacy. However, in an ideal scenario, a user would be able to keep using the current version of WhatsApp without having to agree to the new policy, even though this could mean not having functionalities that the latest version of the app offers. Another option for a user could be to seamlessly transition to another messaging client that would have the same functionalities, user interface look and feel, and would have the ability to port conversations from WhatsApp (this references the right to data portability within GDPR).

We argue that with a right to customization in place, a user should be able to choose from a catalog of variants of an application that would be provided and curated by the data controller, the one that he, she, or they feels the most comfortable with regarding the data processing operations that this variant performs. Note that, since this gives a choice to consumers, it will not increase the total amount of data transferred and therefore will not undermine the principle of data minimization. To this end, data controllers would have the responsibility to be transparent and communicate in a clear manner about the data operations in each variant. Thus, users who enjoy highly personalized content, recommendations, and advertisement can opt for a traditional approach in which their data is transparently used to train machine learning algorithms and is probably shared with third parties that could offer additional recommendations according to their demographics. In contrast, more cautious users will be able to select a variant of the software that not only does not share their data with third-parties, but also uses techniques such as homomorphic encryption [3, 76] for training machine learning algorithms, at the cost of performance or quality of the recommendations.

However, maintaining different versions of a software in order to allow users to decide the data processing activities they feel comfortable with represents a large burden on designers, software engineers, and businesses as a whole, as they would need to implement (and maintain) software that is able to provide similar services while considering such data processing customization. A way to accomplish this customization is to design and implement software on the basis of interchangeable components where, for instance, a (micro)service that analyses personal data for shopping recommendation purposes can be exchanged for one that computes such a recommendation using differential privacy [1] where noise is added to the data at the time of collection, or with a simpler service that uses heuristics without personal data. We expect this to encourage companies to make their software more transparent, in order to allow users to mix and match services according to their data processing preferences. Moreover, a microservice approach could enable the creation of a new marketplace, in which microservices are classified and rated according to their data processing operations. Thus, users wanting to enhance their data privacy but who do not feel educated enough to make such decisions, could follow trusted NGOs, activists, and journalists who publicly share their data processing profiles, and mimic them.

Alternatives

Another option of realizing a right to customization is to supply consumers with alternatives up front. Consider a toy robot that interacts with children and parents at home and is equipped with various sensors and processing techniques (e.g., voice and facial recognition). Different designs of the robot's processing capabilities can be envisaged, ranging from more privacy-invasive options (e.g., external processing and sharing of data with third party providers) to more privacy-friendly ones (e.g., local analysis of data). A robot made following PbD principles [33, 74], would provide a pre-installed face recognition module that runs locally in the robot. In this way, the robot would still be able to personalize its content (albeit with lower accuracy). However, requiring data controllers to create an undefined amount of variants for each software application would require mandating what such variants should look like, the data they are allowed to collect, process and store, which might put innovation at risk. Moreover, the burden in understanding and choosing the best variant would be put on the user. Conversely, favoring a total offline approach in which the robot would host multiple variants of learning modules able to provide recommendations for every type of content (e.g., music, video, pictures, stories, etc.) would be infeasible given the limited computational capabilities of such a device. Thus, a way to maintain the same robot functionalities, while sharing data in a controlled manner, is to make users the gatekeepers to their own data. To this end, the Social Linked Data (Solid) project has been proposed. Solid [64] is a Web-based ecosystem that aims at separating data from applications. Currently, when signing up for an application such as the described robot, or for a social media service, users provide their data to a set of data controllers who store, manage, and process it in different ways. Solid provides users with a repository that contains their personal data, referred to as a podPods can be hosted online by trusted providers or by users on their own premises. Solid differs from other pod-based solutions [25] in the way that it takes advantage of technologies and protocols that already exist (e.g., Linked Data [7]) and are well-known in the computer science community. Moreover, it does not require software providers to install and run software on the user's pod, avoiding infrastructure complications. In Solid, a user grants read, write, or control permissions to an application to use explicitly identified data items in their pod. Thereby, an application obtains controlled access to the specific data that the user has explicitly decided to share with the application [11, 64].

In the robot scenario, using a Solid ecosystem, a child would be identified via a WebID, which is a Uniform Resource Identifier (URI) that points to the child's personal profile containing his, her, or their data. Likes, dislikes, age, and current interests are expressed in a structured machine-readable format and are hosted in the pod along with a set of pictures of the child's face. Moreover, users can fragment their data by topic to minimize and explicitly target the data they share with different applications. Thus, a parent can decide to share with the robot vendor the interests of the kid, but not the list of WebIDs of the kid's school friends or medical records. However, parents can decide to share medical information with a new telemedicine app that the kid's pediatrician uses for follow-ups. The permissions for applications to access a user's data are granted using a mechanism that is based on Web Access Control (WAC)[11].

Towards exercising a right to customization, solutions such as Solid could be extended with means to grant applications permissions to perform specific data processing operations (this could, for instance, be based on the catalog created by P3P). A similar mechanism as WAC could be put in place, in which users are able to create a data processing profile that specifies the type of processing they allow over their data. To this

---

[11] https://www.w3.org/wiki/WebAccessControl.

end, vocabularies such as the Data Privacy Vocabulary (DPV)[12] could be used, given that it provides a machine-readable representation of terms relevant to personal data handling, in adherence to the EU GDPR. This vocabulary specifies different processing activities with various concepts (e.g., Remove, Use) that contain various subclasses (e.g., Destruct or Erase, or Analyze, Consult, Profiling). Although this hierarchy comprises several processing activities, this is not an exhaustive list. Designers and software engineers could be in need of a not-yet-specified processing activity. Thus, it is important to stick to standardized and well-known vocabularies that are kept up to date by a community e.g., the W3C DPV community. Moreover, in order to support users in making decisions on what and how to share data with the different data controllers, a folksonomy that exposes profiles of trusted NGOs and public figures could be implemented for users to follow and mimic such profiles.

5.3 Restricting a Right to Customization to 'Reasonable Customizations'

From the discussion above it becomes clear that a right to customization could be interpreted in a way that places a (sometimes unjustifiably) large burden on businesses. The right to customization is thus not to be understood as an overarching right but must come with restrictions. We postulate that these restrictions will depend on how 'reasonable' a customization demand is. The term reasonable is consciously broad, since different contexts will require different thresholds. Clearly, the described technologies—requiring modifications at the data controller or modifying how liberally a data controller can access user data—already trigger different discussions on reasonableness. Demanding the creation of variants is costly, time-intensive, and against the business interests of data controllers and must thus be weighed against the interests of data subjects to customize the processing of their personal data. While the analysis that follows is by no means exhaustive, it provides insights on how to determine what falls under 'reasonable customizations'. Needless to say, it would be desirable to have a set of objective criteria, so as to prevent interpretations of the criterion 'reasonable' that would result in a worsening of the position of the end user. However, for the establishment of concrete criteria, further discussion is essential. Such a discussion cannot be held without involving more stakeholders to the debate, including researchers from other fields, activists, industry representatives, and policymakers.

First, we can learn from the discussion on the right to repair. The Directive 2019/771, for instance, states in Recital 48: "The consumer's choice between repair and replacement should only be limited where the option chosen would be legally or factually impossible or would impose costs on the seller that would be disproportionate, compared to the other option available." This shows clearly that there are costs that are disproportionate, especially when the costs of repair would be unreasonably high compared to other alternatives [54] (ECJ, C-65/09 and C-87/09). Moreover, repair cost can be attributed to the customer. Also the right for customization could, especially in the case of variant-building by data controllers, come with a cost that is passed on to users. While this would enable more privacy-aware users to pay for customizing consent, others might

---

[12] https://dpvcg.github.io/dpv/.

not do so. Of course, such a development could lead to even greater disparity between the 'privacy-haves' and 'privacy-have-nots'.

Second, we can learn from debates surrounding the right to data portability enshrined in Article 20 GDPR, which aims to enhance user control and minimize lock-in effects by facilitating the transfer of data. Despite that many aspects of Article 20 GDPR leave room for interpretation [41], it, as well as the discussions about its shortcomings, can serve as inspiration for possible constraints on the right to customization. This is due to the circumstance that enabling data portability imposes additional costs and efforts on data controllers (with some arguing that it would especially negatively affect small and medium-sized enterprises and would serve as a barrier to market entry, resulting in a negative impact on innovation and competition [78]). Accordingly, limits to this right must reasonably exist. Recital 68 of the GDPR states that the data subject should only have the right to have personal data transferred directly from one controller to another if this is technically feasible. From this it follows that since there is no obligation to establish or maintain processing systems that are technically compatible with those of other controllers, the full exercise of users' right to data portability may be restricted by data controllers if they demonstrate that their organization's technological deployment level makes direct transfer of data to another controller technically infeasible [24]. However, demonstrating such infeasibility might prove hard. Moreover, one has to consider that "what is technically feasible for one data controller might not be technically feasible for another data controller" [27 p. 13]. Against this background, it can be argued that restrictions should be asymmetric, i.e., the obligations applicable to a company would be based on its market share or the scope of its activities. Consequently, entities that have significant market power from a competition law perspective would be subject to stricter obligations to provide for data portability [34]. Lastly, the right to data portability needs to be balanced against other rights. According to Article 20(4) of the GDPR, the right to data portability shall not adversely affect the rights and freedoms of others. This also includes the freedom to conduct a business of data controllers [24].

Finally, the freedom to conduct business should set limits to the right to customization as latter would make the development and deployment of technology more costly and thus harder for providers to compete in the market. The freedom to conduct business (as enshrined in Article 16 of the Charter of Fundamental Rights), includes the right of any company or individual to be able to freely use its economic, technical, and financial resources ([60] with reference to ECJ, C-314/12). Yet, also the freedom to conduct a business is not an absolute right but can be subject to restrictions, "provided that such restrictions correspond to objectives of general interest pursued by the EU and do not constitute a disproportionate and intolerable interference in relation to the aim pursued, impairing the very substance of the rights guaranteed" [32 p. 23]. How to determine what are reasonable customizations and what boundaries the freedom to conduct business sets will have to be evaluated on a case-by-case basis. Potentially, courts could draw insights from other domains, such as in copyright enforcement, where platforms can be required to implement at their own expense upload filters, but where courts have also set limits to such requirements (e.g., SABAM v. Netlog).

6 Discussion and Conclusion

In this article, we have started by describing the limitations of consent in the digital economy and how DPbDD could be seen as a stepping stone for demanding the customization of data processing practices. However, because such an interpretation of DPbDD so far does not exist, we introduce the concept of the (reasonable) right to customization. This right, understood as an individual right to be included within an amended data protection regulation, would empower data subjects to demand more customizable services from data controllers. While acknowledging that technology-driven solutions so far have failed to provide greater user control, there is a new hope for regulation-based engineering approaches that have been developed world-wide. Upon this basis, and inspired by the right to repair which is being interpreted more broadly to include software updates in recent policy making documents, we postulate the right to reasonable customization. Both, the right to repair and the right to customization strive to enable better user control over devices or software and strive to fulfill greater ideals, such as sustainable developments, and privacy-friendly technology developments. Moreover, the stakeholders are similar: On the one hand, individuals (striving for a green planet or more privacy-friendly environments) and on the other hand, large corporations, wanting to continue with their current business model (e.g., increasing revenue, profiling for targeted advertising and content).

A central question that remains is: How does the right to customization address the failures of consent mentioned above in practice? The main advantage of our conceptualization of the right to repair approach is that it moves away from the binary or 'take-it-or-leave-it' approach; this approach is dominant with consent, but becomes also apparent when processing is necessary for the performance of a contract or when legitimate interests of a (big tech) data controller are evoked. Specifically, the right to customization demands from data controllers to provide either reasonable variants or alternatives to users. This reasoning is in line not only with the aspiration of DPbDD but also currently enacted individual rights such as the right to data portability. In addition, the right to customization can permit the creation of more open ecosystems, with the hope that these lead to more transparent systems that enable users to engage with it. It could also incentivize data controllers to be more transparent about their services (and variants thereof), and to create more privacy-friendly variants of their services from the start, in order not to risk having users demand their right to customization. Such right to customization requests would then require a re-design of data processing practices, which would be more costly than having thought about them before a product or service launch, thus supporting the core ideals of PbD. In that sense, the right to customization might address some of the information asymmetries and lack of control discussed above (see Sect. 2). Yet, the right to customization is by no means an ultimate remedy to those challenges, as they are systemic to the current digital economy. For instance, enabling more granular designs of services is not going to prevent the trend of manipulating users to choose the data controller's favorite option over others (in the extreme by means of dark patterns). In addition, critics will likely point out that the proposed technical solutions to enable a right to customization fall within the dream of 'techno-solutionism,' which stands for finding technical remedies to societal problems without taking the bigger picture into account [43]. However, as discussed in Sect. 4, we believe that regulation-based engineering (i.e., engineering that facilitates the exercise of rights) is in principle better able to achieve the objectives of the proposed right to customization. Moreover, looking at the current draft of the ePrivacy Regulation[13], one can observe that EU policymakers are aware of the pressing issues concerning end-user consent and are seeking to address the problem. Recital 20a states that "[i]mplementation of technical means in electronic communications software to provide specific and informed consent through transparent and user-friendly settings, can be useful to address this issue. Where available and technically feasible, an end user may therefore grant, through software settings, consent to a specific provider for the use of processing and storage capabilities of terminal equipment for one or multiple specific purposes across one or more specific services of that provider." This approach seems to be heading in the same direction as the herein proposed right to customization. However, a right to customization would go a step further by not only providing the possibility to grant or deny consent through software settings, but by allowing users to mix and match services according to their data processing preferences.

Moreover, while striving for more user control is not per se a faulty quest, we are continuing to try to solve systemic and collective problems of the digital economy through individual means. To steer away from this problem, we see a need to re-calibrate such approaches and enable more community and collective redress actions. For instance, we need to enable activists of NGOs to facilitate access to widely applicable customizations to users. Hence, similar to how 'repair cafés' enable users to exercise their right to repair by giving them access to and support by enthusiasts, online or offline 'customization communities' would help individuals to exercise their right to customization. This could induce a folksonomy-based approach to the customization of frequently used services, i.e., a situation where specific customization solutions would be shared among a community of participants.

References

1. Abadi, M., et al.: Deep learning with differential privacy. In: Proceedings of the ACM SIGSAC Conference on Computer and Communications Security, pp. 308–318. Association for Computing Machinery (2016)
2. Acquisti, A., Brandimarte, L., Loewenstein, G.: Privacy and human behavior in the age of information. Science **347**(6221), 509–514 (2015)
3. Agrawal, N., Binns, R., Van Kleek, M., Laine, K., Shadbolt, N.: Exploring design and governance challenges in the development of privacy-preserving computation. arXiv preprint arXiv:2101.08048 (2021)
4. Article 29 Working Party: WP29 Opinion 15/2011 on the definition of consent (WP 187) (2011). https://ec.europa.eu/justice/article-29/documentation/opinion-recommendation/files/2011/wp187_en.pdf

---

[13] Council of the European Union, Draft regulation concerning respect for private life and the protection of personal data in electronic communications and repealing directive 2002/58/EC (regulation on privacy and electronic communications) – Council mandate <https://data.consilium.europa.eu/doc/document/ST-6087-2021-INIT/en/pdf>.

5. Berliner Beauftragte für Datenschutz und Informationsfreiheit: Berliner Datenschutzbeauftragte verhängt Bussgeld gegen Immobiliengesellschaft, 5 November 2019 (2019). https://www.datenschutz-berlin.de/fileadmin/user_upload/pdf/pressemitteilungen/2019/20191105-PM-Bussgeld_DW.pdf
6. Bietti, E.: Consent as a free pass: platform power and the limits of the informational turn. Pace Law Rev. **40**, 307–397 (2020)
7. Bizer, C., Heath, T., Berners-Lee, T.: Linked data: the story so far. In: Semantic Services, Interoperability and Web Applications: Emerging Concepts, pp. 205–227. IGI global (2011)
8. Borgesius, F., Kruikemeier, S., Boerman, S., Helberger, N.: Tracking walls, take-it-or-leave-it choices, the GDPR, and the ePrivacy regulation. Eur. Data Protect. Law Rev. **3**, 353–368 (2017)
9. Brownsword, R.: Consent in data protection law: privacy, fair processing and confidentiality. In: Gutwirth, S., Poullet, Y., de Hert, P., de Terwangne, C., Nouwt, S. (eds.) Reinventing Data Protection?, pp. 83–110. Springer, Dordrecht (2009). https://doi.org/10.1007/978-1-4020-9498-9_4
10. Burkert, H.: Privacy-enhancing technologies: typology, critique, vision. In: Agre, P., Rotenberg, M. (eds.) Technology and Privacy: The New Landscape, pp. 126–143. MIT Press, Boston (1997)
11. Buyle, R., et al.: Streamlining governmental processes by putting citizens in control of their personal data. In: Chugunov, A., Khodachek, I., Misnikov, Y., Trutnev, D. (eds.) EGOSE. CCIS, vol. 1135, pp. 346–359. Springer, Cham (2020). https://doi.org/10.1007/978-3-030-39296-3_26
12. Bygrave, L.A.: Hardwiring privacy. In: Brownsword, R., Scotford, E., Yeung, K. (eds.) The Oxford Handbook of Law, Regulation, and Technology, pp. 754–775. Oxford University Press, Oxford (2017)
13. Bygrave, L.A.: Privacy-enhancing technologies: caught between a rock and a hard place. Priv. Law Policy Rep. **9**, 135–137 (2002)
14. Bygrave, L.A.: Article 25 data protection by design and by default. In: Kuner, C., Bygrave, L.A., Dockyes, C. (eds.) The EU General Data Protection Regulation (GDPR): A Commentary, pp. 571–581. Oxford University Press, Oxford (2020)
15. Carolan, E.: The continuing problems with online consent under the EU's emerging data protection principles. Comput. Law Secur. Rev. **32**(3), 462–473 (2016)
16. Cavoukian, A.: Privacy by design: the 7 foundational principles, August 2009 (2011). https://www.ipc.on.ca/wp-content/uploads/Resources/7foundationalprinciples.pdf
17. Choi, H., Park, J., Jung, Y.: The role of privacy fatigue in online privacy behavior. Comput. Hum. Behav. **81**, 42–51 (2018)
18. Clifford, D., Graef, I., Valcke, P.: Pre-formulated declarations of data subject consent: citizen-consumer empowerment and the alignment of data, consumer and competition law protections. German Law J. **20**(5), 679–721 (2019)
19. Custers, B., Dechesne, F., Pieters, W., Schermer, B., van der Hof, S.: Consent and privacy. In: Müller, A., Schaber, P. (eds.) The Routledge Handbook of the Ethics of Consent, pp. 247–258. Routledge, London (2018)
20. Custers, B.: Click here to consent forever: Expiry dates for informed consent. Big Data Soc. **3**(1), 1–6 (2016)
21. Danezis, G., et al.: Privacy and data protection by design - from policy to engineering, European Union Agency for network and information security, ENISA, 12 January 2015 (2014). www.enisa.europa.eu/activities/identity-and-trust/library/deliverables/privacy-and-data-protection-by-design
22. Datatilsynet: Advance notification of an administrative fine, 20/02136-5, 24 January 2021 (2021). https://www.datatilsynet.no/contentassets/da7652d0c072493c84a4c7af506cf293/advance-notification-of-an-administrative-fine.pdf

23. De Hert, P., Papakonstantinou, V.: The new general data protection regulation: still a sound system for the protection of individuals? Comput. Law Secur. Rev. **32**(2), 179–194 (2016)
24. De Hert, P., Papakonstantinou, V., Malgieri, G., Beslay, L., Sanchez, I.: The right to data portability in the GDPR: towards user-centric interoperability of digital services. Comput. Law Secur. Rev. **34**(2), 193–203 (2018)
25. De Montjoye, Y.A., Shmueli, E., Wang, S.S., Pentland, A.S.: OpenPDS: protecting the privacy of metadata through safeanswers. PloS One **9**(7), e98790 (2014)
26. De Oliveira Rodrigues, C.M., de Freitas, F.L.G., Spósito Barreiros, E.F., de Azevedo, R.R., de Almeida Filho, A.T.: Legal ontologies over time: a systematic mapping study. Expert Syst. Appl. **130**, 12–30 (2019)
27. Diker Vanberg, A.: The right to data portability in the GDPR: what lessons can be learned from the EU experience? J. Internet Law **21**, 11–19 (2018)
28. Edenberg, E., Jones, M.L.: Analyzing the legal roots and moral core of digital consent. New Media Soc. **21**, 1804–1823 (2019)
29. Efroni, Z., Metzger, J., Mischau, L., Schirmbeck, M.: Privacy icons: a risk-based approach to visualisation of data processing. Eur. Data Protect. Law Rev. **5**(3), 352–366 (2019)
30. European Commission: Circular Economy Action Plan: For a cleaner and more competitive Europe (2020). https://ec.europa.eu/environment/circular-economy/pdf/new_circular_economy_action_plan.pdf
31. European Data Protection Board (EDPB): Guidelines 4/2019 on Article 25 Data Protection by Design and by Default (2019). https://edpb.europa.eu/sites/edpb/files/consultation/edpb_guidelines_201904_dataprotection_by_design_and_by_default.pdf
32. European Union Agency for Fundamental Rights (FRA): Freedom to conduct a business: exploring the dimensions of a fundamental right (2015). https://fra.europa.eu/sites/default/files/fra_uploads/fra-2015-freedom-conduct-business_en.pdf
33. Garcia, K., Zihlmann, Z., Mayer, S., Tamo-Larrieux, A.: Towards privacy-friendly smart products. Manuscript submitted for publication (2021). https://www.alexandria.unisg.ch/262898/
34. Graef, I.: The opportunities and limits of data portability for stimulating competition and innovation. Compet. Policy Int. - Antitrust Chronicle **2**, 1–8 (2020). https://pure.uvt.nl/ws/portalfiles/portal/45777953/CPI_Graef_data_portability.pdf
35. Gray, C., Santos, C., Bielova, N., Toth, M., Clifford, D.: Dark patterns and the legal requirements of consent banners: an interaction criticism perspective. arXiv preprint arXiv:2009.10194 (2020)
36. Grinvald, L.C., Tur-Sinai, O.: Intellectual property law and the right to repair. Fordham Law Rev. **88**(1), 64–128 (2019)
37. Gürses, S., Troncoso, C., Diaz, C.: Engineering privacy by design. In: Fourth Conference on Computers, Privacy and Data Protection, 25–27 January 2011 (2011). www.cosic.esat.kuleuven.be/publications/article-1542.pdf
38. Hartzog, W.: Privacy's Blueprint the Battle to Control the Design of New Technologies. Harvard University Press, Cambridge (2018)
39. Hern, A.: WhatsApp loses millions of users after terms update. The Guardian, 24 January 2021 (2021). https://www.theguardian.com/technology/2021/jan/24/whatsapp-loses-millions-of-users-after-terms-update
40. Hernandez, R., Miranda, C., Goñi, J.: Empowering sustainable consumption by giving back to consumers the 'right to repair'. Sustainability **12**(3), 850 (2020)
41. Janal, R.: Data portability - a tale of two concepts. JIPITEC **8**, 59–69 (2017)
42. Jasmontaite, L., Kamara, I., Zanfir-Fortuna, G., Leucci, S.: Data protection by design and by default: framing guiding principles into legal obligations in the GDPR. Eur. Data Protect. Law Rev. **4**, 168–189 (2018)

43. Johnston, S.F.: The technological fix as social cure-all: origins and implications. IEEE Technol. Soc. Mag. **37**, 47–54 (2018)
44. Kokolakis, S.: Privacy attitudes and privacy behaviour: a review of current research on the privacy paradox phenomenon. Comput. Secur. **64**, 122–134 (2017)
45. Koops, B.-J.: The trouble with european data protection law. Int. Data Priv. Law **4**(4), 250–261 (2014)
46. Koops, B.-J., Leenes, R.: Privacy regulation cannot be hardcoded. A critical comment on the 'privacy by design' provision in data-protection law. Int. Rev. Law Comput. Technol. **28**, 159–171 (2014)
47. Kosta, E.: Consent in European Data Protection Law. Martinus Nijhoff Publishers, Leiden (2013)
48. Kostova, B., Gürses, S., Troncoso, C.: Privacy engineering meets software engineering. On the challenges of engineering privacy by design. arXiv preprint arXiv:2007.08613 (2020).
49. Kotschy, W.: Article 6 lawfulness of processing. In: Kuner, C., Bygrave, L.A., Dockyes, C. (eds.) The EU General Data Protection Regulation (GDPR): A Commentary, pp. 321–344. Oxford University Press, Oxford (2020)
50. Lutz, C., Hoffmann, C.P., Ranzini, G.: Data capitalism and the user: an exploration of privacy cynicism in Germany. New Media Soc. **22**(7), 1168–1187 (2020)
51. Mathur, A., et al.: Dark patterns at scale. In: Proceedings of the ACM on Human-Computer Interaction, pp. 1–32. arXiv preprint arXiv:1907.07032 (2019)
52. McDonald, A.M., Cranor, L.F.: The cost of reading privacy policies. I/S J. Law Policy Inf. Soc. **4**, 540–565 (2008)
53. Montello, S.: The right to repair and the corporate stranglehold over the consumer: profits over people. Tulane J. Technol. Intellect. Prop. **22**, 165–184 (2020)
54. Morais Carvalho, J.: Sale of goods and supply of digital content and digital services – overview of directives 2019/770 and 2019/771. SSRN (2019). https://ssrn.com/abstract=3428550
55. Mourey, J.A., Waldman, A.E.: Past the privacy paradox: the importance of privacy changes as a function of control and complexity. J. Assoc. Consum. Res. **5**(2), 162–180 (2020)
56. Norberg, P.A., Horne, D.R., Horne, D.A.: The privacy paradox: personal information disclosure intentions versus behaviors. J. Consum. Affairs **41**, 100–126 (2007)
57. Norwegian Forbrukerrådet: Deceived by design: How tech companies use dark patterns to discourage us from exercising our rights to privacy (2018). https://fil.forbrukerradet.no/wp-content/uploads/2018/06/2018-06-27-deceived-by-design-final.pdf
58. Nouwens, M., Liccardi, I., Veale, M., Karger, D., Kagal, L.: Dark patterns after the GDPR: scraping consent pop-ups and demonstrating their influence. In: Proceedings of the 2020 CHI Conference on Human Factors in Computing Systems, pp. 1–13. arXiv preprint arXiv:2001.02479 (2020)
59. Raynes-Goldie, K.: Aliases, creeping, and wall cleaning: understanding privacy in the age of Facebook. First Monday **15**(1) (2010). https://firstmonday.org/ojs/index.php/fm/article/view/2775
60. Reda, J., Selinger, J.: Article's 17's impact on freedom to conduct a business - part 2, Kluwer Copyright Blog, 21 January 2021 (2021). https://copyrightblog.kluweriplaw.com/2021/01/19/article-17s-impact-on-freedom-to-conduct-a-business-part-2/
61. Rosa-Aquino, P.: Fix, or toss? The 'right to repair' movement gains ground. New York Times, 23 October 2020 (2020). https://www.nytimes.com/2020/10/23/climate/right-to-repair.html
62. Rubinstein, I., Good, N.: The trouble with Article 25 (and how to fix it): the future of data protection by design and default. Int. Data Priv. Law **10**(1), 37–56 (2020)
63. Šajn, N.: Consumers and repairs of products, Briefing of European Parliamentary Research Service (2019). https://www.europarl.europa.eu/RegData/etudes/BRIE/2019/640158/EPRS_BRI(2019)640158_EN.pdf

64. Sambra, A.V., et al.: Solid: a platform for decentralized social applications based on linked data. MIT CSAIL & Qatar Computing Research Institute, Techical report (2016).
65. Schartum, D.: Making privacy by design operative. Int. J. Law Inf. Technol. **24**, 151–175 (2016)
66. Schaub, F., Balebako, R., Durity, A., Cranor, L.: A Design space for effective privacy notices. In: Selinger, E., Polonetsky, J., Tene, O. (eds.) The Cambridge Handbook of Consumer Privacy, pp. 365–393. Cambridge University Press, Cambridge (2018)
67. Schermer, B., Custers, B., van der Hof, S.: The crisis of consent: how stronger legal protection may lead to weaker consent in data protection. Ethics Inf. Technol. **16**(2), 171–182 (2014). https://doi.org/10.1007/s10676-014-9343-8
68. Schiffner, S., et al.: Towards a roadmap for privacy technologies and the general data protection regulation: a transatlantic initiative. In: Medina, M., Mitrakas, A., Rannenberg, K., Schweighofer, E., Tsouroulas, N. (eds.) APF. LNCS, vol. 11079, pp. 24–42. Springer, Cham (2018). https://doi.org/10.1007/978-3-030-02547-2_2
69. Simonite, T.: Lawmakers take aim at insidious digital 'dark patterns'. WIRED, 29 January 2021. https://www.wired.com/story/lawmakers-take-aim-insidious-digital-dark-patterns/
70. Solove, D.J.: Privacy self-management and the consent dilemma. Harv. Law Rev. **126**, 1880–1903 (2013)
71. Solove, D.J.: The Myth of the Privacy Paradox. George Washington Law Rev. **89**, 1–42 (2021)
72. Svensson, S., Richter, J.L., Maitre-Ekern, E., Pihlajarinne, T., Maigret, A., Dalhammer, C.: The emerging 'right to repair' legislation in the EU and the U.S. Paper presented at Going Green CARE Innovation (2018). https://portal.research.lu.se/portal/files/63585584/Svensson_et_al._Going_Green_CARE_INNOVATION_2018_PREPRINT.pdf
73. Tamò-Larrieux, A.: Designing for Privacy and Its Legal Framework: Data Protection by Design and Default for the Internet of Things. Springer, Cham (2018). https://doi.org/10.1007/978-3-319-98624-1
74. Tamò-Larrieux, A., Mayer, S., Zihlmann, Z.: Softcoding not hardcoding privacy. Workshop Paper Presented at the Digital Legal Talks (2020). https://www.alexandria.unisg.ch/cgi/users/home?screen=EPrint::View&eprintid=262254#t
75. Teletrust and ENISA: IT Security Act (Germany) and EU General Data Protection Regulation: Guideline "state of the art" technical and organisational measures (2020). https://www.teletrust.de/fileadmin/docs/fachgruppen/ag-stand-der-technik/2020-10_TeleTrusT_Guideline_State_of_the_art_in_IT_security_EN.pdf
76. The Royal Society: Protecting privacy in practice: the current use, development and limits of privacy enhancing technologies in data analysis. Technical report. The Royal Society (2019)
77. Utz, C., Degeling, M., Fahl, S., Schaub, F., Holz, T.: (Un)informed consent: studying GDPR consent notices in the field. In: Proceedings of the 2019 ACM SIGSAC Conference on Computer and Communications Security (CCS 2019), pp. 973–990 (2019)
78. Vanberg, A., Ünver, M.: The right to data portability in the GDPR and EU competition law: odd couple or dynamic duo? Eur. J. Law Technol. **8**(1), 1–22 (2017)
79. Van Hoboken, J.V.J.: Privacy disconnect. In: Human Rights in the Age of Platforms, pp. 255–284. The MIT Press, Cambridge (2019)
80. Veltri, G.A., Ivchenko, A.: The impact of different forms of cognitive scarcity on online privacy disclosure. Comput. Hum. Behav. **73**, 238–246 (2017)
81. Waldman, A.E.: Cognitive biases, dark patterns, and the 'privacy paradox.' Curr. Opin. Psychol. **31**, 105–109 (2020)

A Case Study on the Implementation of the Right of Access in Privacy Dashboards

Jan Tolsdorf(✉) ⓘ, Michael Fischer, and Luigi Lo Iacono ⓘ

Data and Application Security Group, H-BRS University of Applied Sciences,
Sankt Augustin, Germany
{jan.tolsdorf,luigi.lo_iacono}@h-brs.de, michaelfischer5@web.de
https://das.h-brs.de/

Abstract. The right of access under Art. 15 of the General Data Protection Regulation (GDPR) grants data subjects the right to obtain comprehensive information about the processing of personal data from a controller, including a copy of the data. Privacy dashboards have been discussed as possible tools for implementing this right, and are increasingly found in practice. However, investigations of real world implementations are sparse. We therefore qualitatively examined the extent to which privacy dashboards of ten online services complied with the essential requirements of Art. 15 GDPR. For this, we compared the information provided in dashboards with the information provided in privacy statements and data exports. We found that most privacy dashboards provided a decent initial overview, but lacked important information about purposes, recipients, sources, and categories of data that online users consider to be sensitive. In addition, both the privacy dashboards and the data exports lacked copies of personal data that were processed according to the online services' own privacy statements. We discuss the strengths and weaknesses of current implementations in terms of their ability to fulfill the objective of Art. 15 GDPR, namely to create awareness about data processing. We conclude by providing an outlook on what steps would be necessary for privacy dashboards to facilitate the exercise of the right of access and to provide real added value for online users.

Keywords: GDPR · Right of access · Privacy dashboards

1 Introduction

The GDPR [11] provides users of online services operating in the European Union (EU) with many rights to maintain control over their personal data. A

Supported by the German Federal Ministry of Education and Research (BMBF) under the research project "TrUSD - Transparente und selbstbestimmte Ausgestaltung der Datennutzung im Unternehmen" (transparent and self-determined design of data use in organizations) (16KIS0899).

ⓒ Springer Nature Switzerland AG 2021
N. Gruschka et al. (Eds.): APF 2021, LNCS 12703, pp. 23–46, 2021.
https://doi.org/10.1007/978-3-030-76663-4_2

prerequisite for the GDPR to be effective, however, is the requirement that controllers comply with their obligations by implementing adequate processes as well as providing their users with tools to exercise their rights. Much of recent work has revealed weaknesses in the implementation of such tools such as intrusive consent forms [45] and incomprehensible privacy statements [15,46]. Certainly, research has merely focused on problems and solutions with regards to ex-ante control and therefore on rights that apply prior to processing. However, the GDPR, and in particular the right of access under Art. 15, aim to ensure that data subjects are aware of the extent of processing at all times: before, during, and after processing. The right of access is special in the sense that it requires data subjects to exercise this right regularly and independently in order to become truly aware of the processing of their personal data. Research suggests, however, that people are either unaware of their rights or reluctant to make the effort to exercise them [2,34]. To address this problem, the use of prominently placed tools for ex-post control in the form of privacy dashboards is gaining traction, since such tools provide users both with transparency and intervention mechanisms. Research suggests that the use of privacy dashboards both facilitates data controllers' obligation to provide transparency and intervention options to their users and ease data subjects' exercise of their rights [5,33,35]. In practice, online services also already refer data subjects to use these tools for exercising their rights in privacy statements or FAQs, in particular with regards to the right of access.[1] Different to ex-ante control, however, there is currently a lack of research about real world implementations of tools for ex-post control.

This paper constitutes a first step towards closing this gap, by providing an overview of privacy dashboards found in practice, with a particular focus on the right of access. More precisely, our contributions are guided by the overall research question *"to what extent are privacy dashboards found in practice used to implement the right of access under Art. 15 GDPR?"*. For this purpose, we evaluated the information provided by privacy dashboards, data exports, formal requests for access, and privacy statements with ten popular online services operating in different business domains in the EU. The key insights are:

- We found that none of the examined privacy dashboards complied with the requirements of the right of access, and that the information provided was incomplete with respect to purposes, external recipients, external sources, and categories of data listed in the respective privacy statements. Overall, privacy dashboards contained rich information about personal data directly related to individuals or their interactions with a service, but lacked most of the information about personal data that are technical in nature and considered as highly sensitive by online users.
- Furthermore we found that all but one online service provided incomplete personal data in their data exports. For 6/10 online services, the data also differed between privacy dashboards and data exports, and the union of both

---

[1] https://privacy.microsoft.com/en-us/privacystatement, https://support.google.com /accounts/answer/162744?hl=en.

increased the overall amount of information. For another 6/10 online services, privacy dashboards provided less information compared to exports.
- We conclude that the privacy dashboards found in practice have the potential to become a good compromise between the time and effort required for exercising the right of access compared to the extent of information provided. However, they leave lay people in an uninformed state due to a lack of important information.

We consider our results a valuable contribution to previous research on the monitoring and examination of the implementation of the right of access by online services, and complement towards a holistic picture of the GDPR in practice [2,4,8,26,44,47]. To the best of our knowledge, we are the first to investigate the use of privacy dashboards found in practice with regards to their compliance with Art. 15 GDPR by conducting a target/actual comparison of the information provided with respect to online services' privacy statements. Researchers, practitioners, and policy makers may use our results as means to become aware of possible pitfalls when using or implementing privacy dashboards, and as a basis for further research and regulation.

The rest of this paper is structured as follows: first, we present related work on the right of access and privacy dashboards. We then provide details on our procedure and methods for investigating the current implementation of the right of access in privacy dashboards for a sample of ten online services. We then present the results of our study for each online service as well as a summary of findings. We finally discuss our findings and give an outlook for future work.

2   Related Work

We discuss related work with a focus on the right of access and the use of privacy dashboards to accommodate the fundamental objectives of the GDPR with regards to transparency and intervention.

2.1   Right of Access

The right of access under Art. 15 GDPR consists of three key paragraphs:

(**Art. 15 para. 1 GDPR**) – The obligation for controllers to inform data subjects whether personal data are processed, including but not limited to details about the categories of data concerned, the purposes of the processing, and the (categories of) recipients to whom the data are disclosed;

(**Art. 15 para. 2 GDPR**) – The obligation for controllers to inform data subjects about the safeguards taken when transferring personal data to third countries or international organizations;

(**Art. 15 para. 3 GDPR**) – And the right of data subjects to obtain a copy of the personal data processed by a controller. If the request is made digitally, the copy must also be provided in a "commonly used electronic form".

The rights described in Art. 15 para. 1 GDPR have been available to EU citizens since 1995, yet they have regained visibility since the GDPR came into force in 2018. Back then, the right of access made headlines with an NGO filing strategic complaints against large online services who did not comply with the new regulation.[2] Lately, academia has also started to explore the implementation of the different rights available to data subjects in more depth, finding that 20% of the most popular online services did not comply with their basic obligations on informing data subjects one year after the GDPR came into force [8].

Moreover, Art. 15 para. 3 GDPR and the novel right of data portability under Art. 20 GDPR drew researchers' attention too. These articles differ in that the former only obliges controllers to supply a copy of the data, whereas the latter also demands the use of structured data formats to allow data subjects reusing their personal data for their own purposes and also in other services. However, previous studies found that controllers provide the same data formats (e.g. JSON, PDF) for both the right of access and the right of data portability [8,47]. Thereby, the data formats are very heterogeneous [8,44,47] and the number of GDPR compliant file formats can be as low as 40% [47]. Research demonstrated that the usability and perceived usefulness of structured data formats are rather low [5]. Also, a recent qualitative survey on consumer expectations of the right of access for a loyalty program in Germany found that data subjects are more interested in what controllers infer from their personal data, rather than simply knowing what personal data are processed [2]. These findings are also supported by work on transparency conducted prior to the GDPR [21].

The right of access is further governed by the provisions of Art. 12 GDPR, which obliges controllers to verify the identity of the person making the request for access. However, there does not exist a uniform process. Instead, data protection authorities provide different recommendations and controllers' authentication procedures were found to be unsafe in practice [6]. Also, previous studies demonstrated that the right of access can be abused to access personal data of foreigners due to flaws in the authentication process of controllers [10,26,31].

Moreover, Art. 12 para. 3 GDPR provides that controllers must respond to requests for access within one month, but may extend this time span by two months if they can demonstrate the high efforts involved. Previous studies revealed a mixed picture in this respect. In [44], 55% out of 38 online tracking companies responded in time, whereas in [8] 89% out of 212 controllers responded in time. Similarly, the authors of [47] examined the right of data portability and found that 70% out of 230 controllers responded in time.

To the best of our knowledge, there is a lack of studies verifying whether the information provided under the right of access is complete with respect to the personal data processed by controllers, and to what extent the provided information differs between different sources. We provide first insights on this matter by systematically comparing the information retrieved when exercising the right of access with the information provided in controllers' privacy statements. Also,

---

[2] https://noyb.eu/en/netflix-spotify-youtube-eight-strategic-complaints-filed-right-access.

we provide insights on the type and amount of information provided to data subjects in privacy dashboards, data exports, and formal requests for access.

2.2 Privacy Dashboards

Privacy dashboards are transparency tools specially adapted to the context of information privacy, and have repeatedly been identified as helpful in the context of the GDPR for implementing legal obligations, including the right of access [5, 35]. Privacy dashboards have been established in the area of (social) online services and are intended to provide their users with an overview and control (through appropriate settings) of their personal data processed by a controller [35, 48]. They are classified as transparency-enhancing tools (TETs) and constitute proven patterns for the implementation of privacy-friendly systems, so-called privacy transparency patterns (PTPs) [39]. Privacy dashboards are special in the sense that they comprise multiple different PTPs appropriate to the context and in order to provide functions to promote transparency. They may provide the following essential privacy controls [5, 39, 48]:

1. *Overview* – All personal data available to a controller about a data subject together with the associated information (e.g., recipients, purposes) and data flow are presented in a clearly understandable and structured manner. This makes it possible to sensitize users to the extent of their data disclosures and potential consequences for privacy [7].
2. *Verifiability* – Data subjects may understand the current and future processing (e.g., collection, use) of their personal data. This enables data subjects to check the lawfulness of processing and to hold data processors liable in the event of violations [20].
3. *Intervention* – Data subjects may actively influence the processing of their personal data. In particular, they are provided with control over the data stored, and may also initiate corrections or deletions on their own [3, 5, 35].

Academia has recognized and discussed the value of tools similar to privacy dashboards to support online users in their information privacy a long time before the GDPR came into force (e.g. [3, 7, 22, 38]). However, their implementation as a means to accommodate the legal requirements of the GDPR has gained popularity in recent years, including contexts other than online services [5, 24, 27, 33, 35, 43]. As a result, research has defined several requirements for privacy dashboards that provide guidance on (1) how to accommodate legal requirements [5, 35], (2) the architecture and technical prerequisites [5, 27, 32], and (3) the constraints for usability and stakeholder requirements [5, 32, 35, 43]. In conclusion, Raschke et al. [35] postulated that privacy dashboards must implement four tasks to support data subjects in their rights: **(T1)** Execute the right of access; **(T2)** Obtain information about involved processors; **(T3)** Request rectification or erasure of data; **(T4)** Consent review and withdrawal.

In terms of benefits to controllers, research suggests that providing privacy dashboards increase user trust in online services [9, 18]. This increase is attributed to the tools' transparency properties in particular. A case study on the Google dashboard demonstrated that privacy dashboards may also increase users' willingness to disclose personal data [9]. However, limited intervention options or information known to be lacking may have adverse effects [18].

A look at real world data controllers reveals that the majority of online services only recently started implementing different forms of privacy dashboards themselves. However, investigations on these tools are strongly limited to the Google dashboard so far and focused on user attitudes [9] and theoretical concepts [29,48]. To the best of our knowledge, we are the first to systematically examine the scope of information and functions provided by multiple different privacy dashboard implementations found in practice, and with special regards to their compliance with the right of access Art. 15 GDPR. We highlight existing problems and discuss possible solutions to increase the value of privacy dashboards for both data subjects and controllers.

3   Methodology

We conducted a qualitative study to examine the extent to which privacy dashboards found in practice already accommodate the right of access with ten popular online services during the period October and December 2020. For this purpose, we created accounts with these online services and simulated their use with different devices and recorded all activities in a logbook. We then analyzed the information provided by dashboards with controllers' privacy statements and information obtained from data exports. In the following, we provide details on the applied methodology and evaluation of the data. An overview of our methodology is shown in Fig. 1.

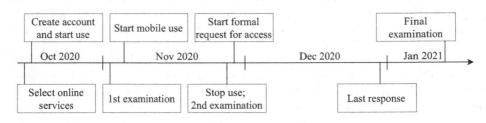

Fig. 1. Chronology of online service use and examination of provided information.

3.1   Selection of Online Services

For our case study, we aimed to gain an overview of the use of privacy dashboards by online services operating in different fields and contexts that online users in the EU frequently interact with. According to the Digital Economy and Society Index [41] and the annual survey on Information and Communication

Technologies [40], the top six categories of online services used by European internet users are music, videos and games (81%), email and communication (75%), news (72%), shopping (71%), banking (66%), and online social networks (65%). For further investigation, we excluded news and banking services because the former often does not require the creation of accounts nor the provision of personal data, whereas the latter requires high efforts for the creation of accounts. We therefore focused on providers of music streaming, video streaming, email, shopping, and social online networks.

We used the Tranco list[3] [23] created on 14 October 2020 to screen the top 100 online services for possible candidates for our investigation. First, we excluded services that are unavailable in German, and then extracted possible candidates for each of the five categories. Next, we reviewed the different services in order of appearance in the Tranco list and examined whether a service offered a privacy dashboard or at least similar functionalities with regards to Art. 15 GDPR. For this purpose, we inspected a provider's website and privacy statement, and signed up for an account if we were unsure about the provided functionality. If a service did not conform with our requirements, we continued with the next service in the list. After we successfully identified a candidate for each category, we stopped our screening. We then repeated the previously described steps for online services that were less popular, but offered similar services compared to the five selected online services. To do this, we conducted a partial online search to find suitable candidates. Based on our screening, we have ultimately picked the following online services:

- Audio streaming: Spotify (Tranco: 80), Deezer (Tranco: 1461)
- Video streaming: Netflix (Tranco: 8), Rakuten TV (Tranco: 43297)
- Shopping: Amazon (Tranco: 18), Zalando (Tranco: 7439)
- Email and search engine: Google (Tranco: 1), Yahoo (Tranco: 17)
- Social network: Facebook (Tranco: 2), LinkedIn (Tranco: 9)

3.2   Sign-Up and Use of Online Services

We created accounts for each online service and provided information about basic demographics (e.g., age, sex), contact data (e.g., name, address), and financial information (e.g., credit card) if applicable. When possible, we used the web version of a service as well as the mobile app (Android) in order to allow the processing of additional meta data (e.g., device ID). We interacted with each service at multiple different points in time in order to generate data about community and service interactions (e.g., creating playlists, streaming media, sending emails, liking groups). We monitored our interactions with a service for the upcoming examination step. More precisely, we recorded the details of the personal data we disclosed along with information about our technical devices in a logbook.

---

[3] https://tranco-list.eu/list/W3W9.

3.3 Examination of the Right of Access

After we successfully set up all the accounts, we aimed for examining which information and functionality are provided by privacy dashboards. First, we extracted required information from privacy statements of online services and then exercised the right of access using (1) privacy dashboards, a user generated (2) data export, as well as a (3) formal request for access. Our investigation consisted of the various steps described below.

Preparation Phase – We started our investigation by inspecting each providers' privacy statement with particular attention to the different recipients, data sources other than the data subject, purposes for processing, and categories of data claimed to be processed. We extracted this information for each provider and double checked our findings with the information provided by Pribot[4], a tool that analyzes privacy statements based on deep learning [17]. Next, we consolidated our findings and identified commonalities between the different privacy statements of all online services. For this, we built a union list of all purposes, recipients, sources, and data categories.

In order to allow drawing conclusions about the expected user perceived sensitivity of the different data, we classified the data into six different groups, following the identified clusters by Milne et al. [28]: Basic demographics (low sensitivity), personal preferences (low to medium sensitivity), community and service interaction (medium sensitivity), financial information (medium to high sensitivity), contact information (medium to high sensitivity), and technical identifiers or data (high sensitivity). While Milne et al. focused on online users in Brazil and the U.S., there is evidence that data sensitivity does not differ significantly for European online users [25,36].

Examination of Dashboards – For each online service, we examined the information and functions provided in the respective dashboards with a particular focus on the tasks T1–T4 defined by Raschke et al. [35] (cf. Sect. 2.2). We examined whether and which information about purposes, recipients, data sources, and personal data was displayed or referenced in the privacy settings and additional info texts. We documented our findings using the lists created during the preparation phase. Furthermore, we examined whether the dashboards provided functions for (1) downloading a copy of the data, (2) restricting or at least limiting data processing, and (3) editing and deleting personal data. Here, we only checked whether the function was present or not, but did not quantify our findings for the different categories of data.

Examination of Data Exports – When possible, we downloaded a copy of personal data using the dashboard at the beginning of our study and again after two weeks to compare the different data exports (cf. Fig. 1). We manually examined each export and extracted the different categories of data. Again, we documented whether and which data were present or missing based on our logbook and the

---

[4] https://pribot.org/polisis.

list of categories of data created during the preparation phase. We also recorded the response formats and response time.

Formal Request for Access – After we finished examining the data exports and identified missing information or personal data, we started a formal request for access by contacting each provider via email or online-forms. We specifically asked for the categories of data that were missing from the exports with respect to their privacy statements and our logbook. Once we received the final response to our request, we repeated the steps taken for analyzing exports described above.

4   Results

In the following section, we present the results of our investigation. First, we report our findings on the information provided in privacy statements, followed by the results of our investigation of the different dashboards for each online service. We then summarize our findings and report on the overall completeness of information found in privacy dashboards.

4.1   Information in Privacy Statements

Recipients and Sources – In total, we identified 13 categories of recipients, and six categories of external data sources. Half the privacy statements listed at least six recipients ($min = 4$, $max = 9$) and two sources ($min = 0$, $max = 4$). All online services stated their *corporate group* and *public authorities* as recipients. Seven online services each also mentioned *advertisers*, *owners*, or *service providers*, and five online services mentioned *third-party providers*. Three of the examined online services even provided the exact (company) name of the recipients. With regards to external sources, five online services each referred to *third-party providers* and *service providers*, four online services mentioned *advertisers*, and three online services stated that they also process *publicly accessible information*.

Purposes – We extracted 22 different purposes for processing from the privacy statements provided by the online services. Half the online services listed at least 11 purposes ($min = 9$, $max = 17$). The five purposes included in all privacy statements comprised *providing the service, troubleshooting and improving the service, customizing the service experience, advertising*, and *preventing fraud*. Moreover, only two providers, namely Spotify and Deezer, clearly stated which personal data were processed for each purpose.

Categories of Data – Looking at the individual online services, we found that each privacy statement listed 32 different categories of data on average ($min = 21$, $max = 48$, $sd = 7$). Yet, only eight categories of data were processed by all service providers, from which five categories belonged to technical data. In total, we extracted 77 different categories of data from all privacy statements. The proportion according to the applied classification (cf. Sect. 3.3) is as

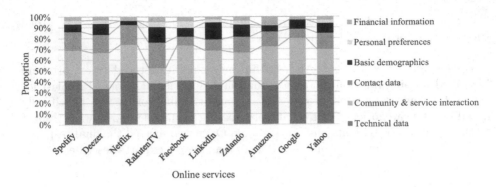

Fig. 2. Proportion of categories of data processed by each online service as defined in privacy statements. Categories of data were classified into groups according to [28].

follows: 37.6% technical data, 35.1% community and service interaction, 9.1% basic demographics, 9.1% contact information, 5.2% personal preferences, and 3.9% financial information. Consequently, technical data together with information about community and service interaction already accounted for two thirds of all data processed by online services, whereas personal data with a clear and direct personal reference accounted for only one third of the data.

Based on this classification, 59.5% of the data belonged to the high–medium sensitivity segment, 31.2% belonged to the medium–low sensitivity segment, and 9.3% belonged to the low sensitivity segment. Based on previous research [25,36], we conclude that online users would perceive the processed data to be of medium to high sensitivity if they were aware of its extent. An overview of the distribution of the different groups of data for each online service is provided in Fig. 2.

4.2 Information in Privacy Dashboards and Exports

In the following, we summarize the functions and information provided by the privacy dashboards for each provider, together with details on the information obtained in data exports.

Spotify – For one thing, the dashboard provided comprehensive overview and control over contact data, basic demographics, and financial information. On the other hand, however, information about technical data and personal preferences were lacking completely. The dashboard made aware of advertisers and third-party services as recipients. Spotify was also one of two providers who made visible the processing of data from linked online social network accounts. The data export was requested via the dashboard and consisted of two parts. The first part became available after three days and the second part after 16 days. The information was provided in JSON format. Whereas the first part lacked technical data and service interaction data with respect to the items mentioned by the privacy statement, the second export was complete. We therefore refrained from sending a formal request.

Deezer – The dashboard provided an overview and control over most groups of personal data, but lacked information about service interaction and all technical data. Furthermore, it made aware of advertisers as recipients. According to their privacy statement, they did not process data from external sources. Also, it was not possible to request an export via the dashboard, but only by email. We received a response after one day containing a TXT-file that included less information than the dashboard for three groups of data, and still lacked technical data. Upon request, we were provided with login credentials for a FTP-server to download an extended data export, however, we were unable to access the server due to technical issues. The problem persisted despite support request.

Netflix – The dashboard provided an overview and control over all groups of personal data, but lacked some technical data and information about service interaction. Furthermore, the dashboard made aware of third-party services as possible recipients as well as a source for personal data. A data export was requested via the dashboard and became available after eight hours. Again, the CSV-files lacked technical data (e.g., advertising IDs). Upon request, we received a response after 29 days, in which we were, again, referred to the data export.

Rakuten TV – The dashboard provided very limited overview and control over personal data, and also lacked all technical data, personal preferences, and some information about community interaction. Nevertheless, the dashboard made aware of advertisers as recipients. According to their privacy statement, they did not process data from external sources. As with Deezer, a data export had to be requested via email. After two days, we received several PDF-files, which, however, did not include any information about personal preferences and also lacked some information about technical data and community interaction.

Facebook – The dashboard provided an overview and control over the different data processed, but lacked mostly technical data. The various data categories were divided into groups and could be inspected individually. A privacy wizard guided us through the different privacy settings. The dashboard made aware of advertisers, third-party services, as well as internal and external users as recipients, but lacked information about external sources. The data export was requested via the dashboard and became available after 30 min. We could choose between HTML and JSON format. Yet again, technical data were incomplete. We obtained a response to our formal request after two days. However, we were again referred to the dashboard and data export only.

LinkedIn – Similar to Facebook, the dashboard provided overview and control over different data by dividing them into different groups. Privacy settings provided control over the processing. The dashboard made aware of third-party services and other users as recipients, but lacked information about external sources. The export was requested via the dashboard and became available on the next day. The provided CSV-files also lacked technical data (e.g. cookie IDs). Upon request for access, we received the same export again.

Zalando – The dashboard provided an overview and control over most groups of data, but lacked some information about service interaction and all technical data. Furthermore, no information was provided about recipients and sources. The export was downloaded via the dashboard and became available after three days. Data subjects may choose between a single PDF-file or multiple CSV-files. The export contained less information compared with the dashboard. Upon a formal request for access, we received a second export on the next day that still lacked technical data, contact data, and information about service interaction.

Amazon – The official web form for requests for access informed data subjects about the possibility to access personal data via the user account dashboard. The dashboard summarized the different services for which personal data are processed, however, largely lacked technical data. Also, it only made aware of third-party services as recipients, but completely lacked information about external sources. The export was available after four days and consisted of CSV-files. Again, technical data were incomplete (e.g., ISP, URL clickstream). We received a response to our formal request after eight days, but no additional data were made available and we were referred to the web form again.

Google – The dashboard provided an overview of the different services and personal data used in connection with the Google account (e.g. browsing history), as well as control over the processing of some personal data (e.g. location tracking, YouTube history). A "privacy checkup"-wizard guided us through the different privacy settings. The dashboard made aware of third-party services and external entities as recipients, but completely lacked information about external sources. The data export was requested via the dashboard and became available after 30 min. While most of the data were provided as JSON-format, some data were provided using common file formats for specific data (e.g. calendar, contacts). We found that technical data (e.g., cookie IDs) as well as basic demographics (e.g., date of birth) were incomplete. In response to our formal request for access, Google referred us to the dashboard. After we pointed out the missing data, we received an archive after 16 days, but no further data were made available.

Yahoo – The dashboard was similarly structured to that of Google and provided an overview and control over the different services and personal data used in connection with the Yahoo account. Furthermore, the dashboard only made aware of advertisers as recipients, but completely lacked information about external sources. The export was requested via the dashboard and became available after eight days. The JSON-files lacked technical data (e.g., cookie IDs), but also contact data and service interactions, which both were available in the dashboard.

4.3　Summary of Findings

Privacy Dashboards – Overall, we found that all examined privacy dashboards implemented the tasks T1 – T4 defined by Raschke et al. [35] to at least some extent (cf. Table 1). With regards to intervention mechanisms (T3 & T4) we

Table 1. Summary of findings for privacy dashboards of ten online services: completeness of information with regards to Art. 15 GDPR (left hand side) and available ex-post controls (right hand side).

	Recipients (all)	Recipients (ext.)	Ext. sources	Cat. of data	Period	Profiling	Safeguards	Download data	Restrict use	Delete data	Edit data
Spotify	◗	◗	◗	◗	✗	✓	✗	✓	✓	✗	✓
Deezer	◗	◗	n.a.	◗	✗	✓	✗	✗	✓	✓	✓
Netflix	◗	◗	◗	◗	✗	✓	✗	✓	✓	✗	✓
Rakuten TV	◗	◗	n.a.	◗	✗	✓	✗	✗	✓	✓	✓
Facebook	◗	◗	◗	◗	✗	✓	✗	✓	✗	✓	✓
LinkedIn	◗	◗	◗	◗	✗	✓	✗	✓	✓	✓	✓
Zalando	○	○	◗	◗	✗	✓	✗	✓	✗	✓	✓
Amazon	◗	◗	◗	◗	✗	✓	✗	✓	✓	✓	✓
Google	◗	◗	◗	●	✗	✓	✗	✓	✓	✓	✓
Yahoo	◗	◗	○	●	✗	✓	✗	✓	✓	✓	✓

$$\text{◗} = \frac{PDB \cap (PRI \cup LOG)}{(PRI \cup LOG)}$$

✗: missing; ✓: present; n.a.: not in privacy statement
PDB: privacy dashboard; PRI: privacy statement; LOG: logbook

found that all dashboards allowed the editing of personal data that were disclosed directly or were related to community interactions. Also, eight dashboards each supported deleting data, restricting the processing of data, and downloading a copy of the personal data. With regards to Art. 15 para. 1 GDPR (T1 & T2), however, we found that none of the privacy dashboards provided complete information. In fact, no dashboard informed about the period of storing personal data as well as the safeguards taken for transferring personal data to servers outside the EU. Also, no dashboard explicitly presented the purposes of the processing other than targeted advertising. A number of other purposes may also be indirectly identifiable, but we were unable to perform unambiguous comparisons with our previously compiled lists. In order to prevent conflicting interpretations, we refrained from a detailed analysis of the purposes in the further evaluation.

On a positive side, however, all dashboards informed about some form of profiling or automated decision-making taking place, in particular with regards to targeted advertisements. With regards to recipients, we found that no dashboard informed about personal data becoming available to public authorities and the corporate group, and only one dashboard made visible that data may be shared between services of the same company. However, we found that information about external recipients tended to be more complete (cf. Table 1). Five dashboards each made visible that data were shared with third-party applications or advertisers, and two dashboards each made visible that other users (including users outside the service) and external service providers (e.g., payment service) may have access to personal data. With respect to external data sources, only two dashboards made visible that the online service consumed data from third party services (e.g., access profile information from Facebook).

Table 2. Completeness of personal data provided in privacy dashboards and data exports compared to the information provided in privacy statements and our logbook.

	Source	Technical data	Commu- nity & service in- teraction	Contact data	Basic demo- graphics	Personal prefer- ences	Financial informa- tion
Spotify	PDB	◔	◑	●	●	◔	
	Exp	◑	◑	●	●	●	
	Exp*	●	●	●	●	●	
Deezer	PDB	◔	◑	●	●	●	
	Exp	◕	◑	●	◑	◔	◑
Netflix	PDB	◑	◑	●	n.a.	n.a.	
	Exp	◕	●	●	n.a.	n.a.	
Rakuten TV	PDB	◔	◕	●	n.a.	◔	
	Exp	◕	◑	●	n.a.	◔	
Facebook	PDB	◕	◕	●	●	n.a.	
	Exp	◑	●	●	●	n.a.	
LinkedIn	PDB	◕	●	●	◑	◔	
	Exp	◑	●	●	◑	●	
Zalando	PDB	◔	◑	●	●	●	
	Exp	◔	◕	◑	●	●	
	Exp*	◑	◑	◑	●	●	
Amazon	PDB	◔	◑	●	●	n.a.	
	Exp	◕	●	●	●	n.a.	
Google	PDB	◑	●	●	●	n.a.	
	Exp	◑	●	●	◑	n.a.	
Yahoo	PDB	◕	●	●	●	●	
	Exp	◕	◑	◑	●	●	
Avg. Information $\Delta = PDB - EXP$		-19%	+7%	+9%	+3%	-1%	0%

$$\text{◑} = \frac{SRC \cap (PRI \cup LOG)}{(PRI \cup LOG)}, \quad SRC \in \{PDB,\ EXP,\ EXP^*\}$$

PDB: privacy dashboard; EXP: standard data export; EXP*: extended data export; PRI: privacy statement; LOG: logbook

We further found that, on average, 53% ($min = 27\%$, $max = 81\%$, $sd = 17\%$) of personal data listed in the respective privacy statements were accessible through dashboards. Yet we observed distinct differences between different groups of personal data (cf. Table 2). First, financial and contact data were complete for all providers, and basic demographic data were likewise complete apart from one exception. With regards to information about community and service interaction, seven dashboards were missing one or two categories of data, whereas three dashboards provided complete information. Interestingly, the former seven dashboards belonged to online services that processed less data about community and service interaction compared with the latter three online services. In terms of technical data, we found that no dashboard provided complete information and four dashboards even lacked this information altogether. In fact, on average, 96% ($min = 82\%$, $max = 100\%$, $sd = 6\%$) of all missing data belonged to the group of technical data.

Table 3. Summary of the completeness of personal data provided in privacy dashboards, data exports, and upon request for ten online services.

Online Service	Completeness of personal data by source							
	PDB		EXP		EXP*		Total	
Spotify	8/21	38% ◑	11/21	52% ◑	21/21	100% ●	21/21	100% ●
Deezer	8/19	42% ◑	8/19	42% ◑	same as EXP		10/19	52% ◐
Netflix	15/23	65% ◑	20/23	87% ◕	same as EXP		20/23	87% ◕
Rakuten TV	4/15	27% ◔	11/15	73% ◕	same as EXP		11/15	73% ◕
Facebook	22/37	59% ◑	30/37	81% ◕	same as EXP		30/37	81% ◕
LinkedIn	16/27	59% ◑	19/27	70% ◕	same as EXP		21/27	78% ◕
Zalando	7/18	39% ◑	5/18	28% ◔	11/18	61% ◑	12/18	67% ◕
Amazon	9/23	39% ◑	20/23	87% ◕	same as EXP		20/23	87% ◕
Google	22/27	81% ◕	22/27	81% ◕	same as EXP		23/27	85% ◕
Yahoo	19/27	70% ◕	19/27	70% ◕	same as EXP		23/27	85% ◕

$$\bullet = \frac{SRC \cap (PRI \cup LOG)}{(PRI \cup LOG)}, \ SRC \in \{PDB, EXP, EXP^*\}$$

PDB: privacy dashboard; EXP: standard data export; EXP*: extended data export;
PRI: privacy statement; LOG: logbook

Data Exports – Seven online services provided the data exports in a structured data format (JSON, CSV), whereas the remaining services responded with HTML, TXT, or PDF files. With regards to the response time, exports provided through download facilities in dashboards became available within a few hours or at the same day in four cases, whereas the other exports only became available after three to eight days. In case the export consisted of multiple parts, the second part became available between five and 16 days. Concerning formal requests for access, six online services responded within two days, whereas the others responded within 8 to 29 days.

We found that, on average, the default data exports contained 67% ($min = 27\%$, $max = 87\%$, $sd = 19\%$) of the categories of data mentioned by the respective privacy statement. The extended data exports, as provided by some online services, further increased the amount of data to 75% ($min = 42\%$, $max = 100\%$, $sd = 15\%$). However, responses to formal requests for access were more complete than standard exports in two cases only. With regards to the different groups of data, we found the following: Two exports each lacked data on personal preferences and contact data. Three exports also missed out on information about basic demographics, and four exports lacked data on community and service interaction. All but one export also lacked technical data. Concluding, only one controller, namely Spotify, provided complete information with respect to the categories of data listed in their privacy statement and our logbook.

Comparison of Exports and Dashboards – Overall, data exports contained 14% to 22% more personal data compared to privacy dashboards. Only in one case, the dashboard provided more data (cf. Table 3). Moreover, the data obtained via the separate sources differed. Exports containing the same amount or more data compared to dashboards did not necessarily contain all data provided by dashboards, and vice versa. In six cases, the union set of exports and dashboards yielded more data than the individual sources. In the remaining four cases, exports included all data available in dashboards. On average, exports contained 19% more technical data than dashboards. Nevertheless, dashboards contained more or the same amount of data for all other data categories (cf. Table 2).

5   Discussion

For as long as dashboards have existed, their purpose has been to make all the information required for a decision accessible to laypersons, preferably at a glance [12]. Certainly, this requires the careful selection of content in order to find the right amount of information required. The problem, however, is that the filtering of information is always done by experts, or as with privacy dashboards, by controllers. In order to ensure the objective of awareness of the right of access, it is therefore crucial that the information presented actually addresses the decision-making process of data subjects in a holistic manner. The numerous theories on decision-making about the privacy of online users under the research stream on the privacy paradox show that this may be difficult to achieve in practice [14]. Yet, with regards to the right of access, the well-known framework contextual integrity can act as a foundation [30]. Contextual integrity emphasizes on the appropriate flow of information based on a tuple comprising sender, data subject, recipient, data, and context. Taking into account social norms for a particular context, different transmission principles apply to a tuple. Consequently, people's privacy decision making process heavily rely on implicit rules. Applying this framework to our results, we find that the balancing of information is fair for some information provided by privacy dashboards, but also has some flaws for other information. Both aspects are discussed in the following sections.

5.1   Information About Purposes, Recipients, and Sources

Regarding recipients, it is probably fair to assume that users of online services are generally aware of public authorities and the corporate group to possibly become recipients of their personal data. Therefore, while their omission from privacy dashboards conflicts with legal requirements to disclose such information, it still seems plausible as to not overload dashboards with information. However, the omission of external recipients are grave enough to conclude that the examined tools undermine most online users' decision making processes. That is, ordinary online users have poor understanding of the online world [19] and simplified mental models let people overlook entities involved in the background of data processing routines, even if they are well aware of the processing in general [1,42]. For example, consumers may overlook service providers such as payment services who get hold of their personal data [1]. Moreover, while online users may be aware of their data being shared with the corporate group, they may be unaware of the different rules that apply to personal data processed outside the EU. Other information deficits relate to the lack of explicit purposes in privacy dashboards and the lack of details in privacy statements. This likely increases the sharing of sensitive data by consumers for purposes for which they do not want their data processed [34]. In contrast, a clear mapping between personal data and purposes, as implemented by Spotify and Deezer, would allow consumers to make informed choices that meet their protection goals. Furthermore, omitting data sources and technical data, but, at the same time, providing almost complete overview and access to user supplied data, pretends a false sender according to contextual integrity. The lack of use of simple but proven privacy patterns, such as personal data tables, which are well known to be very effective for such purposes and have been studied for years [39], constitutes a serious gap. Regarding the extensive functions that some online services made available to their users in the dashboards, it is therefore surprising to find that none of the providers simply displayed all the information in a clear manner in accordance with Art. 15 GDPR.

5.2 Information About Categories of Data

With regards to the information provided about categories of data, our findings are somewhat ambivalent. On the positive side, categories of data that users consciously disclosed themselves (e.g., contact information) or that relate to the main purpose of an online service were almost in all cases completely mapped in the dashboard. On the other hand, however, technical data were generally missing. This is problematic in that online users perceive many technical data such as IP addresses, device IDs, cookie data, and location data to be highly sensitive [25,36]. Also, online users are very concerned if such information is passed on to third-party providers, such as online advertisers [28]. For one thing, current privacy dashboards simply do not take into account much of the data classified as sensitive. On the other hand, it is of course questionable to what extent such information influences users in their data protection decisions. Nevertheless, this decision must not be made by online services. Awareness always requires complete information and therefore requires at least the visibility of the processing of numerous technical data. Thus, while making self-reported data accessible appears reasonable, this could be a false prioritization in terms of the actual perceived sensitivity of data. In this context, online providers can already rely on a plethora of TETs for making sensitive technical data transparent [29]. Here, of course, the effort required on the part of the controller must be weighed against the added value for data protection of providing real time copies of technical data. Clearly, complying with the GDPR must not jeopardize the availability of the actual services. The somewhat long response times of several days for data exports with technical data let us assume that the providing of such data cannot be achieved in real time. Yet this may not even be necessary for the purpose of awareness, since already visualizing the different amount of personal data supports online users in drawing conclusions about the processing [37]. Since technical data accounted for almost 40% of all personal data across all services examined, the current state represents a clear imbalance in information content.

Also, another problem constitutes the lack of self-reported data in privacy dashboards (e.g. community and service interaction) or data assumed to be present (e.g. personal preferences). In such cases, online services risk losing a considerable amount of trust among their customers [9,18]. Online services would be well advised to correct these deficiencies in order to counteract a loss of trust and at the same time provide users with more complete information.

5.3   Copy of Personal Data

Studies have shown that the usability of JSON documents is very poor, and, for lay users in particular, the use cases for the right of access are strictly limited to simple text searches [5]. Instead, visualizations of the data using graph views have been shown to facilitate understanding of recipients, sources, and data flow [3,5,13]. While some of these tools are available to the public[5], they are unlikely to be widely used in practice, since some users are ignorant about their rights [2], or may even refrain from downloading a copy of their personal data due to security concerns [21]. Either way, users expect tools for inspecting data to be provided by online services themselves [21]. It follows that providing structured documents without further ado and without any means to inspect the information offers little value to data subjects. Consequently, current practice reduces the principles of Art. 15 to absurdity, in particular with regards to Recital 63 GDPR claiming that exercising the right must be easy and should enable data subjects "to be aware of, and verify, the lawfulness of the processing." While data exports undoubtedly constitute an important instrument for self-determined privacy, the right to a copy of the data seems to offer little added value in its current form and interpretation. We argue that providing a copy of the data under Art. 15 should be distinct from exports under Art. 20, as they address fundamentally different concerns. To add value to the right to a copy of personal data for awareness, we argue, in line with other work [2,16], that online services should explain the information provided to strengthen the trust relationship with online users. We believe that privacy dashboards as knowledge conversion tools could serve as powerful tools in this regard too.

---

[5] https://transparency-vis.vx.igd.fraunhofer.de/.

6   Ethical Considerations

In the scope of this work we never tried to get hold of any personal data of any natural person other than the authors of this work. However, since our formal request for access involved interaction with people working for the different online services, we identified possible ethical issues. We did not collect nor analyze any of our respondents' personal data. Furthermore, we were only interested in receiving a copy of the personal data processed. If we found discrepancies between data exports and data protection statements, we disclosed this in mail correspondence. We therefore see no need to explicitly report our investigations to the providers again.

7   Limitations and Outlook

Our case study of privacy dashboards from ten online services certainly represents only a small subset of all online services frequently used in practice. However, when selecting these services we found that extensive privacy tools are not yet widely available, which limits the number of possible candidates. Our investigation also already included some of the most popular online services for the most common online activities in the EU. Since we also found the same discrepancies for missing information between privacy dashboards, data exports, and privacy statements from market leaders as well as from less popular providers, we believe that our results offer a solid basis for future quantitative analysis. Yet, privacy dashboard analyses can likely only be conducted qualitatively in the foreseeable future, since it requires manual inspection of UI elements. Different though, automatized verification checks based on privacy statements and data exports would already be possible using the tools available. For example, existing inspection tools for data exports may make users aware of missing categories of data, utilizing deep learning capabilities to automatically extract and compare information from privacy statements and data exports [17].

Furthermore, we did not verify whether personal data were missing from the privacy statements, that is, whether a provider processed more categories of personal data than specified in the statement. Nevertheless, our results indicate that already now controllers have difficulties providing complete information.

Last but not least, our evaluation of privacy dashboards was conducted by experts. Real online users may actually perceive the information provided differently, and future studies should examine in how far privacy dashboards actually make users aware of purposes, recipient, sources, and categories of data.

8   Conclusion

Privacy dashboards are promising tools to meet legal obligations for providing transparency and intervention mechanisms to data subjects, and to ease the exercise of their rights [5,33,35]. However, our review of ten online services indicates that the extent to which real-world implementations already address the right of access is insufficient at present. Despite our small sample, we found rather clear and systematic differences for the amount and completeness of information provided concerning different subjects covered by Art. 15 GDPR. In particular, we found that information about storage period and safeguards were generally missing, while information about data sources, recipients, and technical data were at least incomplete. In contrast, however, information about personal data entered by data subjects themselves were mostly complete, accessible, and editable. Aside from the limited information provided in privacy dashboards, our findings also suggest that the current implementation of the right of access itself is flawed, since only one of ten online services provided a complete copy of personal data with respect to their own privacy statement. Also, for users to become aware of the extent to which their data are processed, they would need to combine the information from privacy dashboards and data exports in most cases. Nevertheless, the objective of Art. 15 to increase awareness would not be achieved because both sources lack some information that is considered highly sensitive by users. Online services should address this issue in order not to lose the trust of their customers. Furthermore, it seems unreasonable to provide incomplete information via several different channels. We therefore advocate – in context of Art. 15 – replacing or at least supplementing the provision of less user-friendly JSON and CSV file downloads with better and complete preparation of the data in the privacy dashboards themselves. Here, it is the developers' task to integrate the tools provided and evaluated by the scientific community. In doing so, they should consider the extent to which all legally required information can be provided and be considerably more cautious in deciding to omit information. Moreover, while the provision of structured data formats is essential for the right to data portability, the usefulness of such copies in the context of Art. 15 is questionable, as they do not effectively facilitate the understanding of personal data processing without appropriate tools. Therefore, in order to facilitate the exercise of the right of access, policymakers should consider clearly separating the concerns of Art. 15 and Art. 20 and emphasize the need to provide copies under Art. 15 in an intelligible manner.

References

1. Acquisti, A., Grossklags, J.: Privacy and rationality in individual decision making. IEEE Secur. Priv. **3**(1), 26–33 (2005). https://doi.org/10.1109/MSP.2005.22
2. Alizadeh, F., Jakobi, T., Boden, A., Stevens, G., Boldt, J.: GDPR reality check - claiming and investigating personally identifiable data from companies. In: 2020 IEEE European Symposium on Security and Privacy Workshops (EuroSPW), pp. 120–129. IEEE (2020). https://doi.org/10.1109/EuroSPW51379.2020.00025
3. Angulo, J., Fischer-Hübner, S., Pulls, T., Wästlund, E.: Usable transparency with the data track: a tool for visualizing data disclosures. In: Proceedings of the 33rd Annual ACM Conference Extended Abstracts on Human Factors in Computing Systems, pp. 1803–1808. Association for Computing Machinery (2015). https://doi.org/10.1145/2702613.2732701

4. Arfelt, E., Basin, D., Debois, S.: Monitoring the GDPR. In: Sako, K., Schneider, S., Ryan, P.Y.A. (eds.) ESORICS 2019. LNCS, vol. 11735, pp. 681–699. Springer, Cham (2019). https://doi.org/10.1007/978-3-030-29959-0_33

5. Bier, C., Kühne, K., Beyerer, J.: PrivacyInsight: the next generation privacy dashboard. In: Schiffner, S., Serna, J., Ikonomou, D., Rannenberg, K. (eds.) APF 2016. LNCS, vol. 9857, pp. 135–152. Springer, Cham (2016). https://doi.org/10.1007/978-3-319-44760-5_9

6. Boniface, C., Fouad, I., Bielova, N., Lauradoux, C., Santos, C.: Security analysis of subject access request procedures. In: Naldi, M., Italiano, G.F., Rannenberg, K., Medina, M., Bourka, A. (eds.) APF 2019. LNCS, vol. 11498, pp. 182–209. Springer, Cham (2019). https://doi.org/10.1007/978-3-030-21752-5_12

7. Buchmann, J., Nebel, M., Roßnagel, A., Shirazi, F., Simo, H., Waidner, M.: Personal information dashboard: putting the individual back in control. In: Digital Enlightenment Yearbook 2013, pp. 139–164. IOS Press (2013)

8. Bufalieri, L., Morgia, M.L., Mei, A., Stefa, J.: GDPR: when the right to access personal data becomes a threat. In: 2020 IEEE International Conference on Web Services (ICWS), pp. 75–83 (2020). https://doi.org/10.1109/ICWS49710.2020.00017

9. Cabinakova, J., Zimmermann, C., Mueller, G.: An empirical analysis of privacy dashboard acceptance: the google case. In: Proceeding of the 24th European Conference on Information Systems (ECIS). Research Papers, vol. 114, pp. 1–18. AIS Electronic Library (AISeL) (2016)

10. Cagnazzo, M., Holz, T., Pohlmann, N.: GDPiRated – stealing personal information on- and offline. In: Sako, K., Schneider, S., Ryan, P.Y.A. (eds.) ESORICS 2019. LNCS, vol. 11736, pp. 367–386. Springer, Cham (2019). https://doi.org/10.1007/978-3-030-29962-0_18

11. European Parliament and Council of European Union: Regulation (EU) 2016/679 (2016). https://eur-lex.europa.eu/legal-content/EN/TXT/HTML/?uri=CELEX:32016R0679&from=EN

12. Few, S.: Information Dashboard Design: The Effective Visual Communication of Data. O'Reilly Media, Inc. (2006)

13. Fischer-Hübner, S., Angulo, J., Pulls, T.: How can cloud users be supported in deciding on, tracking and controlling how their data are used? In: Hansen, M., Hoepman, J.-H., Leenes, R., Whitehouse, D. (eds.) Privacy and Identity 2013. IAICT, vol. 421, pp. 77–92. Springer, Heidelberg (2014). https://doi.org/10.1007/978-3-642-55137-6_6

14. Gerber, N., Gerber, P., Volkamer, M.: Explaining the privacy paradox: a systematic review of literature investigating privacy attitude and behavior. Comput. Secur. **77**, 226–261 (2018). https://doi.org/10.1016/j.cose.2018.04.002

15. Gluck, J., et al.: How short is too short? Implications of length and framing on the effectiveness of privacy notices. In: 12th Symposium on Usable Privacy and Security (SOUPS), pp. 321–340. USENIX Association (2016)

16. Goodman, B., Flaxman, S.: European union regulations on algorithmic decision-making and a "Right to Explanation". AI Mag. **38**(3), 50–57 (2017). https://doi.org/10.1609/aimag.v38i3.2741

17. Harkous, H., Fawaz, K., Lebret, R., Schaub, F., Shin, K.G., Aberer, K.: Polisis: automated analysis and presentation of privacy policies using deep learning. In: 27th USENIX Security Symposium (USENIX Security), pp. 531–548. USENIX Association (2018)

18. Herder, E., van Maaren, O.: Privacy dashboards: the impact of the type of personal data and user control on trust and perceived risk. In: Adjunct Publication of the 28th ACM Conference on User Modeling, Adaptation and Personalization (UMAP), pp. 169–174. Association for Computing Machinery (2020). https://doi.org/10.1145/3386392.3399557

19. Kang, R., Dabbish, L., Fruchter, N., Kiesler, S.: "My data just goes everywhere:" user mental models of the internet and implications for privacy and security. In: 11th Symposium On Usable Privacy and Security (SOUPS), pp. 39–52. USENIX Association (2015)

20. Kani-Zabihi, E., Helmhout, M.: Increasing service users' privacy awareness by introducing on-line interactive privacy features. In: Laud, P. (ed.) NordSec 2011. LNCS, vol. 7161, pp. 131–148. Springer, Heidelberg (2012). https://doi.org/10.1007/978-3-642-29615-4_10

21. Karegar, F., Pulls, T., Fischer-Hübner, S.: Visualizing exports of personal data by exercising the right of data portability in the data track - are people ready for this? In: Lehmann, A., Whitehouse, D., Fischer-Hübner, S., Fritsch, L., Raab, C. (eds.) Privacy and Identity 2016. IAICT, vol. 498, pp. 164–181. Springer, Cham (2016). https://doi.org/10.1007/978-3-319-55783-0_12

22. Kolter, J., Netter, M., Pernul, G.: Visualizing past personal data disclosures. In: 2010 International Conference on Availability, Reliability and Security (ARES), pp. 131–139. IEEE (2010). https://doi.org/10.1109/ARES.2010.51

23. Le Pochat, V., Van Goethem, T., Tajalizadehkhoob, S., Korczyński, M., Joosen, W.: Tranco: a research-oriented top sites ranking hardened against manipulation. In: Proceedings of the 26th Annual Network and Distributed System Security Symposium (NDSS). The Internet Society (2019)

24. Mannhardt, F., Oliveira, M., Petersen, S.A.: Designing a privacy dashboard for a smart manufacturing environment. In: Pappas, I.O., Mikalef, P., Dwivedi, Y.K., Jaccheri, L., Krogstie, J., Mäntymäki, M. (eds.) I3E 2019. IAICT, vol. 573, pp. 79–85. Springer, Cham (2020). https://doi.org/10.1007/978-3-030-39634-3_8

25. Markos, E., Milne, G.R., Peltier, J.W.: Information sensitivity and willingness to provide continua: a comparative privacy study of the United States and Brazil. J. Public Policy Market. **36**(1), 79–96 (2017). https://doi.org/10.1509/jppm.15.159

26. Martino, M.D., Robyns, P., Weyts, W., Quax, P., Lamotte, W., Andries, K.: Personal information leakage by abusing the GDPR 'Right of Access'. In: 15th USENIX Symposium on Usable Privacy and Security (SOUPS). USENIX Association (2019)

27. Matzutt, R., et al.: myneData: towards a trusted and user-controlled ecosystem for sharing personal data. In: 47. Jahrestagung Der Gesellschaft Für Informatik, pp. 1073–1084 (2017). https://doi.org/10.18420/in2017_109

28. Milne, G.R., Pettinico, G., Hajjat, F.M., Markos, E.: Information sensitivity typology: mapping the degree and type of risk consumers perceive in personal data sharing. J. Consum. Aff. **51**(1), 133–161 (2017). https://doi.org/10.1111/joca.12111

29. Murmann, P., Fischer-Hübner, S.: Tools for achieving usable ex post transparency: a survey. IEEE Access **5**, 22965–22991 (2017). https://doi.org/10.1109/ACCESS.2017.2765539

30. Nissenbaum, H.: Privacy as contextual integrity. Washington Law Rev. **79**(1), 1119–157 (2004)

31. Pavur, J., Knerr, C.: GDPArrrrr: Using Privacy Laws to Steal Identities. arXiv:1912.00731 [cs] (2019)

32. Polst, S., Kelbert, P., Feth, D.: Company privacy dashboards: employee needs and requirements. In: Moallem, A. (ed.) HCII 2019. LNCS, vol. 11594, pp. 429–440. Springer, Cham (2019). https://doi.org/10.1007/978-3-030-22351-9_29

33. Popescu, A., et al.: Increasing transparency and privacy for online social network users – USEMP value model, scoring framework and legal. In: Berendt, B., Engel, T., Ikonomou, D., Le Métayer, D., Schiffner, S. (eds.) APF 2015. LNCS, vol. 9484, pp. 38–59. Springer, Cham (2016). https://doi.org/10.1007/978-3-319-31456-3_3

34. Presthus, W., Sørum, H.: Consumer perspectives on information privacy following the implementation of the GDPR. Int. J. Inf. Syst. Project Manag. (IJISPM) **7**(3), 19–34 (2019)

35. Raschke, P., Küpper, A., Drozd, O., Kirrane, S.: Designing a GDPR-compliant and usable privacy dashboard. In: Hansen, M., Kosta, E., Nai-Fovino, I., Fischer-Hübner, S. (eds.) Privacy and Identity 2017. IAICT, vol. 526, pp. 221–236. Springer, Cham (2018). https://doi.org/10.1007/978-3-319-92925-5_14

36. Schomakers, E.M., Lidynia, C., Müllmann, D., Ziefle, M.: Internet users' perceptions of information sensitivity - insights from Germany. Int. J. Inf. Manag. **46**, 142–150 (2019). https://doi.org/10.1016/j.ijinfomgt.2018.11.018

37. Schufrin, M., Reynolds, S.L., Kuijper, A., Kohlhammer, J.: A visualization interface to improve the transparency of collected personal data on the internet. IEEE Trans. Vis. Comput. Graph. **27**(2), 1840–1849 (2021). https://doi.org/10.1109/TVCG.2020.3028946

38. Scudder, J., Jøsang, A.: Personal federation control with the identity dashboard. In: de Leeuw, E., Fischer-Hübner, S., Fritsch, L. (eds.) IDMAN 2010. IAICT, vol. 343, pp. 85–99. Springer, Heidelberg (2010). https://doi.org/10.1007/978-3-642-17303-5_7

39. Siljee, J.: Privacy transparency patterns. In: Proceedings of the 20th ACM European Conference on Pattern Languages of Programs (EuroPLoP), pp. 1–11. ACM (2015). https://doi.org/10.1145/2855321.2855374

40. The European Comission: ICT usage in households and by individuals. Technical report, The European Union (2019). https://ec.europa.eu/eurostat/cache/metadata/en/isoc_i_esms.htm

41. The European Comission: Digital Economy and Society Index (DESI) 2020 - Use of internet services. Technical report. DESI 2020, The European Union (2020). https://ec.europa.eu/digital-single-market/en/use-internet-and-online-activities

42. Tolsdorf, J., Dehling, F.: In our employer we trust: mental models of office workers' privacy perceptions. In: Bernhard, M., et al. (eds.) FC 2020. LNCS, vol. 12063, pp. 122–136. Springer, Cham (2020). https://doi.org/10.1007/978-3-030-54455-3_9

43. Tolsdorf, J., Dehling, F., Lo Iacono, L.: Take back control! the use of mental models to develop privacy dashboards. ITG News **8**(3), 15–20 (2020)

44. Urban, T., Tatang, D., Degeling, M., Holz, T., Pohlmann, N.: A study on subject data access in online advertising after the GDPR. In: Pérez-Solà, C., Navarro-Arribas, G., Biryukov, A., Garcia-Alfaro, J. (eds.) DPM/CBT -2019. LNCS, vol. 11737, pp. 61–79. Springer, Cham (2019). https://doi.org/10.1007/978-3-030-31500-9_5

45. Utz, C., Degeling, M., Fahl, S., Schaub, F., Holz, T.: (un)informed consent: studying GDPR consent notices in the field. In: Proceedings of the 26th ACM SIGSAC Conference on Computer and Communications Security (CCS), pp. 973–990. Association for Computing Machinery (2019). https://doi.org/10.1145/3319535.3354212

46. Wilson, S., et al.: Crowdsourcing annotations for websites' privacy policies: can it really work? In: Proceedings of the 25th International Conference on World Wide Web (WWW), pp. 133–143. International World Wide Web Conferences Steering Committee (2016). https://doi.org/10.1145/2872427.2883035
47. Wong, J., Henderson, T.: How portable is portable? Exercising the GDPR's right to data portability. In: Proceedings of the 2018 ACM International Joint Conference and 2018 International Symposium on Pervasive and Ubiquitous Computing and Wearable Computers (UbiComp), pp. 911–920. Association for Computing Machinery (2018)
48. Zimmermann, C., Accorsi, R., Müller, G.: Privacy dashboards: reconciling data-driven business models and privacy. In: Proceedings of the 9th International Conference on Availability, Reliability and Security (ARES), pp. 152–157. IEEE Computer Society (2014). https://doi.org/10.1109/ARES.2014.27

Consent Management Platforms Under the GDPR: Processors and/or Controllers?

Cristiana Santos[2]([✉]), Midas Nouwens[3], Michael Toth[1], Nataliia Bielova[1], and Vincent Roca[1]

[1] Inria, Paris, France
{michael.toth,nataliia.bielova,vincent.roca}@inria.fr
[2] Utrecht University, Utrecht, The Netherlands
c.teixeirasantos@uu.nl
[3] Aarhus University, Aarhus, Denmark
midasnouwens@cc.au.dk

Abstract. Consent Management Providers (CMPs) provide consent pop-ups that are embedded in ever more websites over time to enable streamlined compliance with the legal requirements for consent mandated by the ePrivacy Directive and the General Data Protection Regulation (GDPR). They implement the standard for consent collection from the Transparency and Consent Framework (TCF) (current version v2.0) proposed by the European branch of the Interactive Advertising Bureau (IAB Europe). Although the IAB's TCF specifications characterize CMPs as data processors, CMPs factual activities often qualifies them as data controllers instead. Discerning their clear role is crucial since compliance obligations and CMPs liability depend on their accurate characterization. We perform empirical experiments with two major CMP providers in the EU: Quantcast and OneTrust and paired with a legal analysis. We conclude that CMPs process personal data, and we identify multiple scenarios wherein CMPs are controllers.

Keywords: Consent management providers · IAB Europe TCF · Data controllers · GDPR · Consent

1 Introduction

To comply with the General Data Protection Regulation (GDPR) [31] and the ePrivacy Directive (ePD) [20], a website owner needs to first obtain *consent* from users, and only then is allowed to process personal data when offering goods and services and/or monitoring the users' behavior. As a result, numerous companies have started providing *"Consent as a Service"* solutions to help website owners ensure legal compliance [60].

A preliminary version of this paper is presented for discussion only, with no official proceedings at ConPro'21: https://www.ieee-security.org/TC/SPW2021/ConPro/.

© Springer Nature Switzerland AG 2021
N. Gruschka et al. (Eds.): APF 2021, LNCS 12703, pp. 47–69, 2021.
https://doi.org/10.1007/978-3-030-76663-4_3

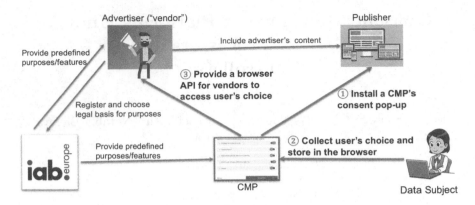

Fig. 1. Actors under IAB Europe TCF ecosystem: IAB Europe, Advertisers (called "endors"), Consent Management Providers (CMPs), Publishers, Data Subjects. The IAB Europe defines the purposes and features that are shown to users. Registered vendors declare purposes and legal basis and the features upon which they rely. CMPs provide consent pop-up, store the user's choice as a browser cookie, and provide an API for advertisers to access this information.

To standardise[1] the technical implementation of these consent pop-ups, the European branch of the Interactive Advertising Bureau (IAB Europe), an industry organisation made up of most major advertising companies in the EU, developed a Transparency and Consent Framework (TCF) [38]. This framework (currently on version 2.0) was developed to preserve the exchange of data within the advertising ecosystem, which now requires being able to demonstrate how, when, from who, and on which legal basis that data is collected. The actors in this ecosystem are IAB Europe, advertisers (called "vendors"), Consent Management Providers (CMPs), publishers, and data subjects (see Fig. 1).

Although recent work has started to address the complex technical and legal aspects of the IAB Europe TCF ecosystem [6,19,35,47,48,50,52], *neither prior work nor court decisions* have so far discussed the role of the CMPs. Therefore, it is currently unclear what the role of these CMPs is under the GDPR, and consequently what their legal requirements and liabilities are.

This paper examines if and when CMPs can be considered a *data controller* – i.e., an actor responsible for determining the purposes and means of the processing of personal data (Art. 4(7) GDPR) – or a *data processor* – i.e., an actor which processes personal data on behalf of the controller (Art. 4(8) GDPR).

Discerning the correct positioning of CMPs is crucial since compliance measures and CMPs liability depend on their accurate characterization (GDPR Recital 79). To determine the role of CMPs under the GDPR, in this paper we answer the following research questions:

Section 2 When are CMPs processing personal data?

---

[1] Standardization is used within the meaning of streamline at scale consent implementation.

Section 3 When do CMPs act as data processors?
Section 4 When do CMPs act as data controllers?

Note that the TCF is a voluntary framework: not all CMPs are part of it and abide by its policies. However, it has become a *de facto* standard used by a growing number of actors [35, Fig. 6]. This means that focusing on the CMPs within this ecosystem provides results that can more easily be generalised, compared to looking at the specific implementations of individual CMPs. Whenever we refer to CMPs in the rest of the article, we are referring to CMPs registered as part of the IAB Europe TCF. Our argumentation is based on:

- legal analysis of binding legal sources (GDPR and case-law) and relevant data protection guidelines from the European Data Protection Board and Data Protection Authorities, document analysis of the IAB Europe TCF,
- empirical data gathered on our own website by deploying Quantcast and OneTrust – the two most popular CMPs in the EU, found respectively on 38.3% and 16.3% of the websites with a EU or UK TLD analyzed by Hils et al. [35].

A legal analysis is done by a co-author with expertise in Data Protection Law, and a technical analysis by Computer Science co-authors.

In this paper, we make the following **contributions**:

- we conclude that CMPs process personal data,
- we analyse what exact behavior qualifies a CMP as a processor,
- we identify several scenarios wherein CMPs can qualify as controllers, and
- we provide recommendations for policymakers.

2 When are CMPs Processing Personal Data?

The *raison d'être* of CMPs is to collect, store, and share a *Consent Signal* [21,38] of a data subject. The Consent Signal is a text-based digital representation of the user's consent in a standardised format, stored in the user's browser, and provided to third-party vendors by the CMP [38, paragraph 17, page 9]. Before discussing whether a CMP can be considered a data controller or processor, we first need to establish whether it even falls under the GDPR, which depends on whether it can be considered to process personal data. To answer this question, we first explain the definition of personal data under the GDPR, and then investigate which data CMPs process in practice and whether such data qualifies as personal data.

2.1 Legal Definitions

Personal data is *"any information relating to an identified or identifiable natural person ('data subject'). An identifiable natural person is one who can be identified, directly or indirectly. In particular by reference to an identifier such as a name, an identification number, location data, an online identifier or to one* *or more factors specific to the physical, physiological, genetic, mental, economic, cultural or social identity of that natural person"* (Article 4(11) GDPR [31]). Recital 30 asserts that online identifiers provided by their devices, such as IP addresses, can be associated to a person, thus making them identifiable.

Processing consists of *"any operation or set of operations which is performed on personal data or on sets of personal data, whether or not by automated means, such as collection, recording, organisation, structuring, storage, adaptation or alteration, retrieval, consultation, use, disclosure by transmission, dissemination or otherwise making available, alignment or combination, restriction, erasure or destruction"* (Article 4(2) GDPR). In practice, this means that almost any imaginable handling of personal data constitutes processing [2].

2.2   Mapping Legal Definitions into Practice

Consent Signal. CMPs provide a consent pop-up, encode the user's choice in a Transparency and Consent (TC) string[2], store this value in a user's browser and provide an API for advertisers to access this information.

IAB Europe TCF specifies that when Consent Signal is "globally-scoped" (shared by CMPs running on different websites), the Consent Signal must be stored in a third-party cookie `euconsent-v2` set with `.consensu.org` domain.

CMPs who register at IAB Europe TCF are provided with a subdomain `<cmp-name>.mgr.consensu.org` that is "delegated by the Managing Organisation (IAB Europe) to each CMP" [37]. "Globally-scoped" Consent Signal allows all CMPs who manage content on their `<cmp-name>.mgr.consensu.org` domains to also have access to the Consent Signal that is automatically attached to every request sent to any subdomain of `.consensu.org`. As a result, other consent pop up providers, who are not registered at IAB Europe, are not in a position to receive the Consent Signal stored in the user's browser because they have no access to any subdomain of `.consensu.org`, owned by IAB Europe. For non-global consent, a CMP can freely choose which browser storage to use for Consent Signal [37]. The Consent Signal contains a non human-readable encoded version (base64 encoded) of:

- the list of purposes and features the user consented to;
- the list of third-party vendors the user consented for;
- the CMP identifier and version, together with other meta-data.

IP Address. While the Consent Signal does not seem to contain personal data, CMPs additionally have access to the user's IP address. In order to include a consent pop-up, publishers are asked to integrate in their website a JavaScript code of a CMP (see step (1) in Fig. 1). Such code is responsible for the implementation of a consent pop-up and in practice is loaded either: (1) directly from the server owned by a CMP (OneTrust's banner is loaded from the OneTrust's domain https://cmp-cdn.cookielaw.org), or (2) from the server

---

[2] For the sake of uniformity, we call it "Consent Signal" in the rest of the paper.

`<cmp-name>.mgr.consensu.org` "delegated by the Managing Organisation (IAB Europe) to each CMP" [37] (Quantcast's script for consent pop-up is loaded from https://quantcast.mgr.consensu.org).

As an inevitable consequence of an HTTP(S) request, the server (of a CMP or controlled by a CMP via a DNS delegation by IAB Europe) is thus able to access the IP address of a visitor in this process. Additionally, CMP declare in their privacy policies the collection of IP addresses [57, ?]. Therefore, from a technical point of view, a CMP is able to record the IP address of the user's terminal in order to fulfil its service. Hereby we conclude that CMPs can have access to the user's IP address.

An IP address can be a cornerstone for data aggregation or identifying individuals. Empirical studies [46,49] found that a user can, over time, get assigned a set of IP addresses which are unique and stable. Mishra et al. [49] found that 87% of users (out of 2,230 users over a study period of 111 days) retain at least one IP address for more than a month. 2% of user's IP addresses did not change for more than 100 days, and 70% of users had at least one IP address constant for more than 2 months. These assertions render IP addresses as a relatively reliable and robust way to identify a user.

Even though these results denote IP address stability (specially static IP addresses), the data protection community and case law diverge in the understanding of "dynamic" IP addresses as personal data. An IP address would be personal data if it relates to an *identified* or *identifiable* person. It was decided [14] that a dynamic IP address (temporarily assigned to a device) is not necessarily information related to an *identified* person, due to the fact that "such an address does not directly reveal the identity of the person who owns the computer from which a website was accessed, or that of another person who might use that computer".

The question that follows is *whether an IP address relates to an identifiable person for this IP address* to be considered personal data. In order to determine whether a person is *identifiable*, account should be taken of *all the means that can reasonably be used* by any entity to identify that person (Recital 26 GDPR). This risk-based approach [14,28] means that anyone possessing the means to identify a user, renders such a user identifiable. Accordingly, CMPs have the means to collect IP addresses (as declared in their privacy policies) and to combine all the information relating to an identifiable person, rendering that combined information (IP address and, in some cases, Consent Signal) personal data.

Since identifiability of a person depends heavily on context, one should also take into account any other reasonable means CMPs have access to, for example, based on their role and market position in the overall advertising ecosystem [28]. One important aspect to consider, then, is the fact that these CMP providers can simultaneously also play a role as an advertising vendor, receiving the Consent Signal provided by their own CMP and (if positive) the personal data of the website visitor. Quantcast, for example, appears in the Global Vendor List (GVL) [39] as registered vendor #11. In the consent pop-up, their Privacy Policy [57], and their Terms of Service [55,56], Quantcast mentions a large number of purposes for processing personal data, such as "Create a personalised ads profile", "Technically deliver ads or content", and "Match and combine offline data sources". The Evidon Company Directory [27] labels Quantcast as "Business Intelligence, Data Aggregator/Supplier, Mobile, Retargeter", and also mentions a large list of possible personal data collection from them. According to the same source, Quantcast also owns a retargeter called Struq. In view of this fact, CMPs seem to have reasonable means to combine information relating to an identifiable person, rendering that information personal data.

Summary. Although a Consent Signal itself does not seem to contain personal data, when the consent pop-up script is fetched from a CMP-controlled server, the CMP also processes the user's IP address, which the GDPR explicitly mentions as personal data. The possibility to combine both types of data renders a user identifiable. This possibility becomes particularly pertinent whenever a CMP also plays the role of a data vendor in the advertising ecosystem, which gives them access to more data that could be combined and increase the identifiability of a user.

3 When are CMPs Data Processors?

3.1 Legal Definitions

A **processor** is an actor that processes personal data *on behalf* of the controller (Article 4 (8) GDPR). The relevant criteria that define this role are: (i) a dependence on the controller's instructions regarding processing activities [2], (Art. 28(3)(a)), Recital 81), and; (ii) a compliance with those instructions [26], which means they are not allowed to go beyond what they are asked to do by the controller [26].

3.2 Mapping Legal Definitions into Practice

The main objectives of CMPs clearly correspond to the definition of data processors, because they act according to the instructions given by the website publisher with regards to the legal bases, purposes, special features, and/or vendors to show to the user in the consent pop-up. IAB Europe TCF also explicitly defines CMPs as data processors in the TCF documentation [38, page 10 (paragraph 8), page 11 (paragraph 11)]. The classification of the CMP as data processors is currently the widely shared consensus about their role.

Responsibility of CMPs as Processors. If a CMP is established as a data processor, it can be held liable and fined if it fails to comply with its obligations under the GDPR (Articles 28(3)(f) and 32–36 GDPR). Moreover, if a false Consent Signal is stored and transmitted, it may well be considered an "unauthorised disclosure of, or access to personal data transmitted, stored or otherwise processed" [31, Art. 32(2)].

Recent works reported numerous CMPs violating the legal requirements for a valid positive consent signal under the GDPR. For example, researchers detected pre-ticked boxes [48,50], refusal being harder than acceptance [50] or not possible at all [48], choices of users not being respected [48], as well as more fine-grained configuration barriers such as aesthetic manipulation [33, Fig. 11], framing and false hierarchy [33, Fig. 12].

4   When are CMPs Data Controllers?

In this section we analyse when CMPs are data controllers. Firstly, in Sect. 4.1 we provide the legal definitions necessary to qualify CMPs as data controllers.

In the following Sects. (4.2–4.5) we will map these legal definitions into practice. Although CMPs are explicitly designated as processors by the IAB Europe TCF specifications [38], we analyse four functional activities of CMPs that enables their qualification as data controllers. We include a technical description of such activities followed by a legal analysis. These activities refer to:

Section 4.2 Including additional processing activities in their tools beyond those specified by the IAB Europe;
Section 4.3 Scanning publisher websites for tracking technologies and sorting them into purpose categories;
Section 4.4 Controlling third-party vendors included by CMPs;
Section 4.5 Deploying manipulative design strategies in the UI of consent pop-ups.

Finally, in Sect. 4.6 we determine the responsibility of a CMPs as data controllers.

4.1   Legal Definitions

The primary factor defining a **controller** is that it "determines the purposes and means of the processing of personal data" (Article 4(7) GDPR). We refer to the European Data Protection Board (EDPB) opinion [2] to unpack what is meant by 1) "determines", and 2) "purposes and means of the processing of personal data".

"Determines' refers to having the "determinative influence", "decision-making power" [2,22,26] or "independent control" [40] over the purposes and means of the processing. This concept of "determination" provides some degree of flexibility (to be adapted to complex environments) and the Court of Justice of the EU (CJEU), Data Protection Authorities (DPAs) and the EDPB describe that such control can be derived from:

– professional competence (legal or implicit) [2];
– factual influence based on factual circumstances surrounding the processing. (e.g. to contracts, and real interactions) [2];
– image given to data subjects and their reasonable expectations on the basis of this visibility [2];

- which actor *"organizes, coordinates and encourages"* data processing [22] (paragraphs 70, 71);
- interpretation or independent judgement exercised to perform a professional service [40].

"Purposes" and "means" refer to "why" data is processed (purposes) and "how" the objectives of processing are achieved (means). Regarding the determination of "purposes", the GDPR merely refers that purposes need to be explicit, specified and legitimate (Article 5(1)(b) [30]. In relation to the determination of "means", the EDPB distinguishes between "essential" and "non-essential means" and provides examples thereof [2,26]:

- "Essential means" are inherently reserved to the controller; examples are: determining the i) type of personal data processed, ii) duration of processing, iii) recipients, and iv) categories of data subjects;
- "Non-essential means" may be delegated to the processor to decide upon, and concern the practical aspects of implementation, such as: i) choice for a particular type of hardware or software, ii) security measures, iii) methods to store or retrieve data.

Important notes on the assessment of controllers are referred herewith. The role of controller and processor are *functional* concepts [26]: the designation of an actor as one or the other is derived from their *factual roles and activities* in a specific situation [2], rather than from their formal designation [3]. Notably, access to personal data is not a necessary condition to be a controller [23,24]. Moreover, the control exercised by a data controller may extend to the entirety of processing at issue, and also be limited to *a particular stage in the processing* [23].

4.2   Inclusion of Additional Processing Activities

Technical Description. When publishers employ the services of a CMP to manage consent on their website, the CMP provides the publisher with the necessary code to add their consent solution to the website. Although this code is ostensibly only for managing consent, it is possible for the CMP to also include other functionality.

As part of our empirical data gathering, we assumed the role of website owner (i.e., publisher) and installed a QuantCast CMP [53] on an empty website. Website owners are instructed by the CMP to "copy and paste the full tag" into their website header and "avoid modifying the tag as changes may prevent the CMP from working properly." [58]: the tag is the minimal amount of code necessary to load the rest of the consent management platform from an external source.

When installing the Quantcast CMP, we discovered that the "Quantcast Tag" script that deploys a consent pop-up on the website also loads a further script `choice.js` that integrates a 1×1 invisible image loaded from the domain `pixel.quantserve.com` (see Fig. 2). When this image is loaded, it also sets a third-party cookie `mc` in the user's browser. By replicating the methodology to

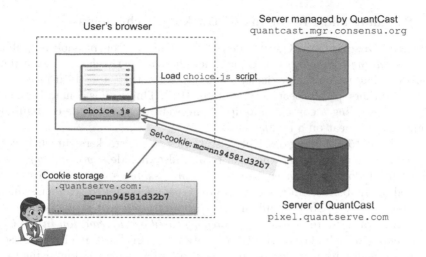

Fig. 2. Loading of invisible pixel by a QuantCast consent pop-up: the pixel sets a third-party cookie `mc` with a user-specific identifier that is further accessible to all subdomains of `quantserve.com`.

detect trackers [29], we analysed the `mc` cookie from `pixel.quantserve.com`; this cookie is *"user-specific"* – that is, its value is different for different website visitors – and comes from a third-party, allowing tracking across all sites where some content from `quantserve.com` or its subdomains is present. Such tracking by `quantserve.com` is prevalent in practice: recent research shows that third-party trackers from QuantCast are in top-10 tracking domains included by other trackers on 9K most popular websites [29, Fig. 6].

In the documentation that describes the QuantCast CMP, they mention that their CMP also contains a "QuantCast Measure" product [58] that is labeled as *"audience, insight and analytics tool"* for *"better understanding of audience"* [59]. The `mc` cookie we detected is the only cookie present on our empty website *before interacting with the QuantCast pop-up*, and thus we conclude that this cookie is likely responsible for the audience measurement purpose of QuantCast.

Legal Analysis. The QuantCast script installs *both a consent pop-up and a tracking cookie*, and its technical implementation makes it impossible for website owners to split these two functionalities. Such joint functionality triggers consequences on its legal status. The tracking cookie enables the QuantCast CMP to process data for its own tracking and measurement purposes, regardless of any instructions from the publisher, nor from the specifications of the IAB Europe TCF. Hence, the independent and determinative influence of a CMP is based on factual circumstances surrounding the processing, which qualifies a CMP in this scenario as a data controller.

4.3   Scanning and Pre-sorting of Tracking Technologies

Technical Description. One of the services CMPs often provide to publishers is a *scanning technology* which identifies the tracking technologies currently installed and active on the publisher's website (e.g., "first- and third-party cookies, tags, trackers, pixels, beacons and more" [12]). This scan is generally the first step when installing a consent pop-up on the website, and can be configured to automatically repeat on a regular basis.

In addition to providing descriptive statistics on the trackers currently active (e.g., what type of tracking), the scan results also include a *pre-sorting* of each of these technologies *into a particular data processing category* which are then displayed in the banner. In the case of OneTrust's CookiePro scanner, which is integrated into the banner configuration procedure when it is performed with an account, trackers are *"assigned a Category based on information in the Cookiepedia database"* [10,11] (a service operated by OneTrust itself). The scanning includes identifying trackers (and matching them with vendors using Cookiepedia) and categorising these trackers/vendors in specific purposes. The four common purposes of trackers of Cookiepedia are i) strictly necessary (which includes authentication and user-security); ii) performance (also known as analytics, statistics or measurement); iii) functionality (includes customization, multimedia content, and social media plugin); and iv) targeting (known as advertising). Any trackers which cannot be found in the database are categorised as "Unknown" and require manual sorting (see Fig. 3). From the setup guides, there seems to be no explicit or granular confirmation required by the publisher itself (although they can edit after the fact): once the scan is complete, the categorisation of trackers is performed automatically and the consent pop-up is updated. In other words, the CookiePro's consent pop-up interface is in part automatically configured by the scanning tool.

This kind of scanning and categorising feature based on a CMPs own database is also offered by several other CMPs such as Cookiebot [9], Crownpeak [15], TrustArc [63] and Signatu [61].

Legal Analysis. In this concrete scenario, through providing the additional services and tooling (besides consent management) of scanning and consequently presorting tracking technologies into pre-defined purposes of data processing, CMPs contribute to the definition of purposes and to the overall compliance of the publisher wherein the CMP is integrated. This level of control of a CMP in determining the purposes for processing personal data and means is a decisive factor to their legal status as data controllers.

Moreover, CMPs that offer this additional service can be potentially be qualified as a *joint controller* (Article 26 GDPR) together with the publisher, as both actors jointly determine the purposes and means of processing. In line with the criteria provided by the EDPB [26], these additional processing operations convey the factual indication of a pluralistic control on the determination of purposes from this concrete CMP and respective publisher embedding these services by default. The acceptance of scanning and categorization of purposes entails i) a

Fig. 3. CookiePro's configuration back-end designed for the publisher, when logged. After completing a scan for trackers on the publisher's website, this screen shows the trackers that were found together with a category they are assigned with.

common and complementing decision taken by both entities, wherein the categorization of purposes ii) is *necessary* for the processing to take place in such manner that it has a *tangible impact* on the determination of the purposes and means of the processing and on the overall and forthcoming data processing.

The provision of both consent pop-up and scanning tool services by a CMP to a publisher creates a situation of *mutual benefit* [23, 24]: CMPs provide a service that creates a competitive advantage compared to other CMP providers, and publishers are relieved of having to manually match trackers with vendors, purposes, and legal bases.

As joint controllers, both entities would then need to make a transparent agreement to determine and agree on their respective responsibilities for compliance with the obligations and principles under the GDPR, considering also the exercise of data subjects' rights and the duties to provide information as required by Articles 13 and 14 of the GDPR. The essence of such arrangement must be made available to the data subject [26].

Such joint responsibility does not necessarily imply equal responsibility of both operators [24], nor does it need to cover all processing, in other words, it may be limited to this particular stage in the processing of scanning and presorting of trackers [23].

4.4 Controlling Third-Party Vendors Included by CMPs

Technical Description. Upon installation of a CMP, the website publisher generally has the possibility to decide which vendors (third-party advertisers) to include in the consent pop-up. From more than 600 vendors currently registered at IAB Europe TCF [39], only the selected vendors will be then stored in the Consent Signal when the user interacts with the consent pop-up. In practice, the way the publisher effectively exercises this choice of vendors depends on the options available in the configuration tool provided by the CMP.

The IAB policies explicitly state that a CMP cannot have preferential treatment for one vendor or another [38, paragraph 6(3)]. Hence, CMPs cannot preselect or treat vendors differently, unless *a publisher explicitly asks* a CMP to include/delete some vendors from the list of all vendors.

Herewith we analyse two case studies of QuantCast and OneTrust. Figure 4 shows an installation process of QuantCast CMP, which gives some power to publishers. It includes by default *around 671 vendors registered in the IAB Europe TCF*, but allows a publisher to remove some of the vendors from this list. This power given to publishers is, however, limited: publishers must either manually search and *select one-by-one the vendors they want to exclude.*

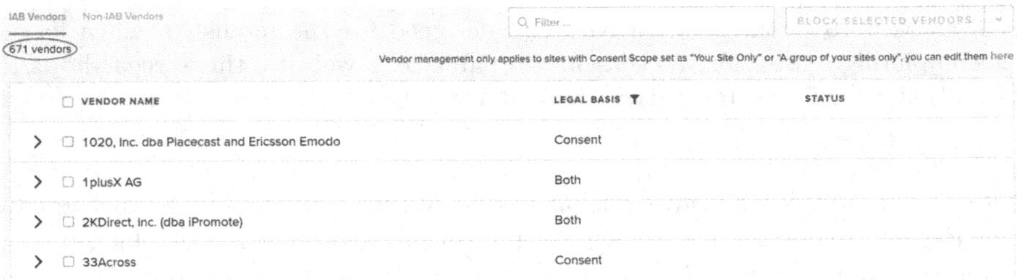

Fig. 4. Installation process of QuantCast CMP [Captured on 5 Feb. 2021]. A publisher has to manually search and exclude one-by-one the vendors from the list of 671 vendors registered in IAB Europe TCF.

Regarding OneTrust's free, open access service called *CookiePro Free IAB TCF 2.0 CMP Builder* [13], it gives no control to the publisher over the list of vendors to include. As a result, when the user clicks "Accept" in a CookiePro banner we installed on our empty website, the Consent Signal contains 2 special features optin, 10 purposes under the legal basis of consent, 9 purposes under legitimate interest, *631 vendors for consent*, and 261 vendors under legitimate interest.

Relying on a publisher to manually remove the vendors with whom it does not have a partnership presupposes that publishers are willing to actively check and configure the list of vendors, which can require an active action from a publisher on a separate screen during the configuration process. Such assumption contends with relevant findings from behavioral studies regarding *default effect bias*, referring to the tendency to stick to default options [1, 42–44]. Thaler and Sunstein concluded that *"many people will take whatever option requires the least effort, or the path of least resistance"* [62]. It seems reasonable to argue that publishers will generally leave the list as is.

Legal Analysis. CMPs are in a position to decide what decision-making power to award to website publishers regarding the selection of specific vendors. By restricting the ability of the publisher to (de)select vendors, the CMP obliges the publisher to present to the user the full list of IAB Europe-registered vendors. We recall that when registering to the IAB Europe, each vendor declares a number of purposes upon which it wishes to operate, and hence it can be concluded that the CMP automatically increases the number of purposes displayed to – and possibly accepted by – the end-user. As a result, a CMP requires the publisher to present more processing purposes than necessary, which has direct consequences on the interface the end-user will interact with.

With such factual decision-making power over the display of purposes rendered to users, it can be observed that CMPs exert influence over the determination of purposes of data processing, turning it to a data controller. Relatedly, deciding on the third-parties that process personal data consists on the determination of *"essential means"* – a competency allocated only to controllers, which again consolidates our conclusion that CMPs are data controllers in the above mentioned scenario.

This practice of including by default hundreds of third-party vendors implies that CMPs seem to breach several data protection principles:

Transparency and fairness principle (Article 5(1)(a) GDPR) which mandates controllers to handle data in a way that would be reasonably expected by the data subjects. When users signify their preferences in the consent pop-up, they are not aware nor expect their data to be potentially shared with around 600 third-parties. Moreover, the inclusiveness by default of this amount of partners seems to trigger severe risks to the rights of users and thus this consent sharing needs to be limited (Recital 75 GDPR).

Minimization principle (Article 5(1)(c) GDPR) provides that data shall be "adequate, relevant and limited to what is necessary in relation to the purposes for which they are processes". This principle is generally interpreted as referring to the need to minimise the quantity of data that is processed. One may, however, also wonder whether the principle extends to other characteristics such as the number of recipients to which data is shared with. Moreover, according to the theory of choice proliferation, a large number of purposes can lead to the user experiencing negative effects. However, in the case of consent pop-ups, the critical threshold of presented purposes beyond which these effects occur is not yet known [45].

4.5   Deployment of Manipulative Design Strategies

Legal Compliance vs. Consent Rates. When designing their consent pop-ups, CMPs have considerable freedom: The only constraint placed on them by the IAB's TCF is that they need to include the purposes and features exactly as defined by the IAB Europe [38]. From a UI perspective, CMPs thus enjoy a design space and can choose *how exactly these choices are presented to the end user*.

The primary service offered by CMPs is to ensure legal compliance, which largely determines how they exercise their design freedom. However, the advertising industry is also incentivised to strive for *maximum consent rates*. This is apparent when looking at how CMPs market themselves. For example, Quantcast describes their tool as able to *"Protect and maximize ad revenue while supporting compliance with data protection laws"* [53] and provides "Choice Reports" that detail "[h]ow many times Choice was shown, Consent rate and Bounce Rate and a detailed breakout if the full, partial or no consent given" [54]. OneTrust advertises that its CMP can *"optimize consent rates while ensuring compliance"*, and *"leverage A/B testing to maximize engagement, opt-ins and ad revenue"* [51]. In other words, although the official and primary service provided by CMPs is legal compliance, in practice, their service consists in *finding the balance between strict legal compliance and maximum consent rates* (considered to be negatively correlated), and this balancing ability becomes a point of competition between them.

Manipulative Design Strategies in Consent Pop-Ups. Recent works denote that many popular CMPs deploy manipulative design strategies in consent pop-ups [33,48,50] and that such strategies influence the users' consent decisions [50,64]. In concrete, recent findings concernedly report the majority of users think that a website cannot be used without giving consent (declining trackers would prevent access to the website) and also click the "accept" button of the banner out of habit [64].

Technical Analysis of Default Consent Pop-Ups. We portray an illustrative example of the use of manipulative design strategies in a consent pop-up. We installed a free version of OneTrust consent pop-up, the *CookiePro Free IAB TCF 2.0 CMP Builder*, on our empty website. During the installation, we chose a default version of the banner without any customization. Figure 5 depicts the 2nd layer of the CookiePro's default banner: the option to "Accept All" is presented on top of the banner, (hence making acceptance to all purposes prioritized), while "Reject All" and "Confirm My Choices" are located at the very bottom of the banner, only made available after scrolling down. This banner includes the dark patterns of "obstruction", "false hierarchy" and "sneaking" [32].

Legal Analysis. From a regulatory perspective, several guidelines have been issued by the EU Data Protection Authorities on consent pop-ups, suggesting UI should be designed to ensure that *user's choices are not affected by interface designs*, proposing a privacy by design and by default approach (Article 25 GDPR), wherein default setting must be designed with data protection in mind. Proposals of such design refer that options of the same size, tone, position and color ought to be used, so as to provide the same level of reception to the attention of the user) [4,7,8,17,34,41]. Although these guidelines are welcomed, they do not have enough legal power to be enforceable in court, and it is unclear whether they impact compliance rates. However, in practice a CookiePro default design convinces the user to select what they feel is either the only option (presented on top), or the best option (proposed in a better position), while other options (to refuse) are cumbersome and hidden.

Determination of Means. The primary service of CMPs is to provide consent management solutions to publishers through consent pop-ups, and thus anything related to this service can be considered as part of the "non-essential means"

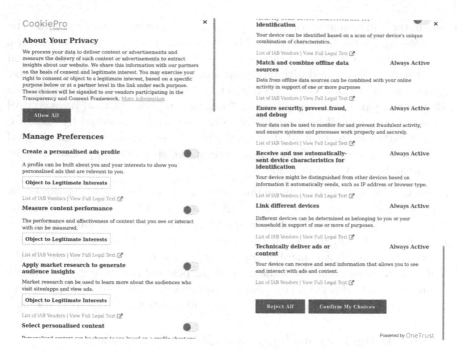

Fig. 5. 2nd layer of the default consent pop-up provided by CookiePro Free IAB TCF 2.0 CMP Builder (owned by OneTrust). [Captured on 13 Jan. 2021]. On the left, the top level of the page, displaying the "Accept All" button. On the right, the bottom of the same screen, displaying the "Reject All" and "Confirm My Choices" buttons, so the user needs to scroll down in order to see them.

that can be delegated to a processor (see Sect. 4.1). However, when CMPs decide to include manipulative design strategies – known as *dark patterns* – to increase consent optimization rate, these can be considered to go beyond their primary goal. Manipulating users decision-making to increase the probability of prompt agreement to consent for tracking is not strictly necessary to provide its consent management service. In particular, resorting to such interface design strategies does not seem to consist of "basic features" or "service improvement" that could be considered as normally expected or compatible within the range of a processor's services [36]. In fact, there are no technical reasons that could substantiate the recourse to these dark patterns. A CMP could devise design banners in a fair and transparent way and which complies with the GDPR. The EDPB [25] refers that *"compulsion to agree with the use of personal data additional to what is strictly necessary, limits data subject's choices and stands in the way of free consent."* We conclude that the use of manipulative strategies does not qualify as a mere technical implementation or operational use to obtain lawful consent, and instead falls inside the *"essential means"* category, making them a data controller.

Determination of Purposes. Following the cognition held by the CJEU on the Jehowa's Witnesses case [22], one decisive factor of the role of a controller consists in the determination of *"who organized, coordinated and encouraged"* the data processing (paragraphs 70, 71). CMPs have exclusive *judgement and control* to adopt manipulative design strategies. Such strategies have a real impact on users' consent decisions and ultimately impact the processing of their data. By deploying such strategies, CMPs do not act on behalf of any other actor (which would lead to them being recognized as "processors"), but instead have control over which purposes will be more likely to be accepted or rejected by users. In practice, CMPs' deployment of *dark patterns* that manipulate the user's final choice evidences a degree of *factual influence or decision-making power* over the processing activities that will follow.

Summary. CMPs exercise a dominant role in the decision-making power on eventual processing activities within the IAB Europe TCF ecosystem. We argue that whenever CMPs impose dark patterns to a publisher and similarly whenever CMPs propose a default banner that features dark patterns to a publisher, these facts strongly indicate a controllership status in its own right due to CMPs' influence on the determination of means and purposes of processing, even if only to a limited extent. However, the afforded discretion availed to CMPs requires a case by case analysis and is more likely to lead to divergent interpretations.

4.6   What Is the Responsibility of a CMP as Controller?

A CMP as a data processor that goes beyond the mandate given by the controller and acquires a relevant role in determining its own purposes, as shown in the scenarios in Sect. 4, becomes a controller with regard to those specific processing operations [2] and will be in breach of its obligations, hence subject to sanctions (Article 28(10)). The breadth of the parties responsibility, including the extent to which they become data controllers, should be analysed on a case by case basis [5] depending on the particular conditions of collaboration between publishers and CMPs, and then should be reflected in the service agreements.

One of their responsibilities as controllers include the obligation to comply with the principles of data protection, thereby they are required to obtain personal data fairly, lawfully and to comply with any transparency requirements with respect to users and obtain a valid consent.

Additionally, CMPs should offer design choices that are the most privacy-friendly, in a clear manner and as a default choice, in line with the principle of data protection by design and data protection by default (Article 25 of the GDPR). Finally, CMPs should respect the minimization principle – the use of compulsion methods (either in the manipulation of purposes, either pre-registering around 600 vendors) *to agree with the use of personal data additional to what is strictly necessary limits data subject's choices and stands in the way of free consent* [25, paragraph 27].

5   Recommendations

In this section, based on our legal and empirical analysis, we propose a number of recommendations for policy makers that could address the current ambiguity revolving the role of CMPs.

Concepts of Controller and Processor in the GDPR Need to be Clarified. We hope to provide influential stakeholders, such as the EDPB, with operational information that can inform its next guidelines on the concepts of controller and processor in the GDPR [26]. In particular, and in the context of the current paper, we would recommend to clarify the following aspects:

1. on defining purposes in practice: our work shows that a CMP influencing users decision-making with respect to accepting or rejecting pre-defined purposes actually renders such entity co-responsible for determining purposes;
2. on the role of deploying manipulative design in CMPs and whether this constitutes "essential means" of processing;
3. on the contractual agreement between publishers and CMPs: such agreement should mirror as much as possible the factual roles and activities they are involved in, pursuant to legal certainty and transparency;

Guidelines Needed on "Provision of Services" for Data Processors. Data processors must limit its operations to carrying out the services for which the controller stipulated in the processing agreement. However, this design space is left to ambiguity and leeway in terms of what "providing the service" entails. Guidance is needed on what is considered to be *compatible and expected purposes* for the provision of their services/operations. For example, while security operations are surely expected, doubts remain regarding the provision of services which include other purposes that go beyond legal provisions and principles such as the compatibility between optimization of consent rate and legal compliance (as mentioned in Sect. 4.5); the EDPB [25, paragraph 27] mentions that such goal cannot be prioritized over the control of an individual's personal data: *an individual's control over their personal data is essential and there is a strong presumption that consent to the processing of personal data that is unnecessary, cannot be seen as a mandatory consideration in exchange for the performance of a contract or the provision of a service.*

DPAs Should Scale Up Auditing of CMPs. Currently, DPAs primarily use labour-intensive, small-sample, qualitative methods to evaluate the legal compliance of CMPs (e.g., the Irish DPA analysed consent pop-ups of 38 websites via a "desktop examination" [18]). Although our normative stance is that compliance evaluations should not be outsourced to algorithms and always involve human oversight, data-driven and automated tools could help DPAs gain a broader understanding of CMP design and compliance trends within their jurisdiction. Auditing can be automated (for example, with scraping technologies) to analyse the presence or absence of certain consent options (e.g., a reject button), interaction flows (e.g., number of clicks to access an option), or default settings (e.g., checked or unchecked choices). Not all requirements for consent are as binary and can be measured in this way (such as the quality of purpose descriptions), but gathering and continuously monitoring those aspects can provide DPAs with initial indications. These insights can be used to decide which follow-up investigations are necessary, and also which aspects might provide the biggest impact if addressed.

Automated Auditing of CMPs Requires Extension of Consent Signal.
The IAB Europe has created a standardised format for consent signals and
successfully implemented APIs that allow various entities to interoperate with
each other. Such consent was created to simplify the exchange of the digital
version of consent between CMPs and advertisers. They do not, however, contain
elements that could help DPAs and users to evaluate the *validity of collected
consent* through automated means. We strongly suggest these standards and
APIs should be expanded (or new ones developed by neutral parties) to include
information about the interface design of a consent pop-up. Such extended digital
format of consent will make consent services computationally legible by more
actors, such as regulators and researchers.

Additionally, in the current IAB Europe TCF system, third-party advertisers
(vendors) just receive a Consent Signal as a part of HTTP(S) request or via
browser APIs, but there is no proof whether such Consent Signal is valid and
whether a vendor actually received it (or, for example, did not generate it by
itself instead). We recommend IAB Europe TCF to change this practice and
to propose solutions that demonstrate evidence of consent collection and its
integrity.

Guidance Needed on Validity of Pre-registration of Vendors. Through
our analysis, we identified that CMPs have the capability to "pre-register" about
600 vendors during the installation process on a website. This pre-registration
of vendors means that if the user accepts some of the purposes presented in
the consent pop up, then all the vendors will be automatically added to a Consent Signal (see an example of OneTrust in Sect. 4.4, where 632 vendors are
allowed when the user clicks "Accept"). Consent stored by CMP in this case
pre-authorizes processing of personal data for around 600 vendors, even if those
vendors are not present on the website, thus making consent being collected *for
future and unforeseen potential processing*. Therefore, such practice may violate
the principles of transparency, fairness and minimization principles. We hope
our analysis of the IAB Europe TCF and the capability of CMPs to pre-register
vendors that do not yet process personal data, will help policy makers to provide
further guidance on the validity of such practice.

**Further Recommendations are Needed Due to the Decision-Making
Power of Consent Pop-Up Providers.** In this article, we have analysed two
most popular CMPs in the EU – QuantCast and OneTrust– and detected several
scenarios when consent pop-up providers can be considered data controllers due
to the enormous power of CMPs that can inject any type of additional functionality at any time in the banner, without the publisher being in position to
technically know or oppose to it. We hope that policy makers take these scenarios into account and provide recommendations for such providers (either withing
or outside of IAB Europe TCF) identifying which practices render them as data
controllers and in which conditions they will be recognized as data processors.

6   Related Work

Previous work analysing the role of CMPs in the advertising ecosystem have examined its technical functioning and interaction designs related to the applicable regulation, but have not inquired how they relate to their role as processors or controllers under the GDPR.

Degeling et al. [19] monitored the prevalence of CMPs on websites from January 2018 until May, when the GDPR came into effect, and measured an overall increase from 50.3% to 69.9% across all 28 EU Member States. Taking a longer view, Hils et al. [35] showed how the rate of adoption doubled year over year between June 2018 and 2020, and that CMPs are mostly used by moderately popular websites (albeit with a long tail of small publishers). Nouwens et al. [50] studied the use of dark patterns in the five most popular CMPs in the UK and estimated that only 11.8% of banners meet minimum legal requirements for a valid consent (reject as easy as accept, no pre-checked boxes, and no implied consent).

Focusing on the programmatic signals rather than user behaviour, Matte et al. [48] analysed 28,000 EU websites and found that 141 websites register positive consent even if the user has not made their choice and 27 websites store a positive consent even if the user has explicitly opted out. Additionally, Matte et al. [47] discuss the purposes and legal basis pre-defined by the IAB Europe and suggest that several purposes might not be specific or explicit enough to guarantee a valid legal basis, and that a large portion of purposes should require consent but are allowed by the TCF to be gathered on the basis of legitimate interest.

Data protection authorities across EU Member States have also reacted to the role and responsibility of CMPs, and issued various guidances. The Spanish DPA [4] asserts that as long as CMPs comply with the requirements for consent, they shall be deemed an appropriate tool. It recommends that CMPs *"must be submitted to audits or other inspections in order to verify that (...) requirements are complied with"*. The Irish DPA [17] reiterates CMPs should be careful to avoid non-compliant designs already explicated as part of GDPR texts (e.g., pre-ticked boxes) and emphasises their accountability and transparency obligations (i.e., consent records) The Danish DPA asserts that whenever any entity integrates content from any third party (including CMPs), it is particularly important to be aware of its role in relation to its processing of personal data that takes place [16].

7   Conclusion

In this paper we discussed the requirements for CMPs to be qualified as processors and as controllers and concluded that such status has to be assessed with regard to each specific data processing activity. From an empirical analysis we concluded that CMPs assume the role of controllers, and thus should be responsible for their processing activities, in four scenarios: i) when including additional processing activities in their tool, ii) when they perform scanning and pre-sorting of tracking technologies, iii) when they include third-party vendors by default, and finally iv) when they deploy interface manipulative design strategies.

Acknowledgements. We would like to thank Daniel Woods, Triin Siil, Johnny Ryan and anonymous reviewers of ConPro'21 and APF'21 for useful comments and feedback that has lead to this paper. This work has been partially supported by the ANR JCJC project PrivaWeb (ANR-18-CE39-0008) and by the Inria DATA4US Exploratory Action project.

References

1. Deceived by design: How tech companies use dark patterns to discourage us from exercising our rights to privacy (2018). https://www.forbrukerradet.no/undersokelse/no-undersokelsekategori/deceived-by-design
2. Working Party: Opinion 1/2010 on the concepts of "controller" and "processor" WP 169 (2010). https://ec.europa.eu/justice/article-29/documentation/opinion-recommendation/files/2010/wp169_en.pdf
3. Advocate General Mengozzi: Opinion of Advocate General Mengozziin Jehovah's witnesses, C-25/17, ECLI:EU:C:2018:57, paragraph 68 (2018)
4. Agencia Española de Protección de Datos (Spanish DPA): Guide on use of cookies (2021). https://www.aepd.es/sites/default/files/2021-01/guia-cookies-en.pdf
5. Article 29 Working Party: Opinion 2/2010 on online behavioural advertising (WP 171) (2010). https://ec.europa.eu/justice/article-29/documentation/opinion-recommendation/files/2010/wp171_en.pdf
6. Bielova, N., Santos, C.: Call for Feedback to the EDPB regarding Guidelines 07/2020 on the concepts of controller and processor in the IAB Europe Transparency and Consent Framework (2020). http://www-sop.inria.fr/members/Nataliia.Bielova/opinions/EDPB-contribution-controllers-processors.pdf
7. Commission Nationale de l'Informatique et des Libertés (CNIL): Shaping Choices in the Digital World (2019). https://linc.cnil.fr/sites/default/files/atoms/files/cnil_ip_report_06_shaping_choices_in_the_digital_world.pdf
8. Commission Nationale de l'Informatique et des Libertés (French DPA): French guidelines on cookies: Deliberation No 2020–091 of September 17, 2020 adopting guidelines relating to the application of article 82 of the law of January 6, 1978 amended to read and write operations in a user's terminal (in particular to "cookies and other tracers") (2020). https://www.legifrance.gouv.fr/jorf/id/JORFTEXT000042388179
9. Cookiebot: Cookie scanner - revealer of hidden tracking, September 2020. https://www.cookiebot.com/en/cookie-scanner/
10. Cookiepedia Official website. https://cookiepedia.co.uk/
11. CookiePro: Lesson 3: Scan Results and Categorizing Cookies, July 2020). https://community.cookiepro.com/s/article/UUID-309d4544-c927-fe00-da50-60ed7668c6b5
12. CookiePro: Scanning a Website, November 2020. https://community.cookiepro.com/s/article/UUID-621498be-7e5c-23af-3bfd-e772340b4933
13. CookiePro by OneTrust: CookiePro Free IAB TCF 2.0 CMP Builder (nd). https://www.cookiepro.com/iab-tcf-2-builder/

14. Court of Justice of the European Union: Case 582/14 - Patrick Breyer v Germany (2016). ECLI:EU:C:2016:779
15. Crownpeak: Vendor categories (nd). https://community.crownpeak.com/t5/Universal-Consent-Platform-UCP/Vendor-Categories/ta-p/665
16. Danish DPA (Datatilsynet): Guide on consent (2019). www.datatilsynet.dk/media/6562/samtykke.pdf
17. Data Protection Commission (Irish DPA): Guidance note on the use of cookies and other tracking technologies (2020). https://www.dataprotection.ie/sites/default/files/uploads/2020-04/Guidance%20note%20on%20cookies%20and%20other%20tracking%20technologies.pdf
18. Data Protection Commission (Irish DPA): Report by the DPC on the Use of Cookies and Other Tracking Technologies (2020). https://www.dataprotection.ie/en/news-media/press-releases/report-dpc-use-cookies-and-other-tracking-technologies
19. Degeling, M., Utz, C., Lentzsch, C., Hosseini, H., Schaub, F., Holz, T.: We value your privacy ... now take some cookies: measuring the GDPR's impact on web privacy. In: Network and Distributed Systems Security Symposium (2019)
20. Directive 2009/136/EC of the European Parliament and of the Council of 25 November 2009. https://eur-lex.europa.eu/legal-content/EN/TXT/?uri=celex%3A32009L0136. Accessed 31 Oct 2019
21. Europe, I: Transparency and consent string with global vendor & CMP list formats (final vol 2.0): About the transparency & consent string (TC String) (2020). https://github.com/InteractiveAdvertisingBureau/GDPR-Transparency-and-Consent-Framework/blob/master/TCFv2/IAB%20Tech%20Lab%20-%20Consent%20string%20and%20vendor%20list%20formats%20v2.md#about-the-transparency-consent-string-tc-string. Accessed 14 Jan 2021
22. European Court of Justice: Case 25/17 Jehovan todistajat, ECLI:EU:C:2018:551
23. European Court of Justice: Case C-40/17 Fashion ID GmbH & Co.KG v Verbraucherzentrale NRW eV, ECLI:EU:C:2019:629
24. European Court of Justice: Case C-210/16 Wirtschaftsakademie Schleswig-Holstein, ECLI:EU:C:2018:388
25. European Data Protection Board: Guidelines 05/2020 on consent, Version 1.1 (2020). https://edpb.europa.eu/sites/edpb/files/files/file1/edpb_guidelines_202005_consent_en.pdf. Accessed 4 May 2020
26. European Data Protection Board: Guidelines 07/2020 on the concepts of controller and processor in the GDPR Version 1.0 (2020). https://edpb.europa.eu/our-work-tools/public-consultations-art-704/2020/guidelines-072020-concepts-controller-and-processor_en
27. Evidon: Quantcast-related pages on Evidon Company Directory (2017). https://info.evidon.com/companies?q=Quantcast. Consulted 8 Jan 2021
28. Finck, M., Pallas, F.: They who must not be identified - distinguishing personal from non-personal data under the GDPR. Int. Data Priv. Law 10 (2020)
29. Fouad, I., Bielova, N., Legout, A., Sarafijanovic-Djukic, N.: Missed by filter lists: detecting unknown third-party trackers with invisible pixels. In: Proceedings on Privacy Enhancing Technologies (PoPETs) (2020). Published online 08 May 2020, https://doi.org/10.2478/popets-2020-0038
30. Fouad, I., Santos, C., Al Kassar, F., Bielova, N., Calzavara, S.: On compliance of cookie purposes with the purpose specification principle. In: 2020 International Workshop on Privacy Engineering, IWPE (2020). https://hal.inria.fr/hal-02567022

31. Regulation (EU) 2016/679 of the European parliament and of the council of 27 April 2016 on the protection of natural persons with regard to the processing of personal data and on the free movement of such data, and repealing directive 95/46/EC (general data protection regulation) (text with EEA relevance). https:// eur-lex.europa.eu/legal-content/EN/TXT/?uri=celex:32016R0679

32. Gray, C.M., Kou, Y., Battles, B., Hoggatt, J., Toombs, A.L.: The dark (patterns) side of UX design. In: Proceedings of the CHI Conference Human Factors in Computing Systems, p. 534 (2018)

33. Gray, C.M., Santos, C., Bielova, N., Toth, M., Clifford, D.: Dark patterns and the legal requirements of consent banners: an interaction criticism perspective. In: ACM CHI 2021 (2020). https://arxiv.org/abs/2009.10194

34. Greek DPA (HDPA): Guidelines on Cookies and Trackers (2020). http://www. dpa.gr/APDPXPortlets/htdocs/documentSDisplay.jsp?docid=84,221,176,170,98, 24,72,223

35. Hils, M., Woods, D.W., Böhme, R.: Measuring the emergence of consent management on the web. In: ACM Internet Measurement Conference (IMC 2020) (2020)

36. Hintze, M.: Data controllers, data processors, and the growing use of connected products in the enterprise: managing risks, understanding benefits, and complying with the GDPR. Cybersecurity (2018)

37. IAB Europe: Transparency and Consent String with Global Vendor and CMP List Formats (Final vol 2.0) (2019). https://github.com/ InteractiveAdvertisingBureau/GDPR-Transparency-and-Consent-Framework/ blob/master/TCFv2/IABTechLab-Consentstringandvendorlistformatsv2.md. Accessed 12 Feb 2021

38. IAB Europe: IAB Europe Transparency & Consent Framework Policies (2020). https://iabeurope.eu/wp-content/uploads/2020/11/TCF_v2-0_Policy_ version_2020-11-18-3.2a.docx-1.pdf

39. IAB Europe: Vendor List TCF v2.0 (2020). https://iabeurope.eu/vendor-list-tcf-v2-0/

40. Information Commissioner's Office: Data controllers and data processors: what the difference is and what the governance implications are (2018). https://ico.org.uk/ for-organisations/guide-to-data-protection/guide-to-the-general-data-protection-regulation-gdpr/controllers-and-processors/

41. Information Commissioner's Office: Guidance on the use of cookies and similar technologies (2019). https://ico.org.uk/media/for-organisations/guide-to-pecr/guidance-on-the-use-of-cookies-and-similar-technologies-1-0.pdf

42. Jared Spool: Do users change their settings? (2011). https://archive.uie.com/ brainsparks/2011/09/14/do-users-change-their-settings/

43. Johnson, E.J., Bellman, S., Lohse, G.L.: Defaults, framing and privacy: why opting in-opting out. Mark. Lett. **13**, 5–15 (2002)

44. Johnson, E.J., Goldstein, D.G.: Do defaults save lives? Science **302**, 1338–1339 (2003)

45. Machuletz, D., Böhme, R.: Multiple purposes, multiple problems: a user study of consent dialogs after GDPR. In: Proceedings on Privacy Enhancing Technologies (PoPETs), pp. 481–498 (2020)

46. Maier, G., Feldmann, A., Paxson, V., Allman, M.: On dominant characteristics of residential broadband internet traffic. In: Proceedings of the 9th ACM SIGCOMM Conference on Internet Measurement Conference, pp. 90–102 (2009)

47. Matte, C., Santos, C., Bielova, N.: Purposes in IAB Europe's TCF: which legal basis and how are they used by advertisers? In: Antunes, L., Naldi, M., Italiano, G.F., Rannenberg, K., Drogkaris, P. (eds.) APF 2020. LNCS, vol. 12121, pp. 163–185. Springer, Cham (2020). https://doi.org/10.1007/978-3-030-55196-4_10. https://hal.inria.fr/hal-02566891

48. Matte, C., Bielova, N., Santos, C.: Do cookie banners respect my choice? Measuring legal compliance of banners from IAB Europe's transparency and consent framework. In: IEEE Symposium on Security and Privacy (IEEE S&P 2020) (2020)

49. Mishra, V., Laperdrix, P., Vastel, A., Rudametkin, W., Rouvoy, R., Lopatka, M.: Don't count me out: on the relevance of IP address in the tracking ecosystem. In: Huang, Y., King, I., Liu, T., van Steen, M. (eds.) WWW 2020: The Web Conference 2020, Taipei, Taiwan, 20–24 April 2020, pp. 808–815. ACM/IW3C2 (2020). https://doi.org/10.1145/3366423.3380161

50. Nouwens, M., Liccardi, I., Veale, M., Karger, D., Kagal, L.: Dark patterns after the GDPR: scraping consent pop-ups and demonstrating their influence. In: CHI (2020)

51. OneTrust PreferenceChoice: Consent management platform (CMP). https://www.preferencechoice.com/consent-management-platform/. Accessed 20 Jan 2021

52. Pawlata, H., Caki, G.: The impact of the transparency consent framework on current programmatic advertising practices. In: 4th International Conference on Computer-Human Interaction Research and Applications (2020)

53. Quantcast: Quantcast Choice (2020). https://www.quantcast.com/products/choice-consent-management-platform/

54. Quantcast: Quantcast Choice - User Guide (2020). https://help.quantcast.com/hc/en-us/articles/360052725133-Quantcast-Choice-User-Guide

55. Quantcast: Quantcast Choice Terms of Service (2020). https://www.quantcast.com/legal/quantcast-choice-terms-of-service/

56. Quantcast: Quantcast Measure and Q for Publishers Terms of Service (2020). https://www.quantcast.com/legal/measure-terms-service/

57. Quantcast: Quantcast Privacy Policy (2020). https://www.quantcast.com/privacy

58. Quantcast: Quantcast Choice - Universal Tag Implementation Guide (TCF v2) (2021). https://help.quantcast.com/hc/en-us/articles/360052746173-Quantcast-Choice-Universal-Tag-Implementation-Guide-TCF-v2-

59. Quantcast: Quantcast Measure (2021). https://www.quantcast.com/products/measure-audience-insights/

60. Santos, C., Bielova, N., Matte, C.: Are cookie banners indeed compliant with the law? Deciphering EU legal requirements on consent and technical means to verify compliance of cookie banners. Technol. Regul. 91–135 (2020). https://doi.org/10.26116/techreg.2020.009

61. Signatu: Trackerdetect (nd). https://signatu.com/product/trackerdetect/

62. Thaler, R.H., Sunstein, C.R.: Nudge: Improving Decisions About Health, Wealth, and Happiness. Yale University Press (2008)

63. TrustArc: Cookie Consent Manager (nd). https://trustarc.com/cookie-consent-manager/

64. Utz, C., Degeling, M., Fahl, S., Schaub, F., Holz, T.: (Un)informed consent: studying GDPR consent notices in the field. In: Conference on Computer and Communications Security (2019)

Improving the Transparency of Privacy Terms Updates
Opinion Paper

Alexandr Railean$^{(\boxtimes)}$ and Delphine Reinhardt

Institute of Computer Science, Georg-August-Universität Göttingen,
Göttingen, Germany
{arailea,reinhardt}@cs.uni-goettingen.de

Abstract. Updates are an essential part of most information systems. However, they may also serve as a means to deploy undesired features or behaviours that potentially undermine users' privacy. In this opinion paper, we propose a way to increase *update transparency*, empowering users to easily answer the question "what has changed with regards to my privacy?", when faced with an update prompt. This is done by leveraging a formal notation of privacy terms and a set of rules that dictate when privacy-related prompts can be omitted, to reduce fatigue. A design that concisely visualizes changes between data handling practices of different software versions or configurations is also presented. We argue that it is an efficient way to display information of such nature and provide the method and calculations to support our assertion.

Keywords: IoT · Privacy · Usability · Updates · Transparency · GDPR

1 Introduction

Although updates are an inherent part of the lifecycle of most information systems, the update process is affected by a number of technical and usability issues, which can be seen in contexts ranging from mobile and desktop applications, to embedded systems and Internet of Things (IoT) appliances [13,34]. As a result, many systems remain insecure, while users are frustrated and may lose interest in the maintenance of their systems [13,34]. Among these update-related issues, we focus on *transparency*, discussed in Art. 12(1) of the General Data Protection Regulation (GDPR), which requires that information addressed to users should be *"concise, easily accessible and easy to understand, and expressed in clear and plain language"*, such that they can figure out *"whether, by whom and for what purpose* personal data are collected" [12,14]. Prior research has shown that the current level of transparency is inadequate and that in many cases end users cannot exercise their rights [8,26]. Users face problems such as excessive length of privacy policies, complex language, vagueness, lack of choices, and fatigue [31]. The need for improvements is also motivated by estimations that show that

N. Gruschka et al. (Eds.): APF 2021, LNCS 12703, pp. 70–86, 2021.
https://doi.org/10.1007/978-3-030-76663-4_4

the expectation for users to fully read and understand privacy policies is not realistic, as it would take circa 201 h for a typical American user to read the privacy policies they are exposed to in the course of a year [19]. Moreover, even when users read policies, they are often confronted with "opaque transparency" - a practice of deliberately designing user experiences in a way that obfuscates important information [5,18]. This suggests that end-users are in a vulnerable position and that their privacy is undermined.

In this paper we focus on the scenario in which a user is notified about an update for an IoT device they own, prompting them to consider potential privacy implications of installing the update. We propose a set of measures that simplify this analysis, and posit that a net gain in transparency can be attained by (1) avoiding unnecessary prompts, (2) showing less information, (3) displaying it in a common form, and by (4) decoupling feature, security and privacy updates. As a result, end-users can increase awareness of how data collection may affect their privacy, and thus be in a better position to make informed decisions.

In what follows, we elaborate on each of the points above. Section 2 provides a high-level overview of our approach. Section 3 introduces a formal notation of privacy terms, which is then used in Sect. 4 to determine when update prompts can be omitted. In Sect. 5, we argue that our proposed way of expressing updated privacy terms is more efficient than prose typically used for this purpose. Section 6 describes additional steps that can be taken to further improve transparency. In Sect. 7 we discuss the implications of applying our approach, while Sect. 8 reviews related work. We make concluding remarks in Sect. 9.

2 Proposed Approach

Art. 6(1a) and Art. 7 of the GDPR require informed and freely given consent before the collection of personal data, unless exemptions from Art. 6(1) apply. This is also required when something changes in the way personal data are handled since consent was previously granted [12]. In this paper we explore a scenario where instead of flooding users with information, we show them a minimal subset of facts that are sufficient to make a rough, but actionable assessment. Further refinement can be accomplished by investing more time in the evaluation, should the user wish so.

We assert that this minimal subset of information is a "who gets the data" table shown in Fig. 1, because it is easy to interpret, and it can be used to quickly derive answers to these questions related to transparency:

1. *What* data are collected?
2. *What is the purpose* of collection?
3. *Where* are the data stored?
4. *How long* are they kept?
5. *Who* has access to the data?
6. *How often* are the data sent?

The table in Fig. 1 was originally conceived as a component of an Online Interface for IoT Transparency Enhancement (OnLITE), which summarizes data

Data type	⇅	Purpose	⇅	Company	⇅	Country	⇅	Duration	⇅	Frequency	⇅
🌡 temperature		research		Minerva LTD		🇨🇦 Canada		1y		daily	
💧 humidity		marketing		ThirstFirst LTD		🇺🇸 USA		1y		hourly	

Fig. 1. The "who gets the data" table, adapted from [27]. Note that the table can be configured to show personal and non-personal data (see Sect. 7.5 for details).

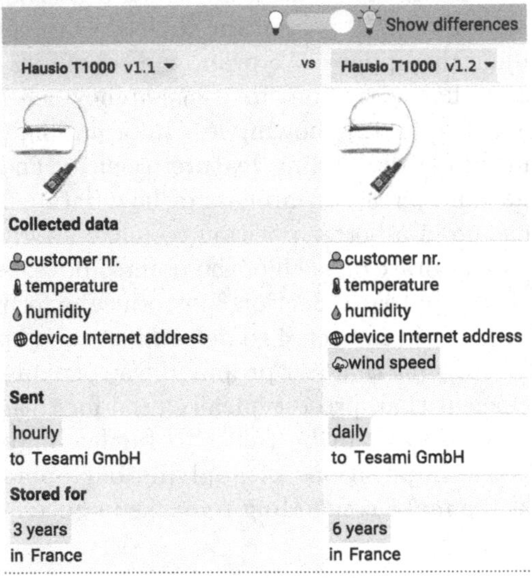

Fig. 2. Comparing two versions of the same device side by side, while highlighting differences (adapted from [27]).

collection practices and privacy information, and makes it easy to compare different IoT devices side by side, as shown in Fig. 2 [27]. Although the aforementioned transparency questions are not directly expressed in the legal requirements, they are derived from Art. 13 of the GDPR, and the results of our previously conducted usability evaluation showed that such a formulation is clear to non-experts [27].

In this work we take the idea further, applying OnLITE when an update is available, enabling users to compare an IoT device, a program, or a web-site against *another version of itself*. Thus, we leverage a design that we evaluated and which received positive feedback from our participants [27]. Considering that the privacy impact variations between updates are expected to be minimal, we have reasons to believe that the proposed UI will focus the users' attention on the few things that have changed, making it more difficult for companies to deploy features that are potentially privacy-abusive.

In the context of consent prompts for updated terms, the earliest time when we can take steps to protect a user's privacy is *before* displaying the prompt. It has been established that exposing a person to frequent stimuli leads to fatigue, making them more likely to dismiss potentially important interactions [7,31]. Such an effect occurs after just two exposures, and grows with repeated exposure [1,2]. Conversely, decreasing the total number of exposures can reduce fatigue. Thus, we have to understand in what circumstances consent prompts can be omitted without undermining users' privacy. To this end, we propose a notation of privacy terms, and then use it to formally define these circumstances.

3   Formal Notation of Privacy Terms

There are multiple factors that can influence a user's privacy. We take a GDPR-centric approach and focus on the items targeted by the transparency questions listed in Sect. 2. For example, privacy is affected if the *retention* period changes from "1 month" to "10 years", or if the collection *frequency*[1] changes from "once per day" to "twice per second" [15]. Thus, our notation aims to capture these parameters, using the following symbols:

Data type Δ type of collected data
Purpose Π purpose of collection
Time T the retention period
Company C a company that gets the data
Location Λ location of said company
Frequency Φ how often the data are transmitted

These symbols are then encapsulated into structures of a higher level of abstraction, such that they are easier to write down and reason about:

Term Θ a tuple of the form $(\Delta, \Pi, C, \Lambda, T, \Phi)$, indicating agreement to sharing a type of data, for a specific purpose, with a company located in a particular country, for the given duration of time, shared at a certain regularity.

Consent K a set of terms accepted by the user, e.g., $K = \{\Theta_1, \Theta_2, \Theta_3, ..\Theta_i\}$.

Thus, when a user gives consent, we formally represent that in an expanded form as: $K = \{(\Delta_1, \Pi_1, C_1, \Lambda_1, T_1, \Phi_1), \ldots, (\Delta_i, \Pi_i, C_i, \Lambda_i, T_i, \Phi_i)\}$. Here is a practical example with some actual values: $K = \{(temperature, research, MinervaLTD, Canada, 1y, daily), (humidity, marketing, ThirstFirstLTD, USA, 1y, hourly)\}$.

This notation facilitates the automatic processing of privacy terms by software and enables us to define a formal set of rules that govern when consent *must* be requested again, and when it can be omitted.

Note that in the example above Λ is a country, but it could also be a less granular value such as "within EU" or "outside EU". At this stage we only argue that a location component must be present in the tuple, without having a strong preference towards one option or the other. Finding the optimal approach is outside the scope of this opinion paper.

---

[1] Art. 13 of the GDPR does not require showing information about how often the data are transferred. We include it, because increasing sampling rates can lead to privacy implications, especially when correlation with other data-sets is possible.

Table 1. Primary filters. If any rule is matched, a consent prompt is unnecessary.

Rule	Logic	Formal notation	Intuition
1	Strict subsets	$K_{new} \subset K_{old}$	I agree to fewer (i.e., more stringent) terms than before
2	Equal sets	$K_{new} = K_{old}$	I still agree to identical terms
3	Shorter duration	$\Theta_i T_{new} \leq \Theta_i T_{old}$	If I agreed to sharing it for 5 years, I agree with sharing it for 3 years (assuming everything else in Θ_i is the same)
4	Reduced frequency	$\Theta_i \Phi_{new} \leq \Theta_i \Phi_{old}$	If I agreed to sharing it every minute, I agree with sharing it every hour (i.e., less often)

4 When to Request Consent Again

In what follows, we propose a set of rules that act as filters, if at least one of them *is matched*, it means that consent *must not* be requested from the user again. Please refer to Table 1, where we denote previously accepted terms with K_{old}, and the new terms that the software wants the user to accept with K_{new}.

We can also apply additional filters, based on the privacy protections offered in different parts of the world (for an example, refer to Table 2). To this end, we propose the concept of a *privacy protection gradient*, which differentiates areas by level of privacy protection mechanisms in place.

In this hypothetical example (Fig. 3), we consider the EU and the European Economic Area (EEA) as the region with the highest level of protection, because the GDPR directly applies here. It is followed by a "second tier", which includes countries considered to provide an adequate level of data protection, per Art. 45 of the GDPR. As of this writing, the list includes Andorra, Argentina, Canada, Faroe Islands, Guernsey, Israel, Isle of Man, Japan, Jersey, New Zealand, Switzerland, Uruguay and South Korea. A hypothetical "third tier" could include countries or states that are said to have legislation comparable to the GDPR (e.g., Brazil with the Lei Geral de Proteçao de Dados, modeled after the GDPR [11], California and its Consumer Privacy Act [36], etc.), followed by the rest of the world, assumed to provide the weakest protections. Note that this is only a simplified model that enables us to reason about the "privacy gradient". Finding the optimal number of tiers and assigning each country to a tier is outside the scope of this paper.

We postulate that "moving up" along the gradient increases privacy, and thus can happen without re-requesting consent. In contrast, moving in the opposite direction would potentially weaken a user's privacy, hence such a transition would require consent to be obtained again.

In our formal notation, the level of protection applicable to a location Λ is written as Λ^π. Thus, if the old location of the data was in an area less secure than the new location, we express that as $\Lambda_{old}^\pi < \Lambda_{new}^\pi$.

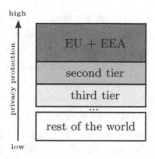

Fig. 3. Privacy protection levels in different political, economic or strategic unions.

Table 2. Secondary filter, subject to discussion, can be deactivated by users.

Rule	Logic	Formal notation	Intuition
5	Go up or sideways on the "privacy gradient"	$\Theta_i \Lambda^\pi_{old} \leq \Theta_i \Lambda^\pi_{new}$	Moving from an area with fewer and weaker protections to an area with more and stronger protections, or to an area with comparable protections (assuming everything else in Θ_i is identical)

Such secondary filters can be controversial. For example, there was an attempt to use the GDPR to silence journalists in Romania [24], therefore some users might rank the privacy protection levels of this EU member differently, while others would prefer to consider the EU as a single entity. A compromise solution might be to let users choose beforehand whether they want to treat such changes as major or minor ones (an example is shown in Fig. 6), or choose other criteria for computing Λ^π, such as the democracy index[2].

5 The Information Efficiency Metric

Since one of the ways in which users' privacy is undermined is through exposure to lengthy privacy policies that are not likely to be read [19, 26], one step towards improving the status quo is to reduce the volume of data users have to analyze when making decisions that can affect privacy. Therefore, we need a way to quantify this volume, in order to objectively compare different representations of privacy terms.

One way to accomplish this is by computing information efficiency, i.e., the ratio between "total" and "useful" information [28]. In what follows, we present an example calculation, using the notation proposed in Sect. 3.

Recall that each term of a privacy policy is a tuple expressed as $\Theta = (\Delta, \Pi, C, \Lambda, T, \Phi)$. For example, Λ represents one of the world's 193 countries[3].

---

[2] eiu.com/topic/democracy-index.

[3] According the to UN un.org/en/member-states.

Therefore, when specifying a country, we choose one of 193 discrete values, i.e., we produce $\lceil log_2 193 \rceil = 8$ bits of *useful* information.

Before this information can be communicated, we must *encode* it [32]. Assume we use an alphabet of 26 letters and that our text is case-insensitive, thus each letter is worth $\lceil log_2 26 \rceil = 5$ bits. Therefore, if we want to encode "Portugal", we need 8 letters, i.e., $8 \times 5 = 40$ bits. Now we calculate the efficiency of our encoding as $\eta = \frac{info_{useful}}{info_{total}} \times 100 = \frac{5}{40} \times 100 \approx 13\%$. This result can be roughly quadrupled by using the ISO 2-letter country code, "PT", instead of the full name. Thus, the ratio makes it obvious that one of the encodings incurs an overhead of circa 80%, prompting a search for better alternatives.

We then quantify the other elements of Θ, by relying on existing terminology that defines types of data, purposes of collection and retention periods [3,4,9], reaching a total of **155 bits**. The complete calculation is omitted for brevity, but is available in Appendix A.

We propose using this metric as a standard practice applied to rule out inefficient representations, because they are likely to lead to poor usability.

Although a high information efficiency is desired, we must consider metrics like the time and the mental effort necessary to interpret the message. For example, replacing country names with flags, or using icons to instead of text to represent data types will improve efficiency, but it might not work well with all users, or it could affect screen readers and automated translation software. Therefore, when reasoning about ways to represent privacy policies, information efficiency should be counter-balanced with a human-centered design process, taking aesthetics, and user satisfaction into account [10].

5.1   Table Benefits and Prose Deficiencies

While our calculations show that expressing privacy terms as a table is more efficient than as prose, we posit that tables may also have the *highest information efficiency* among options. This is due to the fact that tables omit "glue text", which improves the flow of prose, but also constitutes the bulk of the message.

In addition, a tabular layout for privacy terms comes with the following benefits. (1) It is easier to skim through because it is a fixed structure consisting of similar elements. In contrast, prose would have to be read entirely, otherwise users cannot be sure there is no abusive or unfair clause [5]. (2) Tables are easier to translate (even automatically), because they use predefined values, whereas prose is open to interpretation and can be confusing even to native speakers of the language [5,26]. (3) Sorting, grouping and filtering works well with tables, but not with prose. (4) A table does not have to be processed entirely to be useful. For example, the number of rows can be a powerful signal when comparing something that shares data with 3 vs. 150 partners. (5) Tables pave the way for high permission granularity, where users can accept only specific terms while rejecting others. (6) Consequently, this makes possible the automated processing of terms, e.g., by means of trusted AI assistants that act on the user's behalf. (7) No extra training for users is necessary if the table is extended with new

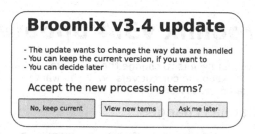

Fig. 4. Hypothetical interface where users indicate whether they want to update without changing the terms. Note the default option is the most conservative, and that there is no "accept terms" option, because the user needs to understand them before accepting, otherwise it would not be an *informed* consent. Clicking "view new terms" opens a "classic OnLITE" page where the current and new versions are compared side by side, with an option to highlight differences (refer to Fig. 2).

columns (e.g., a "condition" column could represent opt-in and opt-out logic, which is not reflected in the example in Fig. 1). Moreover, if a user does not need certain columns, they can hide them.

6   Additional Steps Towards Better Update Transparency

6.1   Distinguishing Feature, Security, and Privacy Updates

Sometimes updates can force users into a "take it or leave it" dilemma [31]. This creates an asymmetry in which vendors can force users into accepting new terms, because otherwise users will not get continued service or remain exposed to security risks. As others suggested, software can be designed in a way that decouples security updates from regular ones [34]. In the same fashion, we advocate the additional decoupling of updates that change the way personal data are handled. If such a level of granularity is achieved, consent forms can be shown less often, thus making it more likely that users will pay attention to one when they see it. In addition, this would mean that end users can exercise the rights enshrined in the GDPR, choosing not to accept the new terms (since consent must be voluntary) and thus continuing to use the software on previously accepted terms. In other words, the "I take it, but I keep the old terms" option becomes possible (as shown in Fig. 4), since we know exactly what terms were previously accepted.

6.2   The Best Time to Ask Permission

Another improvement in the way privacy updates are handled is to consider the best time[4] to display a consent prompt. Usually this happens when it is convenient for the software (e.g., at system boot, at program start-up or at regular

---

[4] Here we mean it in the sense of the Greek word "kairos", which refers to an opportune moment, not to chronology.

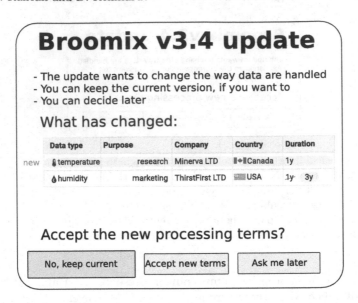

Fig. 5. Hypothetical update featuring an inline consent prompt.

intervals), without regard for the users' preferences. In these circumstances, a consent prompt is likely to interfere with a user's primary task, causing them to either accept the update in order to dismiss the prompt as quickly as possible, or postpone it. Either way, the damage is done - the user was interrupted.

Some operating systems let users decide when to apply updates. While this is done out of reliability considerations (the system must be plugged in, or there must be sufficient battery power left), it can also be done to avoid unnecessary distractions. The operating system could group updates based on their type, as discussed in Sect. 6.1, thus reducing potential interference with users' tasks. Alternatively, it can apply some heuristics to determine whether the user is actively involved in a task, and only display these non-disruptive prompts when the system is idle.

6.3   Inline Differences

We propose an "inline difference" prompt, which does not refer to the new terms in a separate window, but displays them in the prompt itself. This is only applicable when the number of differences[5] between the new and old terms is beneath a threshold. The sweet spot remains to be established experimentally, but a good default value could be Miller's "magic number 7 ± 2" [20]. For example, in Fig. 5 you can see that only 2 differences exist between K_{old} and K_{new}, thus they can be displayed inline.

---

[5] $|K_{old} \Delta K_{new}|$, i.e., the cardinality of the symmetric difference between the old and new terms.

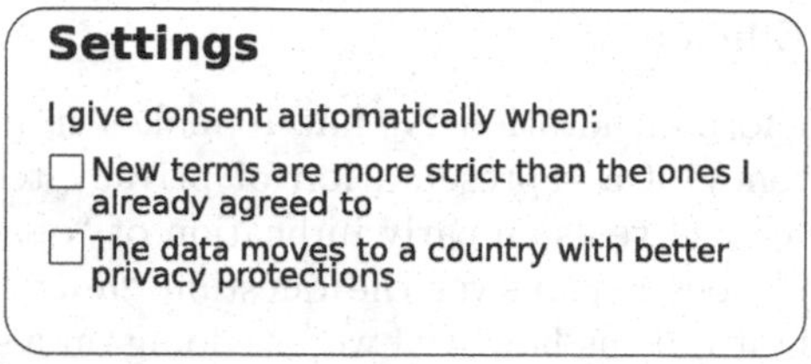

Settings

I give consent automatically when:

☐ New terms are more strict than the ones I already agreed to

☐ The data moves to a country with better privacy protections

Fig. 6. Hypothetical interface where users indicate whether they want to give consent automatically in some cases.

Depending on the user's preferences, a consent prompt may be shown only in a subset of cases. This can be configured in the interface (Fig. 6) or defined when an event occurs: the prompt is always shown the first time, and it contains a checkbox that says "ask me again whenever the data moves within the EU".

7   Discussion

7.1   Reducing Information Asymmetry

Applying the measures outlined in this paper can reduce the information asymmetry between consumers and companies, making data processing practices more transparent and accessible to end users. This can enable users to make decisions based on criteria they may not have been aware of otherwise, and thus reward products that are more privacy-friendly. This, in turn, can incentivise vendors to become more transparent [21].

7.2   Benefits of a Formal Notation

Although the analysis of a privacy policy can be carried out by means of natural language processing and artificial intelligence (AI) tools, such approaches can have accuracy issues and are technically more complex [16, 17]. Moreover, even if human-level general intelligence were available, it is not unreasonable to assume that the AI will have to deal with ambiguities, contradictions or incomplete data, just like humans do when confronted with complex texts. It is also possible that vendors engaged in "opaque transparency" will explore adversarial approaches to deceive such software, akin to methods that trick a program into identifying a deer as an airplane by manipulating a specific pixel [29, 33].

We argue that this problem can be addressed in a simpler way - by mandating vendors to provide the data in a structured format. As we have shown earlier, this information would be easy for humans to comprehend [27], and it would also facilitate automated processing of such data using conventional means. Another benefit is that legal liability can be assigned to the vendor, leaving no wiggle room that would otherwise be created by potentially inaccurate interpretations generated by an AI. Other potential legal ramifications of applying the granular consent notation proposed in this paper will be discussed in our future work.

7.3   Information Efficiency

Another benefit of a formal notation is that it makes it possible to quantify the information efficiency of a representation of privacy terms. The metric is easy to compute and can serve as an early indication of "opaque transparency". Although this method does not answer the question *"how* to do better?", it is still useful because (1) it tells us how well we are doing on a scale from 0 to 100, (2) it can be used to measure improvement during iterative prototyping, and (3) it can be used to objectively compare completely different designs.

7.4   Cross-Context Usage

A unified way of visualizing privacy terms is a major benefit, because end users can leverage their prior experience and apply it in other contexts [23]. For example, once a user familiarizes with the layout of a "who gets the data" table, they can recognize it in a smartphone application marketplace, on web-sites, on IoT devices, and other interfaces.

In such circumstances, one's ability to query the data set can become a general, rather than a specialized skill. This, in turn, can make users more perceptive to the subject of privacy and better equipped to reason about it.

7.5   Listing Non Personally Identifiable Information

Given that the proposed design grew out of IoT-centric research, Fig. 1 contains examples such as temperature or humidity, which do not constitute personal data, at least not without cross-correlating with other data sets. This information is presented for illustrative purposes, and ultimately it is a matter of policy or user preference, whether the table will display strictly personal data, or all collected data in general.

The benefit of listing all types of collected data is that a consumer can make a better judgment. For example, logging room temperature on an hourly basis is less sensitive than doing it every minute. In the latter case, the higher sampling rate can be used to infer whether the room is occupied or empty, how many persons are inside, and whether they sit, stand, or move around [22].

8   Related Work

Several works by Vaniea et al. analyse user behaviour in the context of updates. They found that sometimes prior experience determines users to intentionally ignore updates, in an attempt to avoid negative consequences, such as loss of functionality or undesired changes in the interface. They provide guidelines for improving the update experience through simple steps, such as explaining the changes the update brings or offering a rollback capability. They also advocate the separation of feature and security updates [34,35]. In our paper, we apply some of these ideas to the context of update transparency. We describe a formal method and a UI design for effectively explaining how the changes in an update can influence a user's privacy. In addition, we argue in favour of decoupling privacy updates from other types of updates, with the purpose of reducing unnecessary interruptions.

We also consider relevant the literature related to summarizing privacy policies, because it is a more general form of the "what are the terms I have to accept?" problem users face when dealing with updates. So far this has been attempted through a combination of crowd-sourcing [30], machine learning, and neural networks [16,17,25].

Harkous et al. trained a neural network that analyzes, annotates and summarizes a policy, such that a user would not have to read it entirely. In addition, they provide a chat bot that answers questions about the policy in a natural language [16,17]. While such a mode of interaction reduces the amount of information one has to read at once, a drawback is that some facts will not be revealed unless a user asks about them. Thus, *unknown unknowns* can only be found by stumbling upon them when reading the entire text, hence one cannot rely solely on a dialogue with the bot. Nokhbeh Zaeem et al. propose another automated tool for generating a concise summary of a policy and assign a privacy score to the product or service in question [25]. As in the case of the chat-bot, this approach reduces the volume of text a user has to read, but it is subject to the same limitations as other AI-based methods - a guarantee that the summary is 100% accurate is not provided, which also raises the question of legal liability. In contrast, we propose practical methods of reducing the total volume of text, rather than transforming it and showing a derivative form to the users. Further, the simplicity of our approach makes it immune to adversarial formulations that can trick an AI into misinterpreting a text.

Nevertheless, we believe that our works can complement each other. A chat-bot and a summary screen will be more accurate when they rely on data structured like our "who gets the data" table (versus relying on free-form prose), while the issues of interpretation accuracy and legal liability are also resolved.

Breaux et al. propose a formal language for defining privacy terms. Their notation aims at helping requirements engineers and software developers detect potential contradictions in a policy, especially when the software relies on external services [6]. Their notation differs from the one we describe in this opinion paper in several ways: our proposal is GDPR-centric, hence we include some additional information, e.g., location of collected data. Further, our notation and the logic built upon it is aimed at a wider audience, not only developers.

9   Conclusion

We have described a series of measures that can improve the transparency of updates with respect to data collection practices. The measures rely on a simplified formal notation for privacy terms and heuristics that can be used to reduce the frequency of displaying update prompts. We argue how this approach can reduce habituation effects and we also provide an information efficiency metric that can be used to determine whether privacy terms (or the differences between terms brought by an update) can be expressed in a more concise form. By applying these measures, we believe that the information asymmetry between users and companies can be reduced, putting users in a better position to make informed decisions with respect to their privacy.

Acknowledgments. This research is a continuation of an activity that has originally received funding from the H2020 Marie Skłodowska-Curie EU project "Privacy&Us" under the grant agreement No. 675730.

Appendix A Information Efficiency Calculation Example

We extend the material from Sect. 5 by providing another example. Consider the last term of the tuple, Φ, which represents the frequency with which data are sent. Suppose that in this case we express it as a choice among these options: {*multiple times per second, every second, every minute, hourly, daily, weekly, monthly, on-demand*}. Given that the set has 8 options to choose from, it means that a choice of a specific element yields $\lceil log_2 8 \rceil = 3$ bits of useful information.

Following the same principle, we quantify each component of a privacy term Θ, using terminology adapted from several sources: Platform for Privacy Preferences (P3P) [9], Data Privacy Vocabulary (DPV) [4], and Apple developer guidelines [3], summarized in Table 3. Note that different vocabularies provide a different level of granularity, for example, DPV distinguishes between 161 types of data, while P3P only 16. Since devising a vocabulary is outside the scope of this paper, we err on the safe side and take the maximum values (highlighted in bold) among the considered examples.

Table 3. Summary of discrete choices to indicate the type of collected data, purpose of collection and retention period, using notation proposed by DPV, P3P and Apple developer guidelines.

	DPV		P3P		Apple	
	Items	Bits	Items	Bits	Items	Bits
Data type	**161**	8	17	5	32	5
Purpose	**31**	5	16	4	6	3
Duration	-	-	**5**	3	-	-

After substituting each component, we get: $\Theta = 8+5+20\times6+8+11+3 = 155$ bits. Therefore, the pure information required to express a term is 155 bits, this is how much we would transmit, if we could upload it directly into the conscience of a person. However, some overhead is added because the information is encoded into words, or other forms that have to be perceived by end users.

We argue that the tabular representation is a highly efficient way of encoding privacy terms. This assertion is supported by the following calculation. Suppose

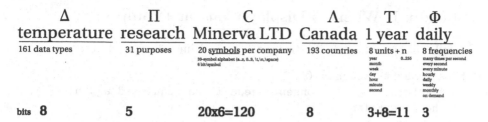

Δ temperature 161 data types	Π research 31 purposes	C Minerva LTD 20 <u>symbols</u> per company 39-symbol alphabet (a..z, 0..9, \t, \n, \space) 6 bit/symbol	Λ Canada 193 countries	T 1 year 8 units + n 0..255 year month week day hour minute second	Φ daily 8 frequencies many times per second every second every minute hourly daily weekly monthly on demand
bits 8	5	20x6=120	8	3+8=11	3

Fig. 7. Annotated calculations that explains how the amount of information in each privacy term is computed, yielding a total of 155 bits.

that the notation consists of 26 small letters of the Latin alphabet, 10 digits, the SPACE, TAB and NEWLINE symbols. The notation has a total of 39 characters, which means that a single character is worth $\lceil log_2 39 \rceil = 6$ bits. In addition, the following conventions apply: a company name is assumed to be a string of 20 characters, thus it is worth up to $20 \times 6 = 120$ bits.

We now apply this encoding to Fig. 7, ignoring the data type icons and the country flags for simplicity. Each line is 49 characters long, yielding $49 \times 6 = 294$ bits. At this stage we can compute the efficiency of this representation: $\eta = \frac{info_{useful}}{info_{total}} \times 100 = \frac{155 \times 2}{294 \times 2} \times 100 \approx 53\%$.

Armed with this number, we can consider various ways to improve efficiency and measure their impact. For example, we can remove the country names and leave only their flags, or use two-letter ISO codes instead of full names. Entries can also be grouped, e.g., all terms related to temperature can skip the word "temperature" in all but the first entry. In addition, search and filter functionality can be used to hide all the rows except the ones the user wants to focus on, thus reducing the total amount of displayed information. With such an efficiency metric at hand, one can argue in favour of one design over another, supporting the choice with hard data.

In addition, we can use the same metric to compare entirely different notations. For example, consider this hypothetical prose version of the terms expressed in Fig. 1: *"We care about your privacy, therefore our smart indoor temperature and humidity meter only collects and shares your data with 2 companies. Temperature data are shared on a daily basis with Minerva LTD, located in Canada. The data are retained for a period of 1 year and are used for research purposes. Humidity is shared on an hourly basis with ThirstFirst LTD, and retained by them for 1 year, in the USA. Humidity data are used for marketing purposes"*. It is 453 characters long, and for the sake of simplicity let us assume that it also uses an alphabet of 39 symbols: 26 lower case Latin letters, 10 digits, space, comma, period. As in the previous case, each symbol is worth 6 bits, therefore $\eta = \frac{info_{useful}}{info_{total}} \times 100 = \frac{155 \times 2}{453 \times 6} \times 100 \approx 11\%$.

The prose version is clearly a step down from an efficiency of 53%! While we acknowledge that this synthetic version of a prose policy could have been shorter, such laconic policies are not the norm [18, 19, 26].

Appendix B When to Display Consent Prompts

The following pseudo-code illustrates the logic defined in Sect. 4 in action:

```
def is_consent_necessary():
    """Returns True if consent needs to be requested again,
    otherwise False"""
    for rule in rules:
        if rule matched:
            return False  # No need to ask for consent

    # if we got this far, re-asking for consent is required
    return True
```

A more granular approach enables us to tell whether a primary or a secondary filter matched, allowing more control (e.g. the GUI can display different prompts, depending on the magnitude of the difference):

```
def is_consent_necessary_granular():
    """Returns a tuple consisting of (necessary, reason),
    where necessary is True or False, while reason is
    one of {MAJOR, MINOR, NONE}."""
    for rule in primary_rules:
        if rule matched:
            # a primary rule was fired, no need to ask
            # consent again. E.g. some terms were removed
            # or made more strict
            return False, MAJOR

    for rule in secondary_rules:
        if rule matched:
            # a smaller change, we don't necessarily need
            # to ask consent again, but we might have to,
            # depending on the user's preferences. E.g.,
            # switch to another EU country, or moving up to
            # a "stronger privacy" place
            return False, MINOR

    # if we got this far, re-asking for consent is required
    return True, NONE
```

References

1. Anderson, B.B., et al.: How polymorphic warnings reduce habituation in the brain: insights from an fMRI study. In: Proceedings of the 33rd Annual ACM Conference on Human Factors in Computing Systems (2015)

2. Anderson, B.B., et al.: Users aren't (necessarily) lazy: using NeuroIS to explain habituation to security warnings. In: Proceedings of the 35th International Conference on Information Systems (2014)
3. App privacy details on the App Store. Apple Developer. https://developer.apple.com/app-store/app-privacy-details/
4. Bos, B.: Data Privacy Vocabulary. W3C Recommendation. W3C (2019). https://www.w3.org/ns/dpv
5. Bösch, C., et al.: Tales from the dark side. In: Proceedings on Privacy Enhancing Technologies (2016)
6. Breaux, T.D., Hibshi, H., Rao, A.: Eddy, a formal language for specifying and analyzing data flow specifications for conflicting privacy requirements. Requirements Eng. 19(3), 281–307 (2013). https://doi.org/10.1007/s00766-013-0190-7
7. Casey, S.M.: Set Phasers on Stun: And Other True Tales of Design, Technology, and Human Error (1993)
8. Cate, F.H.: The limits of notice and choice. IEEE Secur. Priv. Mag. 8, 59–62 (2010)
9. Cranor, L.F.: Web Privacy with P3P (2002)
10. I. DIS. 9241–210: 2010. Ergonomics of Human System Interaction-Part 210: Human-Centred Design for Interactive Systems (2009)
11. Erickson, A.: Comparative analysis of the EU's GDPR and Brazil's LGPD: enforcement challenges with the LGPD. Brooklyn J. Int. Law 44, 859 (2018)
12. European Parliament and Council of European Union. Regulation 2016/679 of the European Parliament and of the Council. In: Official Journal of the European Union (2016)
13. Fagan, M., et al.: A study of users' experiences and beliefs about software update messages. In: Computers in Human Behavior (2015)
14. GDPR Recital 58 - The Principle of Transparency. https://gdpr-info.eu/recitals/no-58/
15. Greveler, U., et al.: Multimedia content identification through smart meter power usage profiles. In: Proceedings of the International Conference on Information and Knowledge Engineering (IKE) (2012)
16. Harkous, H., et al.: Polisis: automated analysis and presentation of privacy policies using deep learning. In: 27th USENIX Security Symposium (2018)
17. Harkous, H., et al.: PriBots: conversational privacy with chatbots. In: 12th Symposium on Usable Privacy and Security (2016)
18. Human, S., Cech, F.: A human-centric perspective on digital consenting: the case of GAFAM. In: Zimmermann, A., Howlett, R.J., Jain, L.C. (eds.) Human Centred Intelligent Systems. SIST, vol. 189, pp. 139–159. Springer, Singapore (2021). https://doi.org/10.1007/978-981-15-5784-2_12
19. Mcdonald, A.M., et al.: The cost of reading privacy policies. J. Law Policy Inf. Soc. 4, 543–568 (2008)
20. Miller, G.A.: The magical number 7±2. In: Psychological Review (1956)
21. Morgner, P., et al.: Opinion: security lifetime labels - overcoming information asymmetry in security of IoT consumer products. In: Proceedings of the 11th ACM Conference on Security & Privacy in Wireless and Mobile Networks (2018)
22. Morgner, P., et al.: Privacy implications of room climate data. In: Foley, S.N., Gollmann, D., Snekkenes, E. (eds.) ESORICS 2017. LNCS, vol. 10493, pp. 324–343. Springer, Cham (2017). https://doi.org/10.1007/978-3-319-66399-9_18
23. Nielsen, J.: Jakob's Law of Internet User Experience. https://www.nngroup.com/videos/jakobs-law-internet-ux/
24. Nielsen, N.: EU warns Romania not to abuse GDPR against press. EUobserver (2018). https://euobserver.com/justice/143356

25. Nokhbeh Zaeem, R., et al.: PrivacyCheck v2: a tool that recaps privacy policies for you. In: Proceedings of the 29th ACM International Conference on Information & Knowledge Management (2020)

26. Okoyomon, E., et al.: On the ridiculousness of notice and consent: contradictions in app privacy policies. In: Workshop on Technology and Consumer Protection (2019)

27. Railean, A., Reinhardt, D.: OnLITE: on-line label for IoT transparency enhancement. In: Asplund, M., Nadjm-Tehrani, S. (eds.) NordSec 2020. LNCS, vol. 12556, pp. 229–245. Springer, Cham (2021). https://doi.org/10.1007/978-3-030-70852-8_14

28. Raskin, J.: The Humane Interface: New Directions for Designing Interactive Systems (2011)

29. Lederman, N.G., Lederman, J.S.: The elephant in the room. J. Sci. Teacher Educ. **26**(8), 669–672 (2016). https://doi.org/10.1007/s10972-015-9446-z

30. Sadeh, N., et al.: Towards usable privacy policies: semi-automatically extracting data practices from websites' privacy policies'. In: Poster Proceedings of the 10th Symposium On Usable Privacy and Security (2014)

31. Schaub, F., et al.: A design space for effective privacy notices. In: Proceedings of the 11th Symposium On Usable Privacy and Security (2015)

32. Shannon, C.E.: A mathematical theory of communication. Bell Syst. Tech. J. **27**, 379–423 (1948)

33. Su, J., et al.: One pixel attack for fooling deep neural networks. IEEE Trans. Evol. Comput. **23**, 828–841 (2019)

34. Vaniea, K., et al.: Betrayed by updates. In: Proceedings of the CHI Conference on Human Factors in Computing Systems (2014)

35. Vaniea, K., et al.: Tales of software updates. In: Proceedings of the CHI Conference on Human Factors in Computing Systems (2016)

36. Voss, W.G.G.: The CCPA and the GDPR are not the same: why you should understand both. In: CPI Antitrust Chronicle (2021)

Privacy Enhancing Technologies

User-Generated Pseudonyms Through Merkle Trees

Georgios Kermezis[1], Konstantinos Limniotis[1,2]($\boxtimes$) iD,
and Nicholas Kolokotronis[3] iD

[1] School of Pure and Applied Sciences, Open University of Cyprus,
2220 Latsia, Cyprus
georgios.kermezis@st.ouc.ac.cy, konstantinos.limniotis@ouc.ac.cy
[2] Hellenic Data Protection Authority, Kifissias 1-3, 11523 Athens, Greece
klimniotis@dpa.gr
[3] Department of Informatics and Telecommunications, University of Peloponnese,
Akadimaikou G.K. Vlachou Street, 22131 Tripolis, Greece
nkolok@uop.gr

Abstract. A pseudonymisation technique based on Merkle trees is described in this paper. More precisely, by exploiting inherent properties of the Merkle trees as cryptographic accumulators, we illustrate how user-generated pseudonyms can be constructed, without the need of a third party. Each such pseudonym, which depends on several user's identifiers, suffices to hide these original identifiers, whilst the unlinkability property between any two different pseudonyms for the same user is retained; at the same time, this pseudonymisation scheme allows the pseudonym owner to easily prove that she owns a pseudonym within a specific context, without revealing information on her original identifiers. Compared to other user-generated pseudonymisation techniques which utilize public key encryption algorithms, the new approach inherits the security properties of a Merkle tree, thus achieving post-quantum security.

Keywords: Data minimisation · General data protection regulation · Merkle trees · Personal data · Pseudonymisation

1 Introduction

Pseudonymisation of personal data constitutes an important privacy enhancing technique that, when appropriately implemented, suffices to provide specific data protection safeguards. More precisely, the data pseudonymisation may give rise to protecting (hiding) the real identities of the individuals (which is related, as a

---

This project has received funding from the European Union's Horizon 2020 research and innovation programme under grant agreement no. 786698. The work reflects only the authors' view and the Agency is not responsible for any use that may be made of the information it contains.

N. Gruschka et al. (Eds.): APF 2021, LNCS 12703, pp. 89–105, 2021.
https://doi.org/10.1007/978-3-030-76663-4_5

data protection goal, to data confidentiality), as well as to unlinkability of individuals across different application domains. Moreover, pseudonyms can also be used in some cases to ensure verification of the actual identity of the individual (which is related, as a data protection goal, to data integrity) [15,16]. Therefore, taking into account the six data protection goals as they have been presented in [19] for addressing the legal, technical, economic, and societal dimensions of privacy and data protection in complex IT systems - namely confidentiality, integrity, unlinkability, availability, intervenablity and transparency - the pseudonymisation may contribute in ensuring (at least) the three of them.

The aforementioned data protection goals of pseudonymisation are implied in the European General Data Protection Regulation (Regulation (EU) 2016/679 or GDPR). There are several references to pseudonymisation within the GDPR, mainly as the vehicle for providing appropriate data protection safeguards in several cases, such as towards achieving the so-called *data protection by design* principle. However, choosing a proper pseudonymisation technique is not always an easy task, since there are different parameters that need to be considered each time, taking into account the specific scenario that the pseudonymisation is to be used [15,16].

One quite challenging use case of pseudonymisation is the one that the user's pseudonym is being generated in the user's environment - i.e. user-generated pseudonyms. In such a scenario, neither the data controller (as is defined in the GPDR) nor any other (trusted or not) third party is actively employed in the process of deriving the pseudonyms; instead, the individuals by themselves, via a specific process in a decentralised approach, generate pseudonyms which in turn are being subsequently used by data controllers.

1.1   Related Work

Several pseudonymisation approaches focusing on deriving user - generated pseudonyms have been proposed in the literature (e.g. [24,34,36]), mainly based on public key cryptographic primitives. One of the most known scenarios of user-generated pseudonyms is the the case of several blockchain systems (such as the case of Bitcoin), in which the users are being identified by a meaningless identifier (i.e. the pseudonym, being called *address* in this case) which is uniquely associated with a relevant cryptographic key corresponding to its owner.

As stated in [24], when designing such a decentralised approach for pseudonym generation, we are mainly interested in fulfilling the following requirements: i) ease of use, ii) linking a pseudonym to its owning user should not be possible for any other than the user herself, unless it is explicitly permitted, iii) in cases that users may have multiple pseudonyms, it should not be possible to identify different pseudonyms as belonging to the same user, iv) injectivity, in terms that the pseudonym generation process should avoid duplicates, v) flexibility, i.e. it should be possible to add new pseudonyms to the user entities with minimal effort.

1.2   Contribution of This Work

In this paper, we explore the notion of the so-called cryptographic accumulators, in order to derive user-generated pseudonyms with some specific properties. Cryptographic accumulators are data structures based on cryptographic primitives to efficiently implement set membership operations [32]. They allow to accumulate a finite set of values $\{x_1, x_2, \ldots, x_n\}$ into a succinct value X. Therefore, they may constitute a convenient tool to derive pseudonyms (corresponding to the relevant succinct values) that are contingent on a set of initial identifiers (corresponding to the relevant set of values), so as to allow extracting the information whether a given identifier corresponds to a given pseudonym. To achieve this goal, we appropriately utilize the Merkle trees [28] - which is a case of a cryptographic accumulator - as the means to provide a new pseudonymisation technique. The generic idea of using Merkle trees for pseudonymisation purposes has been very recently discussed in [17]. In our approach, we propose a new pseudonymisation scheme such as, for a user A with some domain-specific identifiers $\mathrm{id}_{A_0}, \ldots, \mathrm{id}_{A_{n-1}}$, a pseudonym P_A of A can be generated by the user A herself, satisfying the following properties:

P1. The pseudonym P_A depends on all $\mathrm{id}_{A_0}, \ldots, \mathrm{id}_{A_{n-1}}$.

P2. Knowledge of P_A does not allow revealing any of the original identifiers id_{A_i}, $i = 0, 1, \ldots, n-1$.

P3. The user A can prove, whenever she wants, that any id_{A_i}, $i = 0, 1, \ldots, n-1$, corresponds to P_A, without revealing any other information on the remaining identifiers id_{A_j}, $j \in \{0, 1, \ldots, n-1\} \setminus \{i\}$.

P4. The user may generate several such pseudonyms $P_A^{(0)}, \ldots, P_A^{(s)}$, with the above properties, being pairwise unlinkable.

P5. Two different users A and B will always generate different pseudonyms P_A and P_B, regardless the number, the types and the values of their original identifiers.

Therefore, the new pseudonymisation technique satisfies the properties described in [24] (implementation issues will be subsequently analysed), enriched with some additional properties that may be of high importance in specific scenarios, as discussed next. Actually, due to the property **P3**, the user A may prove, if she wants, that two different pseudonyms $P_A^{(1)}$ and $P_A^{(2)}$, even if they have been given to two different organisations Org_1 and Org_2 respectively, correspond to her; such a proof of pseudonym's ownership though (i.e. proving to Org_1 that she owns $P_A^{(2)}$ in Org_2 and/or vice versa), does not reveal any additional information on the original identifiers of A to either Org_1 or Org_2.

Moreover, it should be pointed out that the cryptographic strength of the above properties are strongly related to the cryptographic strength of the Merkle tree as an one-time signature scheme, which is known to be post-quantum secure under specific assumptions on the underlying hash function [9,10] (see Subsect. 3.3). This is an important property, taking also into account that other known techniques on deriving user-generated pseudonyms (such as the aforementioned techniques in [24,34,36])) rely on conventional public key cryptographic schemes which are not post-quantum secure.

The rest of the paper is organised as follows. First, the necessary background is given in Sect. 2, covering both the basic elements of the legal framework (Subsect. 2.1) and the typical Merkle trees (Subsect. 2.2). Next, the basic idea on the proposed pseudonymisation technique is presented in Sect. 3; this section also includes a discussion on the security properties and on implementation issues, as well as on possible application scenarios for this technique. Finally, concluding remarks are given in Sect. 4.

2   Preliminaries

2.1   Pseudonymisation and Data Protection: Legal Framework

The European Regulation (EU) 2016/679 (2016)—known as the *General Data Protection Regulation* or GDPR—constitutes the main legal instrument for personal data protection in Europe, which applies to all organizations that process personal data of individuals residing in the European Union, regardless of the organizations' location, which can be outside European Union.

The term *personal data* refers to any information relating to an identified or identifiable natural person, that is a person who can be identified (being called *data subject*). *Personal data processing* means any operation that is performed on personal data, including the collection, recording, structuring, storage, adaptation or alteration, retrieval, use, disclosure by transmission, dissemination, combination and erasure. The GDPR codifies the basic principles that need to be guaranteed when personal data are collected or further processed and sets specific obligations to the *data controllers* - i.e. the entities that, alone or jointly with others, determine the purposes and means of the processing of personal data. Amongst them, the so-called *data minimisation principle* refers to the necessity that the personal data shall be adequate, relevant and limited to what is necessary in relation to the purposes for which they are processed (art. 5 of the GDPR).

The data minimisation, as a fundamental principle, spans the entire text of the GDPR: for example, is it explicitly mentioned in art. 25 towards ensuring the *data protection by design* principle, which in turn constitutes an important challenge involving various technological and organisational aspects [2]. Moreover, the art. 11 of the GDPR states that if the purposes for which the data controller processes personal data do not or do no longer require the identification of an individual, then the controller shall not be obliged to maintain, acquire or process additional information in order to identify the data subject.

In light of the above requirements, data pseudonymisation plays an important role in data protection. From an engineering perspective, a pseudonym is defined as an identifier of a subject, which is different from the subject's *real name* [1,33], whereas the types of pseudonyms may be distinguished by the context of use [33]. Typically, a pseudonym replaces a data subject's identifier, with the latter one being able to explicitly identify the data subject within a specific context;

for example, the original identifier can be a combination of first name and last name, an e-mail address, or even a device/network identifier (e.g. an IP address, a device ID etc.) which in turn constitute personal data when the device is associated with an individual (see also [12]).

The GDPR also defines pseudonymisation as *the processing of personal data in such a manner that the personal data can no longer be attributed to a specific data subject without the use of additional information, provided that such additional information is kept separately and is subject to technical and organisational measures to ensure that the personal data are not attributed to an identified or identifiable natural person.* As the GDPR explicitly states, pseudonymous data are personal and not anonymous data, despite the fact that there is often a confusion in characterizing pseudonymous data as anonymous (see, e.g., [12] for a discussion on this). However, with a properly implemented pseudonymisation scheme, pseudonymous data should not allow revealing the original identifier without some *additional information*; this piece of information can be, for example, a cryptographic key which is protected - and that's why a pseudonymisation technique often relies on utilizing a cryptographic function to identifiers or other identity-related information (see, e.g., [15,16] and the references therein).

2.2 Merkle Trees

A Merkle tree is a binary tree based on a cryptographic hash function H. Having as starting point N values $y_0, \ldots, y_{N-1}$, where $N = 2^n$ for some integer n, the i-th leaf node is labeled with the corresponding hash value $H(y_i)$ of y_i, whereas every inner node is labeled with the hash value formed from the concatenation of its children's labels. The label of the root node is the accumulated value, which is clearly contingent on all $y_0, \ldots, y_{N-1}$. For example, in Fig. 1 which illustrates a Merkle tree of $2^3 = 8$ leaves (i.e. of height 3), it holds $a_{1,0} = H(a_{0,0} \parallel a_{0,1}) = H(H(y_0) \parallel H(y_1))$, $a_{2,0} = H(a_{1,0} \parallel a_{1,1})$ and $a_{3,0} = H(a_{2,0} \parallel a_{2,1})$.

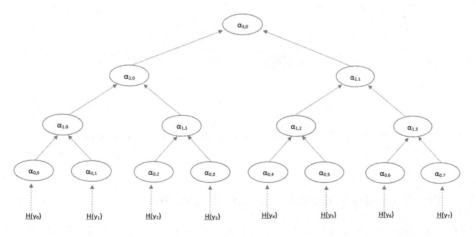

Fig. 1. A classical Merkle tree with 2^3 leaves.

A Merkle tree may be the basis for deriving hash-based one-time signatures [28], generalizing the notion of Lamport's signatures [22]. Each y_i corresponds to a private key that is being used to sign a message, whereas the root of the tree is the signer's public key. Let us assume, for simplicity, the simplest case in which each signature corresponds to a single-bit messages - i.e. either 0 or 1. When such a y_i is to be used for signing one bit (either 0 or 1) of the message, the signer actually signs the message with the pair $(y_i, H(y_i))$ - i.e. the signer reveals the private value y_i which allows for the computation of $H(y_i)$ which in turn is being used for the verification of the signature. More precisely, to allow signature verification, the signer should also reveal the *authentication path* of the tree - i.e. all the necessary labels of the intermediate nodes which are needed to verify the root of the tree, that is the signer's known public key. For example, for the case of the Merkle tree illustrated in Fig. 1, the verification path for the signature corresponding to y_2 consists of the labels $a_{0,3}$, $a_{1,0}$ and $a_{2,1}$ (see Fig. 2). Once a private key is being revealed it should not be used again for signing (and, thus, the number of possible messages that could be signed depends on the size of the tree). Actually, for any pair y_i, y_{i+1}, $i = 0, 2, 4, \ldots$, only one of these private values can be used for signing, depending on the message (i.e. y_i is being used if the current bit of the message is 0 and y_{i+1} if the current bit of the message is 1) and, after its usage, this pair is not being used for future signatures. The Merkle trees constitute the main building blocks for hash-based post-quantum secure signature schemes, such as LMS [26], XMSS [20], and SPHINCS+ [5].

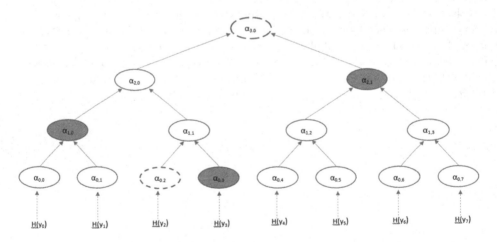

Fig. 2. An authentication path in a Merkle signature scheme.

3   The New Pseudonymisation Technique

In this section, we present how a Merkle tree can be used to generate pseudonyms with the properties **P1–P5** described in Sect. 1.

3.1 Initial Assumptions

Our main initial assumption is that an individual A is being identified by different organisations $\text{Org}_0, \ldots, \text{Org}_{N-1}$ though pairwise distinct identifiers id_{A_i}, $i = 0, 1, \ldots, N - 1$ respectively; for example, depending on the context, such identifiers could be. e.g., a Social Security Number, an Identity Card Number, a VAT Registration Number or even an e-mail address or a device identifier. We are not interested in how each Org_i, $i = 0, 1, \ldots, N-1$, obtains, at the first place, the identifier id_{A_i}; we simply assume that the validity of each such identifier, for the corresponding organisation, is ensured (i.e. through a secure registration procedure). This in general needs to be carefully considered - for example, it may need, depending on the context, a specific architectural structure based on recognised digital certificates; in any case, such an initial secure registration process is out of the scope of this paper.

Actually, the term *identifier* is being used hereinafter to describe any piece of information that allows distinguishing an individual from other individuals; the GDPR (Article 4) provides a non-exhaustive list of common identifiers (such as name, identification number, location data, online identifier). In our scenario, an identifier for each organisation could be of any form. However, our main assumption is that an organisation Org_i should not, by default, be able to link personal information of A with another organisation Org_j (i.e. such a linking would vanish the data minimisation principle); this in turn means that, for any pair i, j, the organisation Org_i should not know that id_{A_j} is associated with the individual A. For example, a hospital may identify a patient though her Social Security Number; however, since there is no need for the hospital to get knowledge of the VAT Registration Number of the patient, this user's identifier should not become known to the hospital.

It should be pointed out that the notion of identifier is not necessarily restricted to a single value, as in the examples presented above; for example, one such identifier id_{A_i} may consist, e.g., of a combination of individual's first name, last name and ID card number; although the ID card number by itself suffices to uniquely identify the individual in a specific context (i.e. it is a single identifier), we may allow incorporating many user's attributes into the definition of a single identifier. By these means, the number of possible single identifiers that may occur does not affect our analysis, since all of them may become part of a new single identifier incorporating all of them. Indeed, re-visiting the above example, the combination of first name and last name could be also an identifier (depending on the context), apart from the ID card number; however, we may define in this case that: $\text{id}_{A_1} = \text{first\_name} \parallel \text{last\_name} \parallel \text{ID\_card\_number}$.

Moreover, in the subsequent analysis, we assume that the organisations Org_i, $i = 0, 1, \ldots, N - 1$ do not secretly exchange information towards getting, for a user A, much more personal information of A than they need for their data processing purposes (i.e. they do not collaborate maliciously in terms of personal data protection requirements). In other words, for any $i \neq j$, Org_i and Org_j do not try to link information relating to id_{A_i} and id_{A_j} - which would also lead in revealing id_{A_i} (resp. id_{A_j}) to Org_j (resp. Org_i). It should be noted that

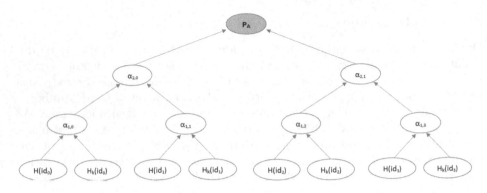

Fig. 3. Generating a pseudomyn depending on $\mathrm{id}_{A_0}, \mathrm{id}_{A_1}, \mathrm{id}_{A_2}, \mathrm{id}_{A_3}$

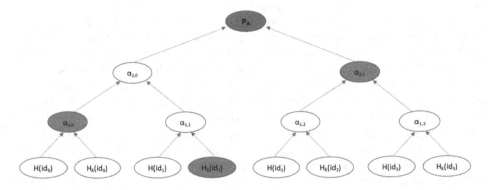

Fig. 4. Proving that the pseudonym P_A corresponds to the known identifier id_{A_1}

such linking attacks, generally, may be possible between different databases, even if the relevant users identifiers are different: this may occur, for example, by comparing the so-called quasi-identifiers of individuals (see, e.g., [18]). In our paper, we do not consider such threats; we simply focus on deriving user-generated different pseudonyms $P_A^{(i)}$ and $P_A^{(j)}$ being pairwise unlinkable - i.e., for any $i \neq j$, $P_A^{(i)} \neq P_A^{(j)}$, whilst knowledge of $P_A^{(i)}$, $i = 0, 1, \ldots, N-1$, does not allow computation of id_{A_i}, as well as computation of any other identifier id_{A_j} of A. Moreover, under the aforementioned assumption of the honest model with respect to the behavior of the parties (organisations), there is no way to establish that $P_A^{(i)}$ and $P_A^{(j)}$ correspond to the same individual - unless the individual A by herself wants to prove it.

3.2 How to Derive a Pseudonym

Let us assume that the user A wants to generate N pseudonyms $P_A^{(i)}$, $i = 0, 1, \ldots, N-1$, each for one different organisation Org_i, where Org_i already knows the identifier id_{A_i} of A. First, for the sake of simplicity, we assume that

$N = 2^n$ for some integer n (and the more general case will be subsequently discussed). For these parameters, each pseudonym is associated with a Merkle tree of height $n+1$ - i.e. with $2N$ leaves. For the i-th such Merkle tree, the labels $a_{0,0}^{(i)}, a_{0,1}^{(i)}, \ldots, a_{0,2N-1}^{(i)}$ of its leaves are constructed via a secret key $k^{(i)}$, which is known only to A, as follows:

$$a_{0,\ell}^{(i)} = \begin{cases} H(\mathrm{id}_{A_{\ell/2}}), & \text{if } \ell = 0, 2, 4, \ldots, 2N-2, \\ H_{k^{(i)}}(\mathrm{id}_{A_{(\ell-1)/2}}), & \text{if } \ell = 1, 3, 5, \ldots, 2N-1 \end{cases}$$

where H is a cryptographic hash function and $H_{k^{(i)}}$ is a keyed hash function with a key $k^{(i)}$ - i.e. a Message Authentication Code (MAC). Actually, in simple words, each pair of leaves of the Merkle tree corresponds to one users's identifier; the first leaf of the pair is labelled by the hashed value of the identifier, whilst the second leaf is labelled by the keyed hashed value of the identifier (i.e. its MAC). Such a Merkle tree is shown in the Fig. 3, with 8 leaves (i.e. $N = 4$); the label P_A of the root corresponds to the pseudonym of the user (for simplicity, we write in this Figure P_A and k instead of $P_A^{(i)}$ and $k^{(i)}$ respectively). Apparently, the root of the tree depends on all its leaves - namely, on all identifiers id_{A_i}, $i = 0, 1, \ldots, N-1$. Moreover, by using different key $k^{(i)}$ for each Merkle tree, a different pseudonym $P_A^{(i)}$ is being generated for each Org_i; all of these pseudonyms $P_A^{(i)}$ though, $i = 0, 1, \ldots, N-1$, share the same properties (i.e. each of them depends on all id_{A_i}, $i = 0, 1, \ldots, N-1$,) and are pairwise unlinkable.

Since we assume that these pseudonyms are being generated in the user's environment, which in turn means that each secret key $k^{(i)}$ is known only to the pseudonym's owner A, it is essential to establish a procedure that the user A proves to an organisation Org_j that she owns the pseudonym $P_A^{(i)}$. Recalling our assumption that Org_j already knows id_{A_j} as an identifier of A, the properties of a Merkle tree as a cryptographic primitive for a digital signature (see Fig. 2) suffice to allow such a proof of ownership. Indeed, let us assume that, for the pseudonym derived in the Fig. 3, that the user A wants to prove to Org_1 that she owns this pseudonym. Then A simply reveals the labels of the authentication path of the tree that allows Org_1 verify that the pseudonym $P_A^{(i)}$ corresponds to id_{A_1} - namely, A reveals the values $H_{k^{(i)}}(\mathrm{id}_{A_1})$, $a_{1,0}$ and $a_{2,1}$ (recall that Org_1 can compute $H(\mathrm{id}_{A_1})$). This is illustrated in Fig. 4. Clearly, a similar procedure may be followed for any identifier id_{A_i}, $i = 0, 1, \ldots, N-1$ or, equivalently, to any organisation Org_i, $i = 0, 1, \ldots, N-1$. Due to the properties of the Merkle tree, no information on other identifiers of A is revealed in this verification procedure. Moreover, for a secure keyed hash function, knowledge of the pair $(\mathrm{id}_{A_i}, H_{k^{(i)}}(\mathrm{id}_{A_i}))$ does not allow computing $k^{(i)}$.

An interesting remark is that the above verification procedure holds for any pair $i, j \in \{0, 1, \ldots, N-1\}$ - i.e. A can always prove to Org_j that $P_A^{(i)}$ corresponds to id_{A_j}, without revealing to Org_j any other information on the remaining identifiers id_{A_ℓ}, $\ell \in \{0, 1, \ldots, N-1\} \setminus \{j\}$. If $i = j$, such a verification procedure is essential in establishing that the pseudonym of A within Org_j will be $P_A^{(j)}$; this is a necessary first step (i.e. a registration process), since a pseudonym $P_A^{(j)}$ may be considered as valid in a specific context only if the relevant organisation Org_j that will use $P_A^{(j)}$ is ensured for its validity. However, if $i \neq j$, then we are in the case that A proves to Org_j that she owns another pseudonym $P_A^{(i)}$ in another organisation Org_i - i.e. the user A allows for linking personal information of herself. Note that, without this intervention (i.e. proof of ownership) of A, such a linking between $P_A^{(i)}$ and $P_A^{(j)}$ is not possible.

Due to the nature of the Merkle tree, which is typically considered as a full balanced binary tree, the number of its leaves is always a power of 2; that's why we first assumed that $N = 2^n$ for some n. However, this may not be always the case. To alleviate this issue, we choose the minimum possible integer m such that $N < 2^m$ and we proceed accordingly by constructing a Merkle tree with 2^{m+1} leaves; the first $2N$ of them correspond to the N user's identifiers as described previously, whereas the remaining $2^{m+1} - 2N$ leaves can be chosen arbitrarily.

3.3   Security Requirements

As in any hash-based post-quantum signature scheme, the security of the described pseudonymisation scheme rests with the cryptographic properties of the underlying hash function H in the Merkle tree [10,11]. In our case, the necessary security requirement for H is collision resistance, which means that finding two inputs with the same hash value is computationally infeasible. Collision resistance implies other weaker security requirements such as one-wayness (i.e. for essentially all pre-specified outputs, it is computationally infeasible to find any input which hashes to that output) and second-preimage resistance (i.e. it is computationally infeasible to find a second input which has the same hash value as that of a specified input). Therefore, if collision resistance is present, an adversary cannot find, for any given pseudonym $P_A^{(i)}$, as well as for any given label of an intermediate node of the tree, any relevant id_{A_ℓ}, $\ell = 0, 1, \ldots, N-1$. Moreover, an adversary cannot find/compute inputs which give rise to the same outputs as the original id_{A_ℓ}, $\ell = 0, 1, \ldots, N-1$.

An important parameter of hash functions towards evaluating the aforementioned collision resistance is the length n of the hash value. As it is stated in [10], the so-called birthday attack, which works for any hash function, finds a collision in time approximately $2^{n/2}$; moreover, in a quantum world, there exists an attack finding a collision in time approximately $2^{n/3}$ [4]. Therefore, today we need $n \geq 256$, whilst for post-quantum security we need $n \geq 384$ [10]. The cryptographic NIST standards SHA-2 [30] and SHA-3 [31] are known to be collision-resistant, also supporting such lengths for their output.

Our pseudonymisation scheme also utilises a keyed hash function. Apparently, the requirement of collision resistance is also necessary for this function. To this end, the HMAC [29] or GMAC [13] cryptographic standards can be, e.g., used. For the case of HMAC, it is well-known [6] that its cryptographic strength depends on the properties of the underlying hash function - whereas the security of HMAC is formally studied in [7]. Therefore, again an appropriate collision resistant hash function, such as SHA-2 or SHA-3, suffices to develop a secure keyed hash function (see also ENISA's report on cryptographic parameters [14]). The security properties of the GMAC, being an information-theoretic authentication code, already assumes an attacker with unlimited computing power and, thus, it provides protection in the post-quantum era (see, e.g., [3]). Regarding the key size, GMAC provides post-quantum security with 128 bits key size [3]. The same key size is also considered as adequate today for HMAC; however, although there is a belief that such a key size will also be adequate for HMAC in the post-quantum era, several post-quantum implementations of HMAC utilize larger key sizes (see, e.g., [23]).

Apart from the properties of the cryptographic primitives that are being used, the following security requirement should also necessarily be in place: When the user A registers her pseudonym $P_A^{(i)}$ to the organisation Org_i, this registration should be authenticated (i.e. the identity of A providing id_{A_i} shall be ensured). Otherwise, an adversary having knowledge of the original identifier id_{A_i} of A could clearly create a fake pseudonym $P_A^{(i')}$ for which he could prove that it stems from id_{A_i}.

In a similar manner, the authentication path needs also to be fully protected; indeed, if an authentication path for a specific identifier is leaked, then this can be subsequently used by an adversary in a type of replay-attack (similarly to the case of post-quantum digital signatures based on Merkle trees, which do not allow the usage of the same authentication path twice for signing). In the same direction, it should be pointed out that the proposed scheme does not alleviate the potential threat of users acting maliciously, in terms of sharing their identifiers and authentication paths with other users (this is an issue that is being discussed in [25] as an important concern for some applications). In any case though, it is logical to assume that, in specific applications, the users do not want to share such information because they do need to protect their personal data.

3.4 Possible Applications

Based on the above properties of the pseudonymisation scheme, several possible application scenarios can be considered, in which the proposed pseudonymisation scheme provides the means to ensure data minimisation. Some indicative applications are given below, actually based on the properties **P1–P5** of the scheme.

Minimizing Information Requested from Another Entity/Data Controller. Let us assume that the individual A is identified by id_{A_1} in Org_1 and by id_{A_2} in Org_2, whereas the organisation Org_1 needs to get some information about A from Org_2. However, Org_1 (resp. Org_2) should not get knowledge of id_{A_2} (resp. Org_1).

As a specific indicative example, Org_1 could be, e.g., a University, using the student number of A as id_{A_1}, whereas Org_2 could be the Finance Ministry, with the Department/Service that is responsible for citizens taxes, using the VAT number as id_{A_2}. Let us assume that the University needs to get knowledge on the annual income of the student A, in order to decide whether the student A deserves some benefits (e.g. housing alliance). Actually, due to the data minimisation principle, if the decision on students benefits is based on a threshold of their annual income, only knowledge on whether this income is higher or lower than the threshold is needed (and not the exact value of the income).

With our pseudonymisation scheme, the user A has already created the pseudonyms $P_A^{(1)}$ and $P_A^{(2)}$ for the University and Finance Ministry respectively, having proved to each of them their ownership. Each of these pseudonyms is the root of a Merkle tree with 4 leaves; the leaves, in both trees, corresponds to the student number and the VAT number. To allow the University obtain the necessary information, the student A may provide to her University her pseudonym $P_A^{(2)}$ that uses for the service of the Finance Ministry, proving also that this pseudonym indeed corresponds to her; note that, for such a proof of ownership, A will provide to the University the authentication path of the Merkle tree of $P_A^{(2)}$ corresponding to her student number and not to the VAT Number (i.e. a different authentication path from the one that A used to prove the ownership of $P_A^{(2)}$ to the Finance Ministry). In other words, the University is able to verify the ownership of $P_A^{(2)}$, without getting any information on the VAT number of A. Then, the University simply asks the Finance Ministry to response whether the annual income of the individual with the pseudonym $P_A^{(2)}$ if higher or lower than the prescribed threshold. By these means, the University receives the minimum possible information that is necessary to perform its tasks.

Clearly, other similar examples as the above may be considered.

Minimizing Exchange of Information Between Joint Data Controllers or Between a Data Controller and a Data Processor. There are also cases in which a specific personal data processing is being somehow shared between different entities - each of them having a specific role in the whole process. Depending on the role, this could be a case of joint controllership (i.e. two or more entities are joint data controllers, that is they jointly determine the purposes and means of processing) or the case that some entities are data processors (i.e. entities which process personal data on behalf of the controller(s)). In any case, there may be necessary that such a single entity should have restricted access to personal data, in the framework of the data minimisation principle. For example, let us assume that one entity (let's say Org_2) may perform analysis on raw data, so as to derive an output for each individual which in turn will be feed to another entity (let's say Org_1). It is probable that, due to the data minimisation principle, Org_2 should not be able to re-identify the individuals, whilst Org_1, being able to re-identify them, should get access only to the outcome of the processing of Org_2 and not to the whole volume of initial raw data.

As a possible application scenario lying in this case, we may refer to data processing based on the Pay-How-You-Drive model. The main idea of this insurance model is that drivers have to pay a premium based on their driving behaviour and degree of exposure, instead of paying a predetermined fixed price. Such a model poses several privacy risks, due to the fact that the evaluation of the driver's behavior typically necessitates tracking of the driver's routes, collecting and/or extracting detailed personal information (speed, harsh braking/acceleration, visited places, trips frequencies and time schedules, number and duration of possible stops etc.). Hence, the proposed pseudonymisation scheme could possibly alleviate such privacy threats as follows:

- The collection of raw data, based on the driver's driving information, is performed by Org_2, which in turn performs the whole analysis in order to derive a scoring for the driver (according to the model). The scoring by itself does not allow going backwards to the detailed personal information.
- Org_2 works on pseudonymised information. For an individual (driver) A, Org_2 uses a user-generated pseudonym $P_A^{(2)}$ based on an identifier id_{A_2} of A which is known only to Org_2. Although it is important that id_{A_2} is unique for A and suffices to discriminate her from any other user, the value id_{A_2} by itself should not be able to allow finding the identity of A. For example, id_{A_2} could be a unique identifier generated by the relevant smart application.
- Org_2 submits the output of its analysis (i.e. scoring of the driver) to the insurance company Org_1, in a pseudonymised form, based on the pseudonym $P_A^{(2)}$. Note that, at this moment, Org_1 is not able to link $P_A^{(2)}$ to any of its insured customers (whereas even id_{A_2} is not known to Org_1).
- Org_2 deletes the raw data.
- The user A proves to the Org_1 that she owns the pseudonym $P_A^{(2)}$. Such a proof of ownership is based on an identifier id_{A_1}, which is known only to Org_1 for identifying its customers, which had been also used, in conjunction with id_{A_2}, for constructing $P_A^{(2)}$. In other words, $P_A^{(2)}$ is the root of a Merkle tree, whose four leaves are based on two identifiers id_{A_1} and id_{A_2} - namely, they are being labelled by id_{A_1}, $H_k(id_{A_1})$, id_{A_2}, $H_k(id_{A_2})$ respectively.
- The user (driver) may create new pseudonyms (i.e. by changing her secret keys) for a new relevant processing by Org_1 and Org_2.

By the above procedure, the insurance company gets the desired information on the evaluation of the driving behavior of its customer A, without obtaining any detailed personal information of her driving habits (trips, speed etc.). Moreover, Org_2 which get (and processes) such detailed personal information, is not able to link this information to an identified individual, unless of course the user A wants to prove her exact identity to Org_2 - e.g. in case of disputing the accuracy of personal data processed (recall also our assumption with respect to the honest model, in the beginning of Sect. 3).

Although the above clearly does not constitute a full solution to the privacy challenges of a Pay-How-You-Drive model, it becomes clear that by utilizing advanced pseudonymisation techniques such the one presented here, more options for alleviating data protection issues in several application scenarios are present.

3.5   Implementation Analysis

The performance of Merkle trees in terms of one-time signature schemes, taking into account both speed and storage, has been widely discussed by several researchers, whereas several improvements deviating from the naive implementation have been also proposed. Namely, there are techniques aiming to generate the signature without saving too many nodes, at a still efficient time - i.e. dealing with the so-called Merkle tree traversal problem (see, e.g., [8,27,35]).

Here, we do not focus on finding the best possible implementation, but we rather discuss several aspects that need to be considered. First, the height of the tree depends fully on the number of leaves - which, in our case, is fully determined by the number N of original user's identifiers id_{A_i}, $i = 0, 1, \ldots, N - 1$. The height in turn determines the total number of the tree's nodes, as well as the length of the verification path (which in general affects network performance). More precisely, in a Merkle tree of height h, the verification path also includes h nodes. For example, if $h = 4$, which means that the number of user's domain-specific identifiers is $N = 8$, and the size of the hash value is 384 bits (i.e. to be consistent with the requirements for post-quantum security), then the size of the verification path, to verify the pseudonym of length 384 bits, is 192 Bytes.

Moreover, as stated above, since the typical form of a Merkle tree implies a balanced tree (i.e. all leaves reside at the bottom level h, where h is the height of the tree), the number of the leaves should be a power of 2, and this forms a restriction of the whole process (it is already discussed that utilizing dummy values could be a way to deal with this issue). Alternatively, this could be alleviated by extending the notion of the Merkle tree so as to be imbalanced (see, e.g., [21]); in such a scenario, no all verification paths will have the same length. In any case though, adding a new leaf (i.e. adding a new identifier) yields a new root of the Merkle tree - i.e. a new pseudonym - and, therefore, an extended verification path. We state the above as possible approaches that could be considered as future research steps.

In any case, it is expected that the utilization of a Merkle tree as a vehicle for pseudonymisation through the proposed approach will not lead to a large tree, since typically the number of individual's identifiers will not be too large (see, e.g., the discussion of possible application areas in Subsect. 3.4). To verify the effectiveness of the approach for small sizes of Merkle trees for N identifiers or, equivalently $2N$ leaves, $2 \leq N \leq 128$, we executed experiments in a typical Windows 10 home computer (AMD Ryzen 3 2200U with Radeon Vega Mobile Gfx 2.5 GHz, with 8 Gb RAM). We utilized Python v.3.8.2 for our implementation of the pseudonymisation scheme, whilst we measured both the time for creating the pseudonym (i.e. to create the Merkle tree) as well as the time for the pseudonym verification (i.e. to verify that the given verification path does yield the pseudonym, for the given identifier). We utilized the SHA-2 hash function, with hash length 256 bits, and the HMAC, via the relevant Python libraries. The results illustrate that, for $N \leq 128$, the time for creating a Merkle tree (without implementing the most effective approach) is less than 1 s (starting from about

15 ms for small values of N), whereas the time for pseudonym verification is less than 40 ms.

4   Conclusion and Future Work

In this paper, we illustrated how a Merkle tree (as a characteristic example of cryptographic accumulator) can be used to provide a pseudonymisation mechanism with specific nice properties in terms of fulfilling the data minimisation principle, which are not easily attained by other known pseudonymisation techniques. Moreover, since the Merkle tree is known to provide post-quantum security, the proposed pseudonymisation scheme suffices to provide long-term security, whereas other known cryptography-based pseudonymisation techniques with similar properties do not provide such post-quantum resistance. The main outcome of the above analysis is that advanced cryptography suffices to provide solutions to personal data protection matters - not only from a security perspective (which is the obvious one) but also from a data minimisation perspective.

The ideas presented in this paper opens several directions for further research. First, for any specific case study utilizing this pseudonymisation scheme, a formal security analysis of the whole procedure is essential to be performed. Furthermore, other extensions of the Merkle trees (as in the cases of post-quantum one time signatures like XMSS or SPHINCS) could be possibly studied in the framework of deriving pseudonymisation schemes. Another interesting direction is to examine how the pseudonym's owner will be able to explicitly define which types of personal data will be exchanged between the two entities (organisations), so as to eliminate the risk that the two organisations exchange more personal data than it is necessary (i.e. to force transparency on the data exchange to the user).

In any case, a general conclusion is that the properties achieved by the proposed technique should be further elaborated, in terms of identifying other application areas in which this technique could be beneficial.

Acknowledgment. The authors would like to thank the anonymous reviewers for their very useful comments which helped to improve the paper.

References

1. Akil, M., Islami, L., Fischer-Hübner, S., Martucci, L.A., Zuccato, A.: Privacy-preserving identifiers for IoT: a systematic literature review. IEEE Access **8**, 168470–168485 (2020). https://doi.org/10.1109/ACCESS.2020.3023659
2. Alshammari, M., Simpson, A.: Towards a principled approach for engineering privacy by design. In: Schweighofer, E., Leitold, H., Mitrakas, A., Rannenberg, K. (eds.) APF 2017. LNCS, vol. 10518, pp. 161–177. Springer, Cham (2017). https://doi.org/10.1007/978-3-319-67280-9_9
3. Bernstein, D.J., Lange, T.: Post-quantum cryptography. Nature **549**, 188–194 (2017). https://doi.org/10.1038/nature23461
4. Brassard, G., Høyer, P., Tapp, A.: Quantum algorithm for the collision problem. In: Kao, M.Y. (ed.) Encyclopedia of Algorithms. Springer, New York (2016). https://doi.org/10.1007/978-1-4939-2864-4_304

5. Aumasson, J.-P., et al.: SPHINCS+ - submission to the 2nd round of the NIST post-quantum project. Specificatin document (2019). https://sphincs.org/data/sphincs+-round2-specification.pdf
6. Bellare, M., Canetti, R., Krawczyk, H.: Keying hash functions for message authentication. In: Koblitz, N. (ed.) CRYPTO 1996. LNCS, vol. 1109, pp. 1–15. Springer, Heidelberg (1996). https://doi.org/10.1007/3-540-68697-5_1
7. Bellare, M.: New proofs for NMAC and HMAC: security without collision-resistance. In: Dwork, C. (ed.) CRYPTO 2006. LNCS, vol. 4117, pp. 602–619. Springer, Heidelberg (2006). https://doi.org/10.1007/11818175_36
8. Berman, P., Karpinski, M., Nekrich, Y.: Optimal trade-off for Merkle tree traversal. Theor. Comput. Sci. **372**(1), 22–36 (2007). https://doi.org/10.1016/j.tcs.2006.11.029
9. Buchmann, J., Dahmen, E., Hülsing, A.: XMSS - a practical forward secure signature scheme based on minimal security assumptions. PQCrypto 2011: Post-Quantum Cryptography, pp. 117–129 (2011)
10. Buchmann, J.A., Butin, D., Göpfert, F., Petzoldt, A.: Post-quantum cryptography: state of the art. In: Ryan, P.Y.A., Naccache, D., Quisquater, J.-J. (eds.) The New Codebreakers. LNCS, vol. 9100, pp. 88–108. Springer, Heidelberg (2016). https://doi.org/10.1007/978-3-662-49301-4_6
11. Buchmann, J., García, L.C.C., Dahmen, E., Döring, M., Klintsevich, E.: CMSS – an improved Merkle signature scheme. In: Barua, R., Lange, T. (eds.) INDOCRYPT 2006. LNCS, vol. 4329, pp. 349–363. Springer, Heidelberg (2006). https://doi.org/10.1007/11941378_25
12. Chatzistefanou, V., Limniotis, K.: On the (non-)anonymity of anonymous social networks. In: Katsikas, S.K., Zorkadis, V. (eds.) e-Democracy 2017. CCIS, vol. 792, pp. 153–168. Springer, Cham (2017). https://doi.org/10.1007/978-3-319-71117-1_11
13. Dworkin, M.: Recommendation for block cipher modes of operation: galois/counter mode (GCM) and GMAC. NIST Special Publication 800–38D (2007)
14. European Union Agency for Cybersecurity: Algorithms, key sizeand parameters report (2014). https://doi.org/10.2824/36822
15. European Union Agency for Cybersecurity: Recommendations on shaping technology according to GDPR provisions - an overview on data pseudonymisation (2018). https://doi.org/10.2824/74954
16. European Union Agency for Cybersecurity: Pseudonymisation Techniques and Best Practices (2019). https://doi.org/10.2824/247711
17. European Union Agency for Cybersecurity: Data Pseudonymisation: Advanced Techniques and use cases (2021). https://doi.org/10.2824/860099
18. Fung, B.C.M., Wang, K., Chen, R., Yu, P.S.: Privacy-preserving data publishing: a survey of recent developments. ACM Comput. Surv. **42**, Article 14 (2010). https://doi.org/10.1145/1749603.1749605
19. Hansen, M., Jensen, M., Rost, M.: Protection goals for privacy engineering. In Proceedings of the 2015 IEEE Security and Privacy Workshops (SPW 2015), pp. 159–166. IEEE (2015). https://doi.org/10.1109/SPW.2015.13
20. Huelsing, A., Butin, D. Gazdag, S.-L., Rijneveld, J., Mohaisen, A.: XMSS: eXtended Merkle Signature Scheme. RFC 8391 (2018). https://rfc-editor.org/rfc/rfc8391.txt

21. Kandappu, T., Sivaraman, V., Boreli, R.: A novel unbalanced tree structure for low-cost authentication of streaming content on mobile and sensor devices. In: 9th Annual IEEE Communications Society Conference on Sensor, Mesh and Ad Hoc Communications and Networks (SECON), Seoul, pp. 488–496 (2012). https://doi.org/10.1109/SECON.2012.6275816

22. Lamport, L.: Constructing digital signatures from a one way function. Technical report SRI-CSL-98, SRI International Computer Science Laboratory (1979)

23. Latif, M.K., Jacinto, H.S., Daoud, L., Rafla, N.: Optimization of a quantum-secure sponge-based hash message authentication protocol. In: 2018 IEEE 61st International Midwest Symposium on Circuits and Systems (MWSCAS), Windsor, Canada, pp. 984–987 (2018). https://doi.org/10.1109/MWSCAS.2018.8623880

24. Lehnhardt, J., Spalka, A.: Decentralized generation of multiple, uncorrelatable pseudonyms without trusted third parties. In: Furnell, S., Lambrinoudakis, C., Pernul, G. (eds.) TrustBus 2011. LNCS, vol. 6863, pp. 113–124. Springer, Heidelberg (2011). https://doi.org/10.1007/978-3-642-22890-2_10

25. Lysyanskaya, A., Rivest, R.L., Sahai, A., Wolf, S.: Pseudonym systems. In: Heys, H., Adams, C. (eds.) SAC 1999. LNCS, vol. 1758, pp. 184–199. Springer, Heidelberg (2000). https://doi.org/10.1007/3-540-46513-8_14

26. McGrew, D., Curcio, M., Fluhrer, S.: Leighton-Micali hash-based signatures. RFC 8554 (2019). https://rfc-editor.org/rfc/rfc8554.txt

27. Merkle, R.C.: A digital signature based on a conventional encryption function. In: Pomerance, C. (ed.) CRYPTO 1987. LNCS, vol. 293, pp. 369–378. Springer, Heidelberg (1988). https://doi.org/10.1007/3-540-48184-2_32

28. Merkle, R.C.: A certified digital signature. In: Brassard, G. (ed.) CRYPTO 1989. LNCS, vol. 435, pp. 218–238. Springer, New York (1990). https://doi.org/10.1007/0-387-34805-0_21

29. National Institute of Standards and Technology: The Keyed-Hash Message Authentication Code (HMAC). FIPS PUB 198-1 (2008). https://nvlpubs.nist.gov/nistpubs/FIPS/NIST.FIPS.198-1.pdf

30. National Institute of Standards and Technology: Secure Hash Standard (SHS). FIPS PUB 80-4 (2015). https://doi.org/10.6028/NIST.FIPS.180-4

31. National Institute of Standards and Technology: SHA-3 Standard: Permutation-Based Hash and Extendable-Output Functions. FIPS PUB 202 (2015). https://doi.org/10.6028/NIST.FIPS.202

32. Ozcelik, I., Medury, S., Broaddus, J., Skjellum, A.: An overview of cryptographic accumulators. In: 7th International Conference on Information Systems Security and Privacy (ICISSP 2021), pp. 661–669 (2021)

33. Pfitzmann, A., Hansen, M.: A terminology for talking about privacy by data minimization: anonymity, unlinkability, undetectability, unobservability, pseudonymity, and identity management. TU Dresden, Dresden Germany, Technical report V0.34 (2010)

34. Schartner, P., Schaffer, M.: Unique user-generated digital pseudonyms. In: Gorodetsky, V., Kotenko, I., Skormin, V. (eds.) MMM-ACNS 2005. LNCS, vol. 3685, pp. 194–205. Springer, Heidelberg (2005). https://doi.org/10.1007/11560326_15

35. Szydlo, M.: Merkle tree traversal in log space and time. In: Cachin, C., Camenisch, J.L. (eds.) EUROCRYPT 2004. LNCS, vol. 3027, pp. 541–554. Springer, Heidelberg (2004). https://doi.org/10.1007/978-3-540-24676-3_32

36. Tunaru, I., Denis, B, Uguen, B.: Location-based pseudonyms for identity reinforcement in wireless ad hoc networks. In: Proceedings of IEEE 81st Vehicular Technology Conference (VTC Spring), pp. 1–5 (2015). https://doi.org/10.1109/VTCSpring.2015.7145918

Towards Improving Privacy of Synthetic DataSets

Aditya Kuppa[1,2]([✉]), Lamine Aouad[2], and Nhien-An Le-Khac[1]

[1] UCD School of Computing, Dublin, Ireland
aditya.kuppa@ucdconnect.ie, an.lekhac@ucd.ie
[2] Tenable Network Security, Paris, France
laouad@tenable.com

Abstract. Recent growth in domain specific applications of machine learning can be attributed to availability of realistic public datasets. Real world datasets may always contain sensitive information about the users, which makes it hard to share freely with other stake holders, and researchers due to regulatory and compliance requirements. Synthesising datasets from real data by leveraging generative techniques is gaining popularity. However, the privacy analysis of these dataset is still a open research. In this work, we fill this gap by investigating the privacy issues of the generated data sets from attacker and auditor point of view. We propose instance level Privacy Score (PS) for each synthetic sample by measuring the memorisation coefficient α_m per sample. Leveraging, PS we empirically show that accuracy of membership inference attacks on synthetic data drop significantly. PS is a model agnostic, post training measure, which helps data sharer with guidance about the privacy properties of a given sample but also helps third party data auditors to run privacy checks without sharing model internals. We tested our method on two real world data sets and show that attack accuracy reduced by PS based filtering.

Keywords: Privacy preserving synthetic data · Generative Adversarial Networks · Privacy audit

1 Introduction

Machine learning (ML) has been widely adopted in a variety of applications across multiple domains. Due to the maturity of large-scale training infrastructure [3], development tools and, the availability of large amounts of training data companies are building huge models with billions of parameters for commercial applications. The training data used to train these models often contain personal or sensitive data [1], which was aggregated from datasets that are used for purposes unknown to the data owner (i.e. the person itself). Unfortunately, end-users who play an active role as data donors lack visibility into how this data is being used/misused by the applications built on top of the data collected. A

ⓒ Springer Nature Switzerland AG 2021
N. Gruschka et al. (Eds.): APF 2021, LNCS 12703, pp. 106–119, 2021.
https://doi.org/10.1007/978-3-030-76663-4_6

growing number of AI incidents[1] show an upward trend of data and model misuses, which include discriminatory hiring decisions, behavioral manipulations, and unethical systems that lack transparency. To gain the trust of users and avoid the privacy implications of data sharing for end users institutions [4–6] and companies [7–14] are adopting synthetic data [15] as a solution to avoid privacy issues.

Synthetic data as an idea was first adopted in designing various imputation methods in the early 90's [15,16]. Raghunathan et al. [29] formally defined a framework to define properties of synthetic data, which was further enhanced in multiple other researchers [17–20,22,30]. Many recent works leveraged traditional statistical techniques and machine learning models to generate synthetic data [21,23–28].

Ideal synthetic data has properties such as handling large datasets with diverse data types (categorical, ordinal, continuous, skewed, etc.), preserving semantic relationships between variables [24] and, underlying algorithms are fairly generalizable and needs a little tuning. ML models trained on synthetic data may have similar performance as original data. Theoretical privacy guarantees can be achieved via "ideal" synthetic data as a synthetic data record is not an actual data record of an individual but reflect the exact data distributions of original data.

In the context of data sharing, the majority of recent methods employ generative models [35,36,41,44,45] to obtain the synthetic data from real data. Popular generative modeling frameworks such as Generative Adversarial Networks (GANs [36]) and Variational Auto-encoders (VAEs) use real data during training to train a model capable of generating (or "synthesising") "fake" data points. Quality metrics such as *fidelity* which measures how "realistic" is the synthetic data when compared to real data and, *diversity* which measures how diverse the generated samples to cover the variability of real data are used to assess quality of the synthetic data.

Measuring the generalization property of synthetic data is very important and often ignored by synthetic data generators. Most of the proposed methods optimize on fidelity and diversity properties ignoring to measure or report, how well the synthetic samples capture the overall distribution including outliers of real data and, not just copies of the (real) samples of training data. Evaluating generalization in generative models is not easy [47,48] when compared to discriminative models which are tested on held-out data.

From compliance and regulation view point, the General Data Protection Regulation (GDPR [37]) gives new rights to citizens regarding transparency around personal data. These include the right of access (knowing which data about the person has been stored) and the right to data erasure, also known as the right to be forgotten (having personal data deleted under certain circumstances). Privacy risk include the *risk of re-identification* and the *risk of inference* [31–34]. When an attacker is able to identify and link individuals within a dataset or across multiple datasets, then these datasets pose the risk of re-identification.

---

[1] https://incidentdatabase.ai/.

These types of attacks can reveal the presence of user [38] or user data was used to train an ML model [39]. Deducing the private information of individuals with high confidence from the linked datasets or ML model fall under the risk of inference.

Motivated by the need from compliance, privacy of the end user and, growing popularity of synthetic data as sharing mechanism both in industry and academia, in this work we aim to investigate privacy properties of synthetic data generated by generative models. First, we propose a novel Membership Inference Attack (MIA), which uses the popular bagging technique to achieve attacker goal of identifying the membership of user in the model trained on synthetic data. Next, a instance level privacy score is calculated to filter the synthctic samples, which could compromise the privacy of the sensitive attributes in the synthetic data to protect from MIAs.

2   Background

We present a brief background on membership inference attacks and generative machine learning models.

Membership Inference Attack (MIA) is one of the most popular privacy attacks against ML models [64–70]. The attacker goal of membership inference (MI) is to determine whether a data sample x is part of the training dataset of a target model $\mathcal{T}$. We define a membership inference attack model $\mathcal{A}_{MemInf}$ as a binary classifier.

$$\mathcal{A}_{MemInf} : x, \mathcal{T} \mapsto \{member, non\text{-}member\} \tag{1}$$

MIA poses severe privacy risks, using a model trained on data samples of people with sensitive information an attacker can execute MIA to successfully infer the membership of person revealing the person's sensitive information. To achieve MIA, Shokri et al. [64] train a number of shadow classifiers on confidence scores produced by the target model with labels indicating whether samples came from the training or testing set. MIAs are shown to work in white-box [50] as well as black-box scenarios against a various target models including ML-as-a-service [64] and generative models [49]. Yeom et al. [52] explore overfitting as the root cause of MI vulnerability.

Similarly, a variant of MIA is attribute inference in which sensitive attribute can be inferred from the target model. This sensitive attribute is not related to the target ML model's original classification task. For instance, a target model is designed to classify an individual's age from their social network posts, while attribute inference aims to infer their educational background [62,63]. Some studies [43,51,52] attribute membership inference attacks to the generalization gap, the over-fitting of the model, and data memorization capabilities of neural networks. Deep neural networks have been shown to memorize the training data [55,60,61], rather than learning the latent properties of the data, which means they often tend to over-fit to the training data. Weakness like this, in some cases, can be exploited by an adversary to infer data samples' sensitive attributes.

Given a data sample x and its representation from a target model, denoted by $h = f(x)$, to conduct the attribute inference attack, the adversary trains an attack model $\mathcal{A}_{AttInf}$ formally defined as follows:

$$\mathcal{A}_{AttInf} : h \mapsto s \tag{2}$$

where s represents the sensitive attribute.

Generative Adversarial Network. (GAN) [36] is a type of adversarial training system, where two competing models are trained against each other. They comprise of two components, a discriminator (D), which is trained to differentiate between real generated data; and the generator (G), which creates fake data to fool the discriminator. The generator G takes in a random noise vector Z and parameter vector $theta_g$ and learns to generate synthetic samples very similar to the real data. The resulting $G(Z; \theta_g)$ network is used to generate fake data with data distribution F_g.

Training GAN's on real-world datasets is notoriously hard. One has to carefully tune both generator and discriminator network parameters at training time to avoid conditions like mode collapse and vanishing gradients. Both these conditions affect the quality of synthetic data generated. Choice of loss functions and GAN architectures also play a vital role in avoiding these problems [56].

Tabular Generators. In this work, we deal in the feature space, which is tabular in nature. The values of features are continuous, ordinal, categorical, textual, and/or multi-categorical values. Textual values can be of variable length, high-dimensional due to long-tail distributions of observational data. Textual data is converted into a set of sequences and projected into a trained embedding that preserves semantic meaning similar to methods proposed in Natural Language Processing (NLP) literature. Traditional Generative Adversarial Network (GAN) [36] architectures proposed in literature perform poorly on tabular data [57] due to – (a) Real data often consists of mixed data types. To generate this data simultaneously, a GAN must be able to apply both softmax and tanh on the output; (b) Images pixel values generally follow a Gaussian-like distribution, which can be normalized to $[-1, 1]$, whereas with tabular data, continuous data often have non-Gaussian distributions with long tails that leads to gradient saturation; continuous data type and imbalanced categorical columns need preprocessing steps before feeding into generators.

Recently proposed Conditional Tabular GAN or CTGAN [57] addresses some of the key problems for tabular data synthesis. The training process involves simulating records one by one. It first randomly selects one of the variables, then it randomly selects a value for that variable. Given that value for that variable, the algorithm finds a matching row from the training data. It also generates the rest of the variables conditioning on the selected variable. The generated and true rows are sent to the critic that gives a score. Similarly, modified WGAN-GP [59] changed the generator of the WGAN-GP. Figure 1 summarizes the CTGAN and

WGAN-GP training procedures. to handle continuous variables. Other recently proposed Robust Variational AutoEncoders (R-VAEs) [58], which inherits the properties of typical Variational AutoEncoders, handles the tabular data more efficiently.

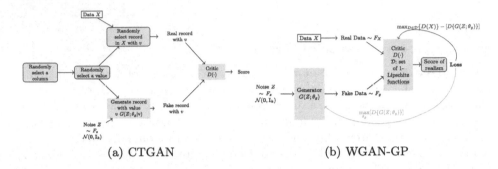

(a) CTGAN   (b) WGAN-GP

Fig. 1. CTGAN and WGAN-GP training dynamics

DPGAN [46] and PATEGAN [54] are popular differentially private GAN's. DPGAN adds noise to the gradient of the discriminator during training to create differential privacy guarantees. PATEGAN first trains multiple teacher models on disjoint distributions of data. At inference time, to classify a new sample it noisily aggerates outputs from previously trained teacher models to generate the final output.

3   Instance Level Privacy Scoring

To avoid MIA type attacks and unintentional leakage of sensitive attributes, we devise an instance level privacy score for generated synthetic data. As shown in previous studies, the main reasons for privacy compromises in generative models is mainly because of over fitting of training data that could lead to data memorization. We empirically measure *memorization coefficient* α_m for each generated sample and use this measure as privacy score. When distributing synthetic data to external third parties, users can filter samples with high privacy score and reduce privacy risks.

Given X_r, X_s real and synthetic data set generated by some generative algorithm Φ respectively. We first convert into latent vectors in embedding space $E(X_r), E(X_s)$. Next, we measure the spherelet distance between each real and generated sample latent vectors. The spherelet distance between $s(X_i)$ and $s(X_j)$ is defined as:

$$d_S = d_R(X_i, X_j) + d_E(X_i, X_j) \tag{3}$$

where d_E is the Euclidean distance between two sets of points, and d_R is Riemannian divergence (geometric) of dataset of X_i and X_j. The intuition behind this is we are measuring the distance between points by projecting the samples on to a sphere centered at c with radius r. Spherelet of X denoted by $s(X) = S(V, c, r)$ where V determines an affine subspace the sphere lies in. The spherical error [53] of X is defined by

$$\epsilon(X) = \frac{1}{n} \sum_{i=1}^{n} (\|x_i - c\| - r)^2 \tag{4}$$

If x_i lie on the sphere then $\epsilon(X) = 0$. Also the distance metric captures (a) which points are found in data manifold in low probability; (b) how close the synthetic and real in nearest neighbour proximity; which can give us a proxy measure for over-fitting and data memorization. *memorization coefficient* α_m for a generated sample X_{g_i} is defined by g_{n_i}/t_{n_i} where t_{n_i} and g_{n_i} are sample counts from training and generated dataset, which have proximity distance lesser than a threshold $> \lambda$. In short, we are measuring the *support set* for the sample X_{g_i} in the training and synthetic set. Samples, which have $\alpha_m < 1$ have large influence of training set and are prone to MI attacks vs samples with $\alpha_m > 1$ capture the underlying distribution of training data without leaking private training set attributes.

The advantage of this method is the model Φ is agnostic and works on data level. Users can discard the samples which cross a certain threshold privacy score to protect privacy of users and, data audit by compliance bodies can be performed without a need to know the model internals and training dynamics.

4   MIA Method

Membership Inference. The goal of a membership inference attack is to create a function that accurately predicts whether a data point belongs to the training set of the classifier. To achieve this, an attacker trains a set of surrogate models [64] on confidence scores produced by the target model and membership as labels to achieve her goal.

Typically, the attacker exploits the model confidence reflecting overfitting to infer membership. [64] first demonstrated MIA with only black-box access to the confidence scores for each input data sample. Their approach involved first training many 'surrogate' ML models similar to the target model and usesthese shadow models to train a membership inference model to identify whether a sample was in the training set of any of the shadow models. MIA is evaluated as a binary classification task, where metrics like false-negative, false-positive rates, and F1 scores reflect the attack success rates of predicting that a given sample is part of the training set.

We adapt 'shadow' training model in our MI attack on synthetic data. Given an auxiliary dataset $\mathcal{D}_{aux}$ similar to the training data distribution, we first randomly sample single data point $\mathbf{L}_t$ and remove it from the dataset. Now, a well-known ensemble learning method Bootstrap aggregating (Bagging) is used to divide remaining dataset $\mathcal{D}_{aux} - 1$ into subsamples with replacement. Generative models are trained on each sub sample and using the trained models

syn_0 synthetic datasets of size k is sampled. These samples as labeled $l_j = 0$ indicating that synthetic data does not contain target sample $\mathbf{L}_t$. Same procedure is repeated by adding $\mathbf{L}_t$ into the dataset $\mathcal{D}_{aux}$ and the synthetic data sets syn_1 of size k is sampled. These samples as labled $l_j = 1$ indicating that synthetic datacontain target sample $\mathbf{L}_t$. Now we have labeled dataset that captures the membership relationship and we train a random forest classifier MI_c, which predicts the probability of a given sample is member or not of the original data set. Given a synthetic dataset S_{Aux}, MI_c predicts the membership of the target record t in the training set of the generative model G that produced S_{Aux}.

5   Experiments

The membership privacy leakage is evaluated through a membership privacy experiment [42,43]. Given a training set D_t which follows a data distribution $\mathcal{D}$ and a learning algorithm ϕ is trained on D_t. We assume the adversary has only access to ϕ via a query interface, which exposes inference and class probability of a given sample. In synthetic data sharing use cases, the adversary has access to synthetic datasets generated by some generative model. Here the goal of the adversary is to discover the membership of a given sample i.e. it belongs to training data or not with access to only synthetic data. We assume domain-dependent data access to the adversary. In our experiments, to measure the strength of the proposed Instance Level Privacy filtering of synthetic data we measure the accuracy drop of MI attack with/without filtering mechanism.

For this work, we use two datasets – First dataset is SIVEP-Gripe database [2] released by Brazilian government with records of 99,557 ICU Covid-19 patients in Brazil, which includes personal information (ethnicity, age and location). A logistic regression (binary classification) model is fit to predict patient-level COVID-19 mortality with 6882 data sample and 25 features. Second dataset is the Brazilian E-Commerce Public Dataset by Olist[2]. It consists of 112,000 customer orders at multiple marketplaces in Brazil. The dataset contains order status, price, payment and freight performance to customer location, product attributes and finally reviews written by customers. Customer and Seller Id's are anonymized, and references to the companies and partners in the review text have been replaced with the names of Game of Thrones great houses. For our experiment we use columns price, customer identifier, customer zip code, customer city as feature columns. A logistic regression model is fit to predict the customer spend by aggregating price column.

We create 5 synthetic datasets using CTGAN, WGAN-GP, PATEGAN, DPGAN, and, RVAE as synthetic data generators for SIVEP-Gripe and E-Commerce data. The training of generator the input dimensions of architecture is adjusted to accommodate the dataset shape. All hidden layers use the ReLU activation function, the final layer uses the sigmoid function. The discriminator network also uses three hidden layers, which are symmetric to the generator. The hidden layers again use ReLU. We train each network with 100

---

[2] https://www.kaggle.com/olistbr/brazilian-ecommerce/.

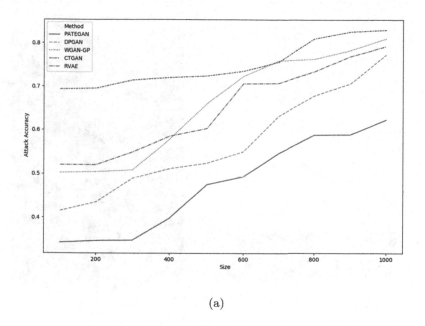

(a)

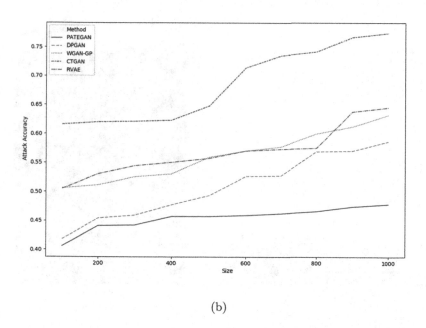

(b)

Fig. 2. Synthetic data size dependency on MIA attack for (a) E-commerce dataset (b) EHR dataset

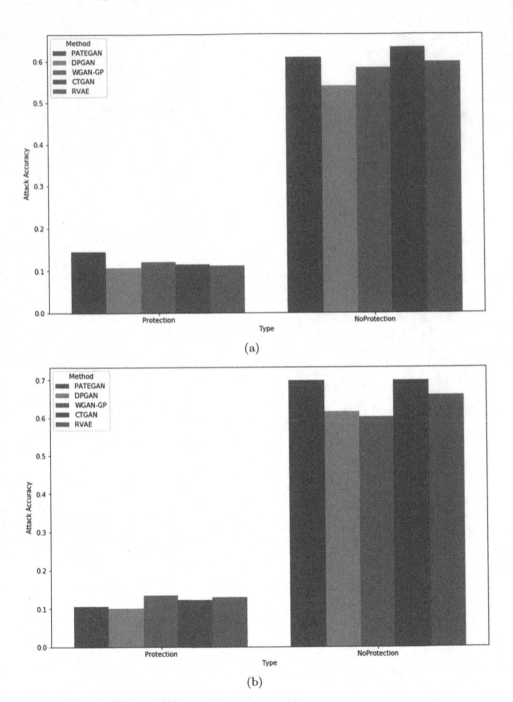

Fig. 3. Attack accuracy drop before and after filtering data points with high privacy scores - (a) EHR dataset (b) E-commerce dataset

epochs. For training differential private GAN's, we used the privacy budgets of $\epsilon = [0.01, 0.1, 0.5, 1.0, 3.0]$. λ is set to 0.5 to reflect the adversary advantage in membership attack. Randomly 1000 samples are sampled from training and marked as $\mathcal{D}_{aux}$. To reflect maximum compromise by adversary as white box setting, we use the same generator to train the shadow model $\mathcal{S}$.

5.1   Experimental Results and Discussion

We first present experimental results of the membership inference attack and the attack accuracy drop before and after we filter the data with α_m method. We measure the accuracy of attack with respect to number of samples in the auxiliary dataset used in the attack mechanism. Figure 2 and 3 summarizes the privacy risk of each synthesising method in terms of MI attack accuracy and auxiliary dataset. We observe that increasing the size of the synthetic dataset increases the risk of privacy leakage. As more information about the data is learnt by adversary the privacy of the data generator weakens. Similarly, differential privacy methods that add noise to the output with some privacy budget ϵ, the attack accuracy decreases showing the value of DP-based generators reduce privacy risks. Increase in privacy strength of the dataset is consistent across datasets and different models highlighting the strength of our proposed method.

5.2   Discussion

To develop good synthetic data generation models we still have some technical hurdles, for example, it is not only hard to exactly predict what data characteristics will be preserved in a model's stochastic output but also appropriate metrics to empirically compare two distributions are lacking. The privacy budgets in terms of perturbations to achieve differential privacy make it even harder to predict which records will remain vulnerable, and might even increase the exposure of some data records. Our work aims to give some direction towards improving synthetic data privacy by assigning instance-level privacy scores. A data auditor or service provider can leverage the scores to remove the data points prone to MI attacks. The advantage of our method is a model agnostic and it can be used in post-hoc fashion. We explored the accuracy drop from the attacker end, but measuring the accuracy-privacy tradeoff due to dropping the data points from the synthetic data on downstream models needs further investigation.

We want to highlight some of the limitations of our work. We only tested our method on tabular data, further investigation is needed to understand the privacy risks of other types of data such as text, images and, audio. Additionally, it can be observed that we use the whole dataset to measure α_m, which may be misleading as pointed out by [40], membership leakage for subgroup may be more vulnerable than others for discriminative models. We plan to address this drawback in our future work. It is also important to point out that the privacy risk measures provided in this analysis are dataset-dependent and *can* be generator-specific. While the proposed method gives some empirical privacy guarantees for generative models and guidance for data sharing use case, we need more detailed analysis on the dependency of α_m against model parameters, and varied dataset distributions. In terms of threat models, our analysis does not take into consideration an attacker who has knowledge of the filtering scheme in advance. A malicious attacker can use only filtered data points to train surrogate models making the proposed scheme invalid.

6   Conclusion

One of the major impediments in advancing ML in security-sensitive domains is the lack of open realistic publicly available datasets. To gain trust and protect the end-user data and, comply with regulations stakeholders are leveraging synthetic data as a tool to share data between third-party aggregators and researchers. However, the privacy analysis of these datasetsis still open research. In this work, we fill this gap by investigating the privacy issues of the generated data sets from the attacker and auditor point of view. We propose an Instance-level Privacy Score (PS) for each synthetic sample by measuring the memorization coefficient α_m per sample. Leveraging, PS we empirically show that the accuracy of membership inference attacks on synthetic data drops significantly. PS is a model agnostic, post-training measure, which helps data sharer with guidance about the privacy properties of a given sample but also helps third party data auditors to run privacy checks without sharing model internals. Finally, there is a lot more work to be done purely within the realm of privacy and our work only addresses a very small issue empirically. Understanding social and legal implications of synthetic data sharing needs inputs and partnerships from policy experts and, compliance officers.

References

1. Carlini, N., et al.: Extracting training data from large language models. arXiv preprint arXiv:2012.07805 (2020)
2. SIVEP-Gripe   (2020).   http://plataforma.saude.gov.br/coronavirus/dados-abertos/. In Ministry of Health. SIVEP-Gripe public dataset, (Accessed 10 May 2020; in Portuguese)
3. Jouppi, N.P., et al.: In-datacenter performance analysis of a tensor processing unit. In: Proceedings of the 44th Annual International Symposium on Computer Architecture, pp. 1–12 (2017)
4. Departement of Commerce, National Institute of Standards and Technology. Differential private synthetic data challenge (2019). https://www.challenge.gov/challenge/differential-privacy-synthetic-data-challenge/. Accessed 19 Feb 2021
5. Olivier, T.T.: Anonymisation and synthetic data: towards trustworthy data (2019).   https://theodi.org/article/anonymisation-and-synthetic-data-towards-trustworthy-data/. Accessed 19 Feb 2021
6. The Open Data Institute. Diagnosing the NHS: SynAE. https://www.odileeds.org/events/synae/. Accessed 19 Feb 2021
7. Hazy. https://hazy.com/

8. AIreverie. https://aireverie.com/
9. Statice. https://statice.ai/
10. One-view. https://one-view.ai/
11. Datagen. https://www.datagen.tech/
12. Synthesize. https://synthezise.io/
13. Cognata. https://www.cognata.com/
14. Mostly-AI. https://mostly.ai/
15. Rubin, D.B.: Statistical disclosure limitation. J. Off. Stat. **9**(2), 461–468 (1993)
16. Little, R.J.: Statistical analysis of masked data. J. Off. Stat. **9**(2), 407–426 (1993)
17. Abowd, J.M., Lane, J.: New approaches to confidentiality protection: synthetic data, remote access and research data centers. In: Domingo-Ferrer, J., Torra, V. (eds.) PSD 2004. LNCS, vol. 3050, pp. 282–289. Springer, Heidelberg (2004). https://doi.org/10.1007/978-3-540-25955-8_22. ISBN 978-3-540-22118-0
18. Abowd, J.M., Woodcock, S.D.: Multiply-imputing confidential characteristics and file links in longitudinal linked data. In: Domingo-Ferrer, J., Torra, V. (eds.) PSD 2004. LNCS, vol. 3050, pp. 290–297. Springer, Heidelberg (2004). https://doi.org/10.1007/978-3-540-25955-8_23. ISBN 3-540-22118-2
19. Reiter, J.P., Raghunathan, T.E.: The multiple adaptations of multiple imputation. J. Am. Stat. Assoc. **102**(480), 1462–1471 (2007)
20. Drechsler, J., Reiter, J.P.: Sampling with synthesis: a new approach for releasing public use census microdata. J. Am. Stat. Assoc. **105**(492), 1347–1357 (2010)
21. Drechsler, J., Reiter, J.P.: An empirical evaluation of easily implemented, non-parametric methods for generating synthetic datasets. Comput. Stat. Data Anal. **55**(12), 3232–3243 (2011)
22. Kinney, S.K., Reiter, J.P., Reznek, A.P., Miranda, J., Jarmin, R.S., Abowd, J.M.: Towards unrestricted public use business microdata: the synthetic longitudinal business database. Int. Stat. Rev. **79**(3), 362–384 (2011)
23. Reiter, J.P.: Using cart to generate partially synthetic, public use microdata. J. Off. Stat. **21**(3), 441–462 (2005)
24. Caiola, G., Reiter, J.P.: Random forests for generating partially synthetic, categorical data. Trans. Data Priv. **3**(1), 27–42 (2010)
25. Drechsler, J.: Synthetic Datasets for Statistical Disclosure Control, vol. 53. Springer, Heidelberg (2011). https://doi.org/10.1007/978-1-4614-0326-5. ISBN 9788578110796
26. Bowen, C.M., Liu, F.: Comparative study of differentially private data synthesis methods. Stat. Sci. (forthcoming)
27. Manrique-Vallier, D., Hu, J.: Bayesian non-parametric generation of fully synthetic multivariate categorical data in the presence of structural zeros. J. Roy. Stat. Soc. Ser. A: Stat. Soc. **181**(3), 635–647 (2018)
28. Snoke, J., Raab, G., Nowok, B., Dibben, C., Slavkovic, A.: General and specific utility measures for synthetic data (2016)
29. Raghunathan, T.E., Reiter, J.P., Rubin, D.B.: Multiple imputation for statistical disclosure limitation. J. Off. Stat. **19**(1), 1 (2003)
30. Kinney, S.K., Reiter, J.P., Berger, J.O.: Model selection when multiple imputation is used to protect confidentiality in public use data. J. Priv. Confident. **2**(2), 3–19 (2010)
31. Article 29 Data Protection Working Party - European Commission. Opinion 05/2014 on anonymisation techniques (2014). https://ec.europa.eu/justice/article-29/documentation/opinion-recommendation/files/2014/wp216_en.pdf
32. Elliot, M., Mackey, E., O'Hara, K., Tudor, C.: The anonymisation decision-making framework. UKAN Manchester (2016)

33. Rubinstein, I.S., Hartzog, W.: Anonymization and risk. Wash. L. Rev. **91**, 703 (2016)
34. Elliot, M., et al.: Functional anonymisation: personal data and the data environment. Comput. Law Secur. Rev. **34**(2), 204–221 (2018)
35. Patki, N., Wedge, R., Veeramachaneni, K.: The synthetic data vault. In: 2016 IEEE International Conference on Data Science and Advanced Analytics (DSAA), pp. 399–410. IEEE (2016)
36. Goodfellow, I.: NIPS 2016 tutorial: generative adversarial networks. arXiv preprint arXiv:1701.00160 (2016)
37. European Commission. Regulation (EU) 2016/679: General Data Protection Regulation (GDPR) (2016)
38. Sweeney, L.: k-anonymity: a model for protecting privacy. Internat. J. Uncertain. Fuzziness Knowl.-Based Syst. **10**(05), 557–570 (2002)
39. Shokri, R., Stronati, M., Song, C., Shmatikov, V.: Membership inference attacks against machine learning models. In: IEEE Symposium on Security and Privacy (S&P) (2017)
40. Yaghini, M., Kulynych, B., Troncoso, C.: Disparate vulnerability: on the unfairness of privacy attacks against machine learning. arXiv preprint arXiv:1906.00389 (2019)
41. Ping, H., Stoyanovich, J., Howe, B.: DataSynthesizer: privacy-preserving synthetic datasets. In: Proceedings of the 29th International Conference on Scientific and Statistical Database Management (2017)
42. Jayaraman, B., Wang, L., Evans, D., Gu, Q.: Revisiting membership inference under realistic assumptions. arXiv preprint arXiv:2005.10881 (2020)
43. Yeom, S., Giacomelli, I., Fredrikson, M., Jha, S.: Privacy risk in machine learning: analyzing the connection to overfitting. In: 2018 IEEE 31st Computer Security Foundations Symposium (CSF), pp. 268–282. IEEE (2018)
44. Zhang, J., Cormode, G., Procopiuc, C.M., Srivastava, D., Xiao, X.: PrivBayes: private data release via Bayesian networks. ACM Trans. Database Syst. **42**, 1–41 (2017)
45. Xu, L., Skoularidou, M., Cuesta-Infante, A., Veeramachaneni, K.: Modeling tabular data using conditional GAN. In: Advances in Neural Information Processing Systems (2019)
46. Yoon, J., Drumright, L.N., Van Der Schaar, M.: Anonymization through data synthesis using generative adversarial networks (ADS-GAN). IEEE J. Biomed. Health Inf. **24**, 2378–2388 (2020)
47. Adlam, B., Weill, C., Kapoor, A.: Investigating under and overfitting in wasserstein generative adversarial networks. arXiv preprint arXiv:1910.14137 (2019)
48. Meehan, C., Chaudhuri, K., Dasgupta, S.: A non-parametric test to detect data-copying in generative models. arXiv preprint arXiv:2004.05675 (2020)
49. Hayes, J., Melis, L., Danezis, G., De Cristofaro, E.: LoGAN: membership inference attacks against generative models. Proc. Priv. Enhanc. Technol. **2019**(1), 133–152 (2019)
50. Sablayrolles, A., Douze, M., Ollivier, Y., Schmid, C., Jégou, H.: White-box vs black-box: bayes optimal strategies for membership inference. In: Proceedings of the 36th International Conference on Machine Learning (ICML), pp. 5558–5567 (2019)
51. Sablayrolles, A., Douze, M., Ollivier, Y., Schmid, C., Jégou, H.: White-box vs black-box: bayes optimal strategies for membership inference (2019)
52. Truex, S., Liu, L., Gursoy, M.E., Yu, L., Wei, W.: Towards demystifying membership inference attacks. ArXiv, vol. abs/1807.09173 (2018)

53. Kuppa, A., Grzonkowski, S., Asghar, M.R., Le-Khac, N.-A.: Black box attacks on deep anomaly detectors. In: Proceedings of the 14th International Conference on Availability, Reliability and Security (2019)

54. Yoon, J., Jordon, J., van der Schaar, M.: PATE-GAN: generating synthetic data with differential privacy guarantees. In: International Conference on Learning Representations (2019). https://openreview.net/forum?id=S1zk9iRqF7

55. Arpit, D., et al.: A closer look at memorization in deep networks. In: Proceedings of the 34th International Conference on Machine Learning - Volume 70, ICML 2017, p. 233–242. JMLR.org (2017)

56. Salimans, T., Goodfellow, I.J., Zaremba, W., Cheung, V., Radford, A., Chen, X.: Improved techniques for training GANs. CoRR abs/1606.03498 (2016)

57. Xu, L., Skoularidou, M., Cuesta-Infante, A., Veeramachaneni, K.: Modeling tabular data using conditional GAN. In: NeurIPS (2019)

58. Eduardo, S., Nazábal, A., Williams, C.K.I., Sutton, C.: Robust variational autoencoders for outlier detection and repair of mixed-type data. In: Proceedings of AISTATS (2020)

59. Camino, R., Hammerschmidt, C., State, R.: Generating multi-categorical samples with generative adversarial networks. arXiv preprint arXiv:1807.01202 (2018)

60. Meehan, C.R., Chaudhuri, K., Dasgupta, S.: A non-parametric test to detect data-copying in generative models. ArXiv, vol. abs/2004.05675 (2020)

61. Izzo, Z., Smart, M.A., Chaudhuri, K., Zou, J.: Approximate data deletion from machine learning models: algorithms and evaluations. ArXiv, vol. abs/2002.10077 (2020)

62. Song, C., Shmatikov, V.: Overlearning reveals sensitive attributes (2020)

63. Melis, L., Song, C., De Cristofaro, E., Shmatikov, V.: Exploiting unintended feature leakage in collaborative learning. In: IEEE Symposium on Security and Privacy (S&P), pp. 497–512. IEEE (2019)

64. Shokri, R., Stronati, M., Song, C., Shmatikov, V.: Membership inference attacks against machine learning models. In: IEEE Symposium on Security and Privacy (S&P), pp. 3–18. IEEE (2017)

65. Chen, M., Zhang, Z., Wang, T., Backes, M., Humbert, M., Zhang, Y.: When machine unlearning jeopardizes privacy. CoRR abs/2005.02205 (2020)

66. Li, Z., Zhang, Y.: Label-leaks: membership inference attack with label. CoRR abs/2007.15528 (2020)

67. Leino, K., Fredrikson, M.: Stolen memories: leveraging model memorization for calibrated white-box membership inference. In: USENIX Security Symposium (USENIX Security), pp. 1605–1622. USENIX (2020)

68. Chen, D., Yu, N., Zhang, Y., Fritz, M.: GAN-leaks: a taxonomy of membership inference attacks against generative models. In: ACM SIGSAC Conference on Computer and Communications Security (CCS), p. 343–362. ACM (2020)

69. Salem, A., Zhang, Y., Humbert, M., Berrang, P., Fritz, M., Backes, M.: ML-leaks: model and data independent membership inference attacks and defenses on machine learning models. In: Network and Distributed System Security Symposium (NDSS). Internet Society (2019)

70. Jia, J., Salem, A., Backes, M., Zhang, Y., Gong, N.Z.: MemGuard: defending against black-box membership inference attacks via adversarial examples. In: ACM SIGSAC Conference on Computer and Communications Security (CCS), pp. 259–274. ACM (2019)

Promoting Compliance with the GDPR

Protection of Personal Data in High Performance Computing Platform for Scientific Research Purposes

Ludovica Paseri[1]([✉]) [iD], Sébastien Varrette[2] [iD], and Pascal Bouvry[2] [iD]

[1] CIRSFID, University of Bologna, Via Galliera 3, 40121 Bologna, Italy
`ludovica.paseri2@unibo.it`
[2] FSTM, University of Luxembourg, 2, Avenue de l'Université,
4365 Esch-sur-Alzette, Luxembourg
`{sebastien.varrette,pascal.bouvry}@uni.lu`

Abstract. The Open Science projects are also aimed at strongly encouraging the use of Cloud technologies and High Performance Computing (HPC), for the benefit of European researchers and universities. The emerging paradigm of Open Science enables an easier access to expert knowledge and material; however, it also raises some challenges regarding the protection of personal data, considering that part of the research data are personal data thus subjected to the EU's General Data Protection Regulation (GDPR). This paper investigates the concept of scientific research in the field of data protection, with regard both to the European (GDPR) and national (Luxembourg Data Protection Law) legal framework for the compliance of the HPC technology. Therefore, it focuses on a case study, the HPC platform of the University of Luxembourg (ULHPC), to pinpoint the major data protection issues arising from the processing activities through HPC from the perspective of the HPC platform operators. Our study illustrates where the most problematic aspects of compliance lie. In this regard, possible solutions are also suggested, which mainly revolve around (1) standardisation of procedures; (2) cooperation at institutional level; (3) identification of guidelines for common challenges. This research is aimed to support legal researchers in the field of data protection, in order to help deepen the understanding of HPC technology's challenges and universities and research centres holding an HPC platform for research purposes, which have to address the same issues.

Keywords: HPC · Scientific research · GDPR · Data protection · Open Science · Sharing data · European institutions

1 Introduction

The digital revolution and the ongoing technological developments are having a considerable impact on the way scientific research is conducted. Both the High Performance Computing (HPC, hereinafter) and the Cloud Computing technologies are increasingly identified as strategic assets and enablers to accelerate the research and the business

© Springer Nature Switzerland AG 2021
N. Gruschka et al. (Eds.): APF 2021, LNCS 12703, pp. 123–142, 2021.
https://doi.org/10.1007/978-3-030-76663-4_7

performed in all areas requiring intensive computing and large-scale Big Data analytics capabilities.

In parallel, the Open Science movement, advocating to make scientific research (including publications, data, physical samples, software, etc.) accessible to all levels, becomes a new strategic priority for both European institutions and Academia. The EU's General Data Protection Regulation (GDPR) [1] which has been in force since 2016, and applicable since May 25, 2018, brings several challenges for Cloud and HPC infrastructures.

In this paper, adopting as a case study the HPC platform located at the University of Luxembourg (ULHPC, hereinafter) the aim is twofold: on the one hand, to shed light on the most problematic aspects related to the GDPR compliance, namely the protection of personal data of data subjects involved in research projects carried out using HPC capabilities; and, on the other hand, to analyse what are the necessary steps to be taken by HPC technologies for the transformation towards the Open Science paradigm.

Large amounts of data are collected, created and manipulated for scientific research purposes, and many of them are personal data. Consider, for instance, the multitude of key research projects related to the COVID-19 pandemic (*e.g.*, vaccine research; investigations on treatments; predictive analyses on the development of infections, etc.): many of these studies have involved not only personal data, but also special categories of personal data, with the strengthened protection according to Art. 9 of the GDPR. In addition, the use of cutting-edge technologies makes processing operations even more complex. For this reason, this study intends to propose an introductory investigation on the use of HPC technologies for scientific research purposes and its relationship with the data protection discipline.

This paper is organised as follows. Section 2 sets the context, providing a description of the HPC capabilities (Sect. 2.1) and an illustration of the Open Science concept (Sect. 2.2). Section 3, then, proposes an overview of the legal framework related to the specific domain of scientific research with reference to the GDPR (Sect. 3.1) and the Luxembourg Data Protection Law (Sect. 3.2). Subsequently, in Sect. 4, the selected case study, *i.e.*, the ULHPC facility, will be explored. The used methodology (Sect. 4.1), the main issues identified by the analysis (Sect. 4.2) and, finally, the proposed solutions (Sects. 4.3 and 4.4) will be highlighted. Finally, Sect. 5 will conclude this study reviewing the open problems left for further investigations.

2   High Performance Computing and Open Science Paradigm

In order to be able to carry out the analysis of personal data protection in HPC platforms, it is essential to focus firstly on what is meant by HPC, and secondly on the scenario within which the use of HPC technologies by researchers develops: the emergence of the new paradigm of science, the so-called Open Science Paradigm, promoted and supported by the European and International institutions.

2.1   High Performance Computing (HPC) Capabilities

Having been used for more than 30 years in climate research, numerical weather prediction, particle and astrophysics, earth sciences and chemistry, HPC is now a cornerstone of all scientific fields and widely recognised as a strategic tool for competitive science. In parallel, the industry and more generally the private sector (including SMEs) are increasingly relying on HPC facilities to invent innovative solutions while reducing implementation cost (through advanced simulations) and time to market.

The following is a broad and general definition of HPC that, although not technically, helps to grasp the gist:

High Performance Computing (HPC) generally refers to the practice of aggregating computing power in a way that delivers much higher performance than one could get out of a typical desktop computer or workstation, in order to solve large problems in science, engineering, or business.

In other words, tasks which would typically require several years or centuries to be computed on a simple desktop computer may only require a couple of hours, days or weeks over an HPC system.

The last decade has seen massive investments in large-scale HPC and storage systems aiming at hosting the surging demand for processing and data-analytics capabilities. The University of Luxembourg operates since 2007 a large academic HPC facility which remains the reference implementation within the country. It offers a leading-edge research infrastructure for Luxembourg's public research while serving as access to the upcoming Euro-HPC Luxembourg supercomputer [2]. This was made possible through an ambitious funding strategy enabled from the early stage of its developments, which was supported at the rectorate level to establish an HPC strategy as transversal to all research domains. The University has invested tens of millions of euro into its own HPC facilities to responds to the growing needs for increased computing and storage capacities, while enabling its researchers to go beyond the limits of traditional simulation. Furthermore, special focus was laid on the development of large computing power combined with huge data storage capacity to accelerate the research performed in intensive computing and large-scale data analytics (Big Data). This joint development is illustrated in the Fig. 1 depicting the characteristics of the ULHPC platform, both in terms of computing power and storage capacity.

Nowadays this initiative accommodates a wide user base (around 1500 registered persons and 600 actives in 2020) ranging from University staff and students to research partners and commercial users. They are given the possibility to run compute- and storage-intensive computations as part of their research or training and, as illustrated on the Fig. 2, this includes computer scientists, engineers, material science researchers, biologists, economists and even historians [3], psychologists and social science researchers working on national and international projects. The University also extends access to its HPC facilities to scientific staff of national public research organizations as well as external partners for the duration of the joint research projects.

As a consequence, the workflow induced by such a large spectrum of users and usage necessarily involves the processing of personal data. Table 1 proposes a list of exemplifying research projects conducting with the use of ULHPC, involving sensitive personal data processing activities. .

Although the aim is to propose an analysis of the challenges that HPC platforms have to face in order to comply with the data protection regulations, this study must

Table 1. Examples of data-sensitive processing activities carried out on the ULHPC facility.

Research project domain	Typology of personal data	Exemplifying processing operations
Systems Biology	Medical and health data	Deep analyse of mixed microbial communities present within human samples from clinical care; Analysis of clinical data for neurodegenerative disorders, primarily for Parkinson's (PD) and Alzheimer's (AD) disease. Personalised medicine development as Proof-of-Concept for its integration into the national healthcare system.
Genetics	Genetic data	Molecular docking and in-vitro experimental drug assessment based on Integrated BioBank of Luxembourg data.
Transportation engineering	Location of personal individuals	Processing activities of geographical locations of specific groups of individuals, aimed at assessing movement flows in Luxembourg to implement shared transport services.
Digital History	Historical data and governmental reports	Personal records of Luxembourg's citizen activity during WW1 and WW2.
Computer science	Images captured by drones of individuals	Surveillance of Luxembourg's Tier-IV data-centres by autonomous drone swarms.

necessarily take into account the scenario in which to place these efforts: the emergence of a new paradigm of science, the Open Science. Over recent years, the University of Luxembourg has launched an ambitious initiative with the aim to refine its digital strategy and to enhance the positioning of the University in the context of various national and international digital transformation trends, in particular as regards the integration of the Open Science paradigm. The ULHPC facility takes a central role in this initiative: the HPC capabilities, in fact, has a holistic view across disciplines, encouraging the sharing of knowledge by its very nature. Let now proceed to shed some light on the concept of Open Science.

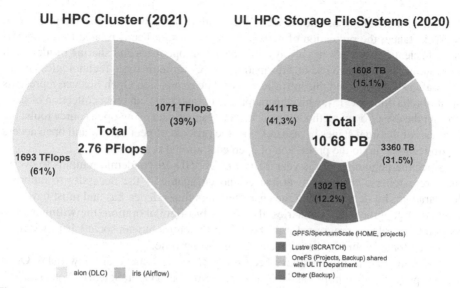

Fig. 1. Overview of the current computing (measured in floating-point operations per second or Flops) and storage (in bytes) capacities of the ULHPC facility.

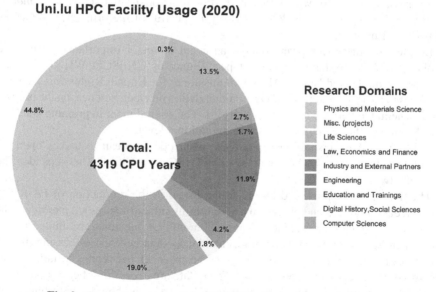

Fig. 2. Computing usage of the ULHPC facility per research domain.

2.2 The New Paradigm of Science: Open Science

The phrase Open Science defines the emerging and new paradigm of science, oriented to the openness of every phase of the research cycle, in accordance with the principle "as open as possible, as closed as necessary" [4]. In other words, it promotes as much as possible the sharing of knowledge, always balancing it with further interests, such as, for instance, the protection of personal data or closure needs related to the ownership. If scientific research has always been based on openness and sharing of ideas and information, the massive use of Information and Communication Technologies (ICTs, hereinafter) has amplified this intrinsic aspect. The expression Open Science represents an "umbrella concept" [5], which encompasses many facets: an open collection of data, through the use of open methodologies; the analysis of data using open source tools; the openness of the final stages of research, *i.e.*, the process of peer review and open access to publications; up to the promotion of open educational resources.

Since the beginning of the year 2020, the COVID-19 pandemic reminds to everyone - researchers, citizens, governments and companies - the necessity to embrace this paradigm by demonstrating the characteristics that science has and must have: the absence of geographical boundaries, the necessity of collaboration, the willingness to cooperate in order to progress, for the benefit of the entire human society [6], as well as the search for solutions to the great challenges of our time.[1]

The European institutions have been promoting for some years now many Open Science projects. Most importantly, consider the European Open Science Cloud (EOSC, hereinafter), namely a trusted ecosystem aimed at sharing research data and publications, for the benefit primarily of researchers, universities and research centers at European level [7, 8]. The purpose of EU institutions is to create a sort of Internet of data and research services [9], which must be FAIR, an acronym that stands for *Findable*, *Accessible*, *Interoperable* and *Reusable* [10], respectful of the principles, values and rights of the European Union.

In line with these European policies, an event of major importance occurred on October 27, 2020: the shared appeal on Open Science by UNESCO, WHO, CERN and the Office of the United Nations High Commissioner for Human Rights was launched. The aim is to issue the first UNESCO recommendation on Open Science, on the occasion of the General Conference of 2021, in Paris [5]. The commitment to promote and foster Open Science is thus emphasised also at international level.

Aside from these institutional initiatives, what does it mean to make "open" the scientific production realised through the use of HPC capabilities? The steps identified are chiefly two.

The first step is represented by the commitment in the production of FAIR data. Research data produced and processed on computing infrastructures are *findable* if they are provided with the necessary identification elements, *i.e.*, metadata and unique and persistent identifier. This aspect raises several challenges for large-scale processing since the transfer toward and from supercomputers assumes network backbones sustaining ultra-high speed low latency interconnectivity. Then, data are *accessible* if easily retrievable through the identifier and they are *interoperable* insofar as they are both human and machine readable [11]. Finally, the *reusability* consists of being richly described (for example, providing indications on their provenance) and reproducible in order to allow reuse by subjects that did not participate in the original collection or creation [10]. The increased security threats targeting ICTs and the continuous updates of systems and

---

[1] While before 2020 it might have seemed a utopian vision of science, the current global effort to find a vaccine for the Covid-19 virus seems to have made this vision more concrete.

applications libraries make this last property particularly challenging: both the storage medium and the processing environment can become obsolete and corrupted in a very short period of time.

The second step is more cultural: for the achievement of a new paradigm of science a corresponding change of mentality among the various actors involved in research domain is essential, avoiding damaging any stakeholder.

In the light of this new scenario of science just described, built on the formula "as open as possible, as closed as necessary", it is crucial to wonder how the fundamental right to the protection of personal data is guaranteed. Accordingly, an overview of the relevant data protection provisions will be useful to investigate the relationship between HPC and data protection, in the field of scientific research.

3 Protection of Personal Data in the Field of Scientific Research: An Overview

Although the GDPR represented a standardisation of data protection regulations at European level, it is essential to note that in some domains Member States (MS, hereinafter) still retain a certain discretion: this is the case for the processing of personal data for scientific research purposes. In this section we will firstly clarify the still discussed concept of scientific research in the field of data protection, starting from the crucial Art. 89 of the GDPR. Then, an overview of the set of rules and exceptions, at European level (GDPR) and at national level (with specific attention to Luxembourg, given the case study), related to the field of scientific research is proposed, according to our perspective.

3.1 Toward a Clearly Defined Concept of Scientific Research

As stated by the European Data Protection Supervisor (EDPS, hereinafter) in its recent preliminary opinion on data protection and scientific research [12], there is no common and globally unequivocal definition of scientific research. Without wanting to fall into the trap of overemphasizing the etymology [13], although everyone has a reasonably clear idea of what scientific research actually is, it is worth clarifying precisely its boundaries, since "(...) it truly is an advantage, legally speaking, to have certain personal data processing formally labelled as scientific research" [14].

As regards the concept of scientific research, it is essential to consider Art. 89 of the GDPR, entitled "Safeguards and derogations relating to processing for archiving purposes in the public interest, scientific or historical research purposes or statistical purposes": multiple and different concepts are combined in this expression[2]. Chiefly, three different purposes can be identified, *i.e.,* (1) archiving; (2) research; (3) and statistics; then, further, the research is divided into two macro-typologies, namely scientific and historical research. This last distinction could be interpreted as a way by which to incorporate research in its overall scope, whether it is derived from the so-called hard sciences or the humanities.

---

[2] Consider that only in recitals 33, 157, 159, 161, the concept of scientific research is considered separately.

Not intending to dwell on the relevant distinction between scientific research and the other two purposes alongside, (archiving and statistics, analysed in [15]), we bring our attention to recital 159 of the GDPR, which gives us a general definition of scientific research, which can be considered a benchmark in the field of data protection:

> For the purposes of this Regulation, the processing of personal data for scientific research purposes should be interpreted in a broad manner including for example technological development and demonstration, fundamental research, applied research and privately funded research. In addition, it should take into account the Union's objective under Article 179(1) TFEU of achieving a European Research Area. Scientific research purposes should also include studies conducted in the public interest in the area of public health.

The GDPR itself, therefore, directs towards a broad interpretation of the concept of processing of personal data for scientific research purposes: the explicit mention of the European Research Area (ERA) is emblematic of the fact that the European legislator is aware of the importance of sharing and exchanging data, at European level, in order to promote the development of research. This concept also clearly emerges in the provisions of recital 157, which recognizes the role of registers (and the data contained in them) for research purposes, stating that, precisely by combining different information, researchers have the opportunity to obtain new knowledge of great value. It was stated in Ienca *et al.* [16] that such records "(...) could include hospital registries for research into widespread medical conditions, as well as social security registries for socio-economic research". It should be noted that the twofold nature of the GDPR, enshrined in Art. 1, is made even more evident in the field of scientific research: on the one hand, the protection of personal data of citizens, a fundamental right as enshrined in Art. 8 of the Charter of Fundamental Rights of the European Union; on the other hand, the enhancement of the free movement of data, identified as the fifth European freedom by the Council of Ljubljana in 2007 with the expression "freedom of knowledge". For the same reason, recital 162 also allows the use of statistical results for scientific research purposes[3].

After clarifying the core concept of the topic under investigation, *i.e.,* scientific research, we move the spotlight on the legal framework inherent to this field.

3.2 EU and Luxembourg Data Protection Rules and Exceptions

In chapter IX GDPR, dedicated to "provisions relating to specific processing situations" is placed the above-mentioned Art. 89, the heart of the discipline of personal data processing in the field of scientific research[4].

---

[3] Remembering, however, that the result of data processing for statistical purposes is data that can no longer be configured as personal or otherwise aggregated.

[4] As mentioned in the previous paragraph, Art. 89 identifies safeguards and exceptions not only for scientific research, but for "processing for archiving purposes in the public interest, scientific or historical research or statistical purposes"; for clearness of exposition, the reference in this paragraph will be limited to scientific research, given the subject under investigation in this paper.

First, consider that the European legislator, although designing a derogatory regime for the processing of personal data for scientific purposes, has taken into consideration that these exceptions are subject to a fundamental condition: the processing in these specific cases should be guaranteed by "appropriate safeguards" for the protection of the rights and freedoms of the data subject. These appropriate safeguards, according to the wording of the provision, must be implemented in the establishment of technical and organisational measures, that "(...) are in place in particular in order to ensure respect for the principle of data minimisation"[5].

Given this fundamental condition for the processing of personal data in the scientific field, two macro-typologies of exceptions can be identified: (a) the exceptions directly provided for within the GDPR; and (b) the exceptions that the GDPR allows MSs to implement. These elements are now detailed.

Exceptions Expressly Established by the GDPR. The first group of exceptions, in order to allow greater freedom in the processing of personal data for scientific research purposes, is represented by a set of provisions that are not organically arranged but can be found in the different chapters of the GDPR, of which a quick overview is presented. First, two exceptions are included in Art. 5 of the GDPR, in relation to the principles: Art. 5(1)b extends the principle of purpose limitation, authorising "further processing" in the case of processing performed for scientific research purposes [16] (while reaffirming the need to ensure compatibility with the safeguards *ex* Art. 89(1), mentioned above)[6]; Art. 5(1)e, instead, as an exception to the principle of data retention, allows the retention for longer periods for data processed for scientific research purposes.

A further exception is, then, provided in Art. 9(2)j: if in the first paragraph of this article the processing of particular categories of data (those that the previous Directive defined as "sensitive data") is prohibited, this rule is mitigated in the next paragraph, which provides an exhaustive list of exceptions to the prohibition, including the purpose of scientific research[7].

In addition, Art. 14(5)b lays down that in the case where the controller obtains the data not directly from the data subject, but from third parties, it is not obliged to provide the information specified in paragraph 1 of the same article, if communication would be impossible or would involve a disproportionate effort, with particular reference to processing for purposes of scientific research.

Finally, two further exceptions are directly foreseen concerning the rights: Art. 17(3)d provides that the right of the data subject to obtain from the controller the erasure of personal data concerning him/her without unjustified delay, limited to the processing for research purposes, is not applicable; likewise, Art. 21(6) allows, substantially, that in the field of scientific research the requests of the data subject to object to the processing can be ignored, if the processing is necessary for the performance of a task of public interest.

---

[5] Art. 89(1) of the GDPR.

[6] "Accordingly, under this exception, medical data collected as part of hospitalisation could not be then used for research purposes without consent".

[7] The *ratio* of the exception, which also emerges in the wording of recital 53, is that of making a public and general interest of the community prevail over the right of the individual to protection of his or her personal data belonging to personal categories.

This assumption is particularly relevant, considering that, in many cases, the processing of data for scientific purposes is carried out on the legal basis of public interest [16].

Scientific Research Derogations within MSs. The GDPR is a European regulation and, therefore, mandatory in all its parts, directly applicable in each MS, pursuant to Art. 179 Treaty on the Functioning of EU [17]. Although it represents a "quasi-federal framework" [18], it also provides a limited number of open clauses that allows and requires the direct regulatory intervention of MSs and one of these is the domain of scientific research[8]. This relatively wide margin of discretion for the MSs inevitably brings with it the risk of providing a fragmentation of the discipline, as it has been repeatedly reiterated [8, 16, 19]. Going beyond this statement, it should be pointed out that such fragmentation is even more risky in an area such as research and the dissemination of knowledge which, by its very nature, has no territorial boundaries and is based on openness.

Considering the case study under investigation, the reference to national legislation, in Luxembourg, goes to chapter 2 of the "Loi du 1er août 2018 portant organisation de la Commission nationale pour la protection des données et du régime général sur la protection des données" (Luxembourg Data Protection Law) [20], represented by Art. 63, 64 and 65[9]. Specifically, the heart of the discipline is expressed by art. 65 which provides a list of "appropriate additional measures" that the controller must necessarily implement in the processing of data for scientific research purposes[10]. What is considerably relevant is the second paragraph of Art. 65: it states that the controller must document and justify, for each research project, every potential exclusion of the measures listed in Art. 65(1)[11]. Such a provision leads to a considerable commitment of skills and time by each research team managing a project involving personal data.

Subsequently, Art. 63 provides that, in the case of processing for scientific research purposes, it is the controller that may derogate from Art. 15 (right of access); 16 (right of rectification); 18 (right of restriction of processing) and 21 (right to object), to the extent that these rights risk making it impossible or considerably damaging the purposes for which the processing is carried out. This wide derogation is in any case subject to the condition of adopting appropriate measures to safeguard the rights of the data subject, referred to in Art. 65.

---

[8] The European Union has competence to establish provisions relating to the protection of individuals with regard to the processing of personal data in the exercise of activities falling within the scope of EU law, pursuant to art. 16(2) TFEU, reiterated in art. 2(2) GDPR, dedicated to defining the material scope of the Regulation. The conjunction of art. 6 TFEU and Title XIX TFEU, entitled "Research and Technological Development and Space", highlights the role of support, coordination and completion of the EU, in relation to the action of MSs in this field.

[9] Also in the Luxembourg national law the reference is always to "*recherche scientifique ou historique ou à des fins statistiques*", and once again for clarity of presentation we simplify the expression, using "scientific research".

[10] They range from the designation of a DPO to the initial determination to the design of a data management plan.

[11] The text of the law states: "*Le responsable de traitement doit documenter et justifier pour chaque projet à des fins de recherche scientifique ou historique ou à des fins statistiques l'exclusion, le cas échéant, d'une ou plusieurs des mesures énumérées à cet article*".

Art. 64, finally, expressly recalling Art. 9(2)j of the GDPR, reiterates that the particular categories of personal data may be processed for research purposes, only if the controller complies with the list of guarantees provided in Art. 65.

Since the legal framework of reference in the field of data protection has been clarified, the attention can be moved to the case study: the ULHPC platform of the University of Luxembourg.

4 Case Study: GDPR Compliance and Open Science Challenges Within the ULHPC

The analysis of the proposed case study, ULHPC, is described starting from the methodology adopted, and then shifting the focus to the major challenges highlighted in terms of the relationship between HPC technology and the data protection. Finally, not pretending to propose a totally exhaustive framework, the paper recommends some suggestions, in response to the challenges raised.

4.1 Methodology

In order to explore the relationship between the European data protection framework and HPC technologies, we started from the analysis of the functioning of the ULHPC platform. It is fundamental to remark that on this aspect, with specific reference to the case of the University of Luxembourg, the Luxembourg Centre for Systems Biomedicine (LCSB) is making great strides forward, carrying out an excellent path of compliance and training in data protection and in the outlining of the Data Protection Impact Assessments (DPIA) [21, 22].

For the aim of this investigation, the first fundamental step consisted in identifying the various phases of research cycle relying on HPC capabilities. The path to be followed to conduct the analysis is that provided by the GDPR, in the wording of Art. 35, concerning the DPIA, which in paragraph 7 indicates the essential elements to be considered in order to realise a proper analysis of the processing of personal data.

The HPC ecosystem developed within the University of Luxembourg was examined following the principles evoked in Art. 35 of the GDPR, across all the computing and data processing workflows performed on the facility as allowed by Art. 35(1)[12]. As shown in Table 1, both users identification details and large-scale research data may contain personally identifiable information (as stored, processed and further shared by the computing facility users).

Figure 3 describes the various interactions that research data may have within an HPC ecosystem and, consequently, also the interactions of any personal data that may potentially be part of a research projects as the ones presented in the Table 1.

---

[12] Art. 35(1) GDPR: "A single assessment may address a set of similar processing operations that present similar high risks".

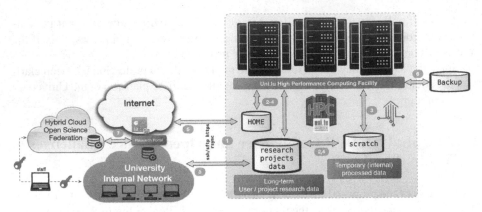

Fig. 3. Data processing interactions for HPC workflows on the ULHPC facility.

As a result, the HPC processing workflow can be designed as follows, in a consistent manner:

(1) data transfer of the input data toward the long-term storage area;
(2) pre-processing phase to prepare the data for research analysis (this may include partial or total data transfer toward the internal scratch area);
(3) job processing on the computing facility, generating both intermediate and final data components;
(4) post processing phase to derive scientific results from the processed data: this typically includes the creation of a metadata catalogue allowing to index and quickly recover scientific data;
(5) data transfer of the output data towards external resources (for instance a laptop of an external server);
(6) archiving of the results, and backup of the long-term storage area;
(7) data replication and synchronization may happen in a federated environment; in parallel, data sharing can be performed in the context of research collaborations; this includes live processing and access by external stakeholders.

This model can be pushed further with regards the input data profiles depending on the data source (*i.e.*, data obtained from an internal resource, an external collaborator, or from an external database or registry), however we assume them as provided from external resources, and that the step 2 comprises an anonymisation phase, if needed and if possible.

4.2 Identified Problems for GDPR Compliance

The analysis of the functioning of the HPC capabilities and their use by researchers depicted in Fig. 3 arises a number of challenges that must be faced by the actors operating in these scenarios: if the aim is to give scientific research increasingly powerful tools, for the benefit of the progress of science and therefore of society, on the other hand it is also necessary to be aware of the need to protect principles and values that characterise the European legal framework.

Based on the ULHPC experience, five challenges can be generalised concerning the processing of personal data in HPC platforms for scientific research purposes:

(1) compliance with the principle of transparency and related information duties;
(2) compliance with the meta-principle of accountability;
(3) ensuring the right of access by the data subjects;
(4) compliance with the principle of data minimisation;
(5) aspects relating to the security of processing, with specific emphasis on data movement.

Regarding the respect of the principles defined by the GDPR, note that although it identifies a number of exceptions for the field of scientific research (as discussed in Sect. 3.2) some pillars of the European data protection architecture must be respected in all circumstances. This is also reiterated by the European Data Protection Board (EDPB), which, recently stressed: "The principles relating to processing of personal data pursuant to Article 5 GDPR shall be respected by the controller and processor, especially considering that a great amount of personal data may be processed for the purpose of scientific research" [23].

The principle of transparency is closely related to the obligation to communicate information, enshrined in Art. 13 and 14 of the GDPR[13], and – in some way – is connected with the more general meta-principle of accountability. The GDPR, in fact, uses the term "principle" to regulate different moments of the processing of personal data: there are principles that determine whether or not it is possible to implement a particular processing; principles that, on the other hand, are intended to determine how certain processing can be conducted; and finally, there are the meta-principles, helping to interpret others [24]. The principle of accountability can be considered as a meta-principle. It is dynamic and it has been identified as "(...) the middle-out interface that strikes the balance between the implementation of rules and principles of the GDPR, and how data controllers should organise themselves, *i.e.,* their own data processing" [25]. This interpretation of the accountability principle is extremely appropriate in a scenario like ours, characterised by a multitude of different subjects and by the possible ambiguity in the identification of the different roles within the domain of scientific research[14].

Among the rights set out by the GDPR, the processing activities performed for scientific research purposes enjoy a privileged position. Some problems arise in relation to the right of access, which grants the data subject the right to obtain from the controller (a) the confirmation that personal data is actually being processed; (b) the access to the personal data concerning him/her and to a set of information expressly listed in Art. 15 of the GDPR. Art. 63 of the Luxembourg Data Protection Law provides that the controller

---

[13] Typically covered at least partially in the Acceptable Use Policy of the ULHPC platform, see: https://hpc.uni.lu/users/AUP.html.

[14] Consider the identification of the controllers and processors: if, generally, for each research project, the individual Principal Investigator (PI) should be considered the controller, and the HPC service provider, *i.e.,* the HPC Team, the processor, it must be emphasised that the situation becomes more complicated when the PI is a researcher at the University which itself provides the HPC service. Although the roles of controller and processor are held by two different subjects, they belong to the same organisation that is responsible for both.

may (not "must") derogate from this principle, to the extent that its compliance makes it impossible to complete the scientific research, while still ensuring compliance with the "additional appropriate safeguards" listed in Art. 65.

A further challenge is the respect of the principle of data minimisation, according to which the personal data collected shall be "adequate, relevant and limited to what is necessary in relation to the purposes for which they are processed"[15], whose respect is also reiterated in Art. 89(1) of the GDPR. The purposes of collection may be generally referred to as "scientific research", but the pragmatic reality is that researchers, at the time of collecting the data they will process through HPC capabilities, may not know precisely the purposes of their research [26].

From the point of view of security – to the extent that it is required by the GDPR – the challenge has been identified in the identification of a precise record of processing activities and in the necessary strengthening of some technical and organisational measures, aimed at ensuring security in accordance with Art. 32 GDPR. One of the major challenges is represented by the complex tracking of data movements, within the platform. Technically speaking, parallel and distributed filesystems used in HPC environments as the ULHPC are not yet fully able to account and log internal data movements[16], as done in the phases 2 to 4 in Fig. 3. With regards the other type of data transfer performed in the considered workflows (*i.e.,* steps 1, 5 and 7), other accountability and monitoring mechanisms can be implemented to fulfil this constraint. Consider that the Luxembourg Data Protection Law, in the list of additional safeguards contained in Art. 65, provides for "the use of a log file enabling the reason, date and time that data is consulted and the identity of the person collecting, modifying or deleting personal data to be retraced"[17], nearly identifying a strengthening of the European regime.

In addition to the issues identified regarding the protection of data processed in HPC environments, consideration must be given to the challenges arising from the scenario in which science operates, *i.e.,* the emergence of the Open Science paradigm.

4.3 Identified Challenges Related to the Open Science Paradigm

Although, as stated in Sect. 2.2, the concept of Open Science is very broad and encompasses multiple aspects of science, in relation to the use of HPC in research projects, fundamental are the FAIR data principles to which the production or collection of processed data needs to adhere.

Complying with the FAIR principles for research data processed on the ULHPC facility brings some challenges for which only partial answers exists today.

With regards the findability, the main issue relates to the fact that most researchers prefer to host their data on their laptop or on the institutional storage systems. The transition to FAIR-aligned data and domain repositories providing core services that help maintain scientific data over time and support data citation, discovery, quality, reuse while developing documentation standards and methodology, is still under investigation.

---

[15] Art. 5(1)c GDPR.

[16] More precisely, changelogs-based auditing capabilities relevant for the GDPR compliance are featured starting recent released versions of Lustre (2.11) and GPFS/Spectrumscale (5.0), the reference filesystems deployed in HPC facilities including the ULHPC.

[17] Art. 65(1)8° Luxembourg law on the protection of personal data.

However, several initiatives are investigated to host such a facility within the University of Luxembourg, complementing the integration of federated infrastructures such as EOSC or Elixir[18].

Regarding accessibility, the main identified limitation is technical and tied to the network backbone capabilities sustaining, as mentioned earlier, ultra-high speed data transfer with low latency from and toward the HPC facility.

Interoperability aspects are facilitated by the emergence of reference standards in scientific data representations such as the Hierarchical Data Format (HDF) or the Common Data Format (CDF).

Finally, reusability and reproducibility were identified as the most difficult issues to tackle for enabling FAIR compliance in the HPC environment. The use of versioned software modules and application containers proved to bring only a partial answer to these questions. Additional efforts are expected from the computer science research community to allow for long-term reproducibility in HPC environments.

Without pretending to provide an all-embracing and exhaustive description, we now proceed to the analysis of the hypothetical and possible solutions to the various challenges just described.

4.4 Some Suggestions to the Challenges Raised

In the first place, consider the issues related to (1) the principle of transparency and information duties, (2) the principle of accountability and (3) the right of access: for those issues an organizational approach is envisaged. Secondly, with regard to (4) the data minimisation and (5) the issue of security, solutions must be sought primarily from a technical point of view.

For the first three issues is suggested a standardisation of procedures, at the internal level. Consider the right of access: it is easily conceivable a scenario in which an individual requests a user of the platform (whether a researcher or a private partner in a research project) to access to data. For instance, in a problematic situation, in which a researcher is accused of having conducted unfair practices related to the research project of which he is part, the right of obtain a copy of the personal data being processed may represent a crucial factor (even judicial) for the individuals involved. For this reason, it is suggested to outline a standard procedure – at an internal level – to deal with possible requests, represented by an internal document or guideline. Standardising a procedure, perhaps by putting it in writing in an internal act, meets two requirements:

1. Continuity of the procedure over time.
2. Demonstrability of accountability, as required by Art. 5(2) of the GDPR.

A successful approach, in this direction, is the one adopted by the University of Leicester, in the definition of internal policies [27].

Similarly, the principle of transparency can be made concrete in a precise description of the information, satisfying the duties *ex* Art. 13 and 14 of the GDPR.

Instead, the meta-principle of accountability should indicate more the approach to be followed in the personal data processing, rather than being considered a provision

---

[18] ELIXIR, a distributed infrastructure for life-science information, https://elixir-europe.org/.

to be respected. The principle of accountability can be fostered firstly by improving the principle of demonstrability, thanks to a set of measures (such as, *e.g.*, the standardisation of the processes of requests to satisfy the rights of data subjects), the controller would strengthen its ability to demonstrate its accountability, as required by Art. 5(2) GDPR; secondly, it is possible to enhance an accountable approach on the training of the different actors involved in the processing of personal data, as a part of the research data internal governance [16]. This last aspect, related to data protection training, has been successfully implemented by the University College of London which provides online courses for all actors in the field, in the research and in the general University' activities [28]. It is fair to admit that very often problems arise because researchers with a scientific background (e.g. medicine, genetics, biology, etc.) may find it difficult to identify, within their own projects, the presence of personal data, as defined by the GDPR.

For the last two issues, (4) data minimisation and (5) security – with specific reference to data movement in HPC – the approach to follow is primarily technical.

Regarding the minimisation, it is generally accepted a two-step strategy: first, for research purposes, it is essential to use personal data only to the extent that they are actually relevant, with a preference for non-personal data [16]; secondly, where possible, it is needed to anonymise or at least pseudonymise personal data processed in the research project [28]. This is typically done during the pre-processing phase (step 3) illustrated in the Fig. 3. However, it is always advisable to embed the general and abstract rule to the relevant context of reference: in the case of ULHPC it should be noted that the infrastructure is held locally and in full control of the university, as public entity.

Then, also the issue of security should be faced primarily at technological level. This aspect is related to the field of information security, namely the general domain of security of technological infrastructures. The concepts of information security and data protection are often confused. Although some aspects of these two domains may overlap, they remain two distinct concepts. Here, the aim is not focus on the purely technical aspects that allow the mitigation of risk and a more effective protection of the security of data subjects, but it is proposed a general analysis relating to the compliance profiles with the GDPR.

In order to address the tracking of data movements, within the platform, in order to guarantee security, many different approaches are viable. An example can be the implementation models of access compartmentalisation[19]. Consider, nonetheless, the risk mitigation policies implemented and applied in the ULHPC facility. From a purely technical point of view – related to the risk assessment and the potential impact on data subjects and the description of risk mitigation measures and safeguards – a holistic, organization-wide risk management process was performed following the US National Institute of Standards and Technology (NIST) Guide for conducting Risk Assessments (NIST 800–30 Rev. 1) [29] grouped according to ISO/IEC 27002 [30]. Below, in Table 2, only an extract of the risk mitigation matrix developed in this work is proposed, which focuses on the items judged to have the highest impact for GDPR compliance. .

---

[19] See CSC, a non-profit state enterprise located in Finland: https://research.csc.fi/data-manage ment-planning.

Table 2. Extract of the technical risk mitigation policy implemented as part of the ULHPC DPIA.

Technical Risk Mitigation Type	ISO 27002	Examples of implemented/planned policy in ULHPC
Management of secret authentication information of use	9.2.4	Temporary secret authentication information sharing with PrivateBin[a]; Initial secure temporary secret authentication information forced to be changed on first use.
Information access restriction	9.4.1	Automated pre-anonymization of research data before injection on ULHPC facility; Protect datasets by appropriate access control lists (ACL). Use of self-encrypting disks (SED) on storage backends.
Secure log-on procedures	9.4.2	2-factor authentication (planned). Secure communication channels (robust Secure Shell). Continuous log of (un)successful logins.
Controls against malware	12.2.1	Automatic security checks and reports. Security patches (system and application level) applied regularly.
Information backup	12.3.1	High-frequency backup. Authenticated encrypted backup for some sensitive project data (as the ones listed in Table 1). Data duplicated on disaster recovery site.

[a]PrivateBin is a minimalist, Open Source utility allowing to securely share online text documents where the server has zero knowledge of pasted data.

5 Conclusions

All the various fields of science make increasingly use of novel and sophisticated computational technologies to implement and accelerate their research projects, taking advantage of the new possibilities offered by the growing computational power enabled by the development of supercomputing facilities. This digital transformation experienced by all scientific domains is considered a real paradigm shift, represented by the Open Science.

In this context, HPC infrastructures are playing a fundamental role as the essential instrument enabling cutting-edge developments in a timely manner. This paper aims to represent a first exploratory investigation of the issues related to the protection of personal data for processing activities carried out through the use of HPC technologies for scientific research purposes. Implementing a GDPR compliance activity of the technology under investigation is an extremely complex operation, which requires – perhaps more than in other circumstances – the adoption of a dynamic approach. To that end, this article focuses on a case study, the HPC platform of the University of Luxembourg, ULHPC to adopt the perspective of the HPC platform operators to tackle both challenges *i.e.,* the compliance to GDPR and the shift to the emerging Open Science paradigm.

A first contribution outlined in this study consists in deepening the concept of scientific research in the field of data protection. Then, an evaluation of the European (GDPR) and national (Luxembourg Data Protection Law) legal framework necessary to explore the compliance of HPC technology was proposed. Finally, the outcomes of the case study analysis were depicted. The results showed that the most problematic aspects are the compliance with: (1) the principle of transparency and the information duties; (2) the general principle of accountability; (3) the right of access; (4) the principle of data minimisation; (5) the implementation of security measures that ensure the control of data movement.

For the first three issues, it is suggested the standardisation of procedures, at an internal level, putting in place policies able to define good practices; for the last two issues, by contrast, solutions are primarily to be sought at a technical-infrastructural level. The most powerful suggestion when analysing GDPR compliance by an HPC platform for scientific research purposes is to consider the principle of accountability as a meta-principle that inspires and guides all others.

In addition, considering similar experiences across Europe[20], a greater cooperation at institutional level would be recommended, with the identification of supportive guidelines for common challenges. Although the intention to promote the use of Cloud Computing and HPC technologies in support of science is repeatedly reiterated at the institutional levels [5], it seems, in practice, to lack effective coordination between the different European HPC platforms, for research purposes, which from a legal point of view are facing the same problems.

As regards the Open Science perspective, furthermore, the focus is mainly on the need to comply with the FAIR data principles enabling findable, accessible, interoperable and reusable data, as output of the scientific research facilitated by supercomputing infrastructures.

Due to the complexity of the topic, many questions remain open, which may be the subject of future research. For instance, a further aspect that needs to be studied in depth, in terms of data protection in HPC platforms, is the relationship between the risk assessment required in the field of information security for HPC and the DPIA, as required by Art. 35 GDPR. Finally, the open challenges identified in the Sect. 4.3 to enable the fulfilment of the FAIR principles at the heart of Open Science developments, need to be explored further, especially in the light of developments in European projects on the subject, which are currently in full progress.

References

1. Regulation (EU) 2016/679 on the protection of natural persons with regard to the processing of personal data and on the free movement of such data. In: OJ L119/1 (2016). https://data.europa.eu/eli/reg/2016/679/oj
2. Council Regulation (EU) 2018/1488, establishing the European High Performance Computing Joint Undertaking. In: OJ L 252 (2018). https://data.europa.eu/eli/reg/2018/1488/oj
3. Beretta, F.: Cycle of (digital) knowledge production in historical sciences. In: Cappelluti, F., et al. (eds.) Open Science: Rethinking Rewards and Evaluation the Key to Change? Zenodo (2020). https://doi.org/10.5281/zenodo.4141447

---

[20] An interesting reflection on these issues has been conducted with the Research Center "Area Science Park", in Trieste (Italy), which holds an integrated environment of cloud computing and HPC capabilities, called "Ecosystem Orfeo": https://www.areasciencepark.it.

4. Commission Recommendation (EU) 2018/790 on access to and preservation of scientific information. In: OJ L 134, 31 May 2018 (2018). https://data.europa.eu/eli/reco/2018/790/oj
5. UNESCO, First draft of the UNESCO Recommendation on Open Science (2020). https://en.unesco.org/science-sustainable-future/open-science/recommendation. Accessed 03 Feb 2021
6. Ayris, P., et al.: Realising the European open science cloud. European Union (2016). https://doi.org/10.2777/940154
7. European Commission, European Cloud Initiative - Building a competitive data and knowledge economy in Europe, COM/2016/178 final (2016). https://eur-lex.europa.eu/legal-content/en/TXT/?uri=CELEX:52016DC0178
8. Saunders, G., et al.: Leveraging European infrastructures to access 1 million human genomes by 2022. Nat. Rev. Genet. **20**(11), 698 (2019). https://doi.org/10.1038/s41576-019-0156-9
9. Budroni, P., Burgelman, J.-C., Schouppe, M.: Architectures of knowledge: the European open science cloud. ABI Tech. **39**(2), 131 (2019). https://doi.org/10.1515/abitech-2019-2006
10. Wilkinson, M.D., et al.: The FAIR guiding principles for scientific data management and stewardship. Sci. Data **3**(1), 4 (2016). https://doi.org/10.1038/sdata.2016.18
11. Hodson, S., et al.: Turning FAIR into reality: final report and action plan from the European Commission expert group on FAIR data. European Union (2018). https://doi.org/10.2777/1524
12. European Data Protection Supervisor (EDPS), A Preliminary Opinion on data protection and scientific research (2020). https://edps.europa.eu/sites/edp/files/publication/20-01-06_opinion_research_en.pdf. Accessed 03 Feb 2021
13. Boniolo, G.: Il pulpito e la piazza. Democrazia, deliberazione e scienze della vita. Cortina Editore, Torino (2010)
14. Sjöberg, C.M.: Scientific research and academic e-learning in light of the EU's legal framework for data protection. In: Corrales, M., Fenwick, M., Forgó, N. (eds.) New Technology, Big Data and the Law, pp. 43–63. Springer, Singapore (2017). https://doi.org/10.1007/978-981-10-5038-1_3
15. Ducato, R.: Data protection, scientific research, and the role of information. Comput. Law Secur. Rev. **37** (2020). https://doi.org/10.1016/j.clsr.2020.105412
16. Ienca, M., et al.: How the general data protection regulation changes the rules for scientific research. European Parliamentary Research Service (EPRS), Scientific Foresight Unit (STOA) (2019). https://doi.org/10.2861/17421
17. Manis, M.L.: The processing of personal data in the context of scientific research. The new regime under the EU-GDPR. Biolaw J. **3** (2017). https://doi.org/10.15168/2284-4503-259
18. Barfield, W., Pagallo, U.: Advanced Introduction to Law and Artificial Intelligence. Edward Elgar Publishing, Cheltenham (2020)
19. Aurucci, P.: Legal issues in regulating observational studies: the impact of the GDPR on Italian biomedical research. Eur. Data Protect. Law Rev. **5**(2), 197–208 (2019). https://doi.org/10.21552/edpl/2019/2/9
20. Loi du 1er août 2018 portant organisation de la Commission nationale pour la protection des données et du régime général sur la protection des données (Luxembourg Data Protection Law) (2018). https://data.legilux.public.lu/eli/etat/leg/loi/2018/08/01/a686/jo
21. Trefois, C., Alper, P., Jones, S., Becker, R., et al.: Data protection impact assessment: general LCSB approach for processing research data. Internal report (2018)
22. Ganzinger, M., Glaab, E., et al.: Biomedical and clinical research data management. In: Systems Medicine: Integrative, Qualitative and Computational Approaches, vol 3. Academic Press (2021)
23. European Data Protection Board (EDPB), Guidelines on the processing of data concerning health for the purpose of scientific research in the context of the COVID-19 outbreak, 03 (2020). https://edpb.europa.eu/our-work-tools/our-documents/guidelines/guidelines-032020-processing-data-concerning-health-purpose_en. Accessed 03 Feb 2021

24. Durante, M.: Computational Power: The Impact of ICT on Law. Society and Knowledge. Routledge, London (2021)
25. Pagallo, U., Casanovas, P., Madelin, R.: The middle-out approach: assessing models of legal governance in data protection, artificial intelligence, and the web of data. Theory Pract. Legislation **7**(1) (2019). https://doi.org/10.1080/20508840.2019.1664543
26. Pagallo, U.: The legal challenges of big data: putting secondary rules first in the field of EU data protection. Eur. Data Prot. L. Rev. **3** (2017). https://doi.org/10.21552/edpl/2017/1/7
27. University of Leicester. https://le.ac.uk/ias/policies-and-resources. Accessed 03 Feb 2021
28. ULC. https://www.ucl.ac.uk/data-protection/data-protection-overview/online-training/data-protection-online-training. Accessed 03 Feb 2021
29. NIST SP 800–30 Rev. 1: Guide for Conducting Risk Assessments, Technical report (2012). https://csrc.nist.gov/publications/detail/sp/800-30/rev-1/final. Accessed 03 Feb 2021
30. ISO/IEC 27002:2013: Information technology, Security techniques, Code of practice for information security controls. https://www.iso.org/standard/54533.html. Accessed 03 Feb 2021

Representing Data Protection Aspects in Process Models by Coloring

Melanie Windrich[1]([✉])(iD), Andreas Speck[1](iD), and Nils Gruschka[2](iD)

[1] Kiel University, 24098 Kiel, Germany
{mwi,aspe}@informatik.uni-kiel.de
[2] University of Oslo, 0373 Oslo, Norway
nilsgrus@ifi.uio.no

Abstract. Business processes typically operate on personal data, e.g., customer data. This requires compliance with data protection regulations, e.g. the European Union General Data Protection Regulation (GDPR). The modeling of business processes is a widespread methodology to visualize and optimize business processes. This should include also data protection concerns. However, standard modeling languages like the Business Process Modeling and Notation (BPMN) do not offer an adequate notation for expressing data protection aspects.

In this paper, we propose a methodology for visualizing privacy concerns in BPMN models. We suggest using colors for marking critical activities and data in the process models. This provides an easy documentation of data protection problems and supports the optimization of processes by eliminating the privacy violation issues.

Keywords: Coloring scheme · Data protection · Privacy visualization · Business process modeling · Process optimization

1 Introduction

Due to the increased efforts to enforce the digital transformation on all levels, more and more business processes are formalized in process models. Process models are an important means in designing and describing information systems as well as in development phase and late in production phase. Many business processes operate on personal data and, therefore, need to comply with data protection regulations, e.g., the General Data Protection Regulation (GDPR) for services offered in the European Union. To identify privacy threats and data protection requirements as early as possible, it makes sense to represent these aspects already in the process model. When potential privacy problems are identified early in the development process the cost for eliminating these flaws may be kept low. Incorporating privacy issues in the process models greatly supports the privacy by design concepts. Also, incorporating privacy issues in the process models greatly supports the privacy by design concepts.

© Springer Nature Switzerland AG 2021
N. Gruschka et al. (Eds.): APF 2021, LNCS 12703, pp. 143–155, 2021.
https://doi.org/10.1007/978-3-030-76663-4_8

The question is how it is possible not only to describe processes but also to detect and mark process elements critical in respect to privacy and data protection. The idea would be a plain and intuitive representation of the states in a process model. In some cases there are activities violating privacy rules. Highlighting these critical activities may help to identify and eliminate the privacy threats. Moreover, such a notation should motivate the users addressing the privacy and data protection problems and to solve them. The desired marking may be applied in business process model notations such as BPMN [19].

In this paper we make the following contributions. We created a concept for user-friendly annotations of business process models with data protection requirements represented with color coding. This concept can be used to meet different goals. First of all, the coloring can help to raise awareness for data protection in the management level of a company. Furthermore, the coloring concept can provide hints for process optimization. Moreover, due to better perception of data protection critical parts of a process, the implementation of security measures can be accelerated. Finally, when a process model is used in early stages of software engineering, the coloring can help implementing privacy by design in the resulting software system. In this paper, we present the results of our ongoing research as work in progress.

The paper is organized as follows. The next section contains the base of the paper which is the coding of coloring, business process modeling and data protection regulations. In Sect. 3, we develop an approach for a colored business model marking different stages of privacy aspects. Section 4 illustrates the concept using a typical example process. In Sect. 5, the related work is presented before concluding the paper in Sect. 6.

2   Background

This section describes the most important basics to understand the approach presented in this paper. These are an introduction in color psychology, a short overview of the used process modeling notation BPMN and some insights in the relevant data protection aspects.

2.1   The Psychology of Colors

The impact of colors on humans has been observed for a long time [12]. This is especially true for the colors red, yellow, green and blue [12,15]. Goldstein, for example, found out that the colors red and yellow have a contrary effect on humans than the colors green and blue [12]. Jacobs and Hustmyer investigated that red is more arousing than the other three colors [15]. Elliot et al. pointed that red compared to green and achromatic colors (black, white, gray) has a significant effect on performance of test subjects and that people tend to avoid red colored things (in this case exercises) [8]. Also one of Goldstein's patients describes red as *"very disagreeable, piercing, obtrusive"* [12] and expresses that yellow has a similar but milder effect. Green is, inter alia, described as *"kind, [...] agreeable, quieting"* [12].

These findings are reasons for the approach of displaying data protection in process models with colors. But despite the usage of the four colors red, yellow, green and blue in literature, we chose to only use the subset red, yellow and green. This set of colors is well known by nearly everyone because they are used as traffic lights [17]. Therfore, the usage is quite intuitive.

2.2 Process Modeling

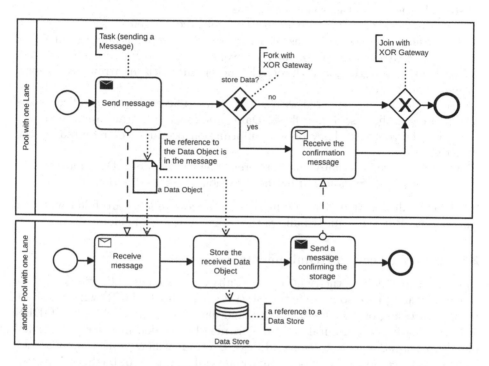

Fig. 1. Example BPMN process (modeled with Camunda)

There are numerous notation types for modeling business processes. An overview of the Fraunhofer Institute for Experimental Software Engineering shows a large number of notations, model types and suites for designing the process models [1]. For our paper, we are using BPMN [19,20]. We have chosen BPMN as modeling notation since this notation is used by a large number of institutions and supported by modeling tools like *Signavio*, *Picture* or *Camunda*. While BPMN provides the notation for different kinds of diagrams, this paper focuses on process diagrams only, since this is the diagram type for modeling the processes. Figure 1 depicts a sample of the usage of the BPMN elements we use in the paper:

- Two pools indicate two actors or organizations concerned with the processes or part of processes. The flow of the process sections are in the lanes of the pools (one pool may contain more than one lane).
- Sequence flows (continuous pointed arrows) connect the activities (rounded rectangles) between the start and end events.
- Activities contain the main functionality of the process. Specializations of activities are atomic tasks and sub-processes (not shown in Fig. 1). Atomic tasks act like leaves in a tree hierarchy which may not call other sub-processes. These sub-processes may be invoked by standard activities like subroutines in programming languages. The example contains general tasks as well as two special types: send tasks and receive tasks.
- The gateways may fork (divergence) or join (convergence) sequence flows. The example shows an exclusive decision and merging. Examples for other gateway control types are parallel, or event-based.
- A dashed line beginning with a circle and ending with an arrow head represents a message flow.
- Data objects are associated with dotted lines. The arrow head indicates the direction of the association flows. Data objects may contain a single object or may be complex. They provide information produced or required by the activities.
- The data store is actually only a reference on such a store. Data may flow in or out of the store indicated by the direction of the association.

By default, all notation elements in BPMN process models are filled white or transparent. But the standard allows the usage of other fill colors [19].

2.3 Data Protection Requirements

The GDPR [10] defines the rights of data subjects as well as obligations for data controllers and processors inside the EU/EEA (Article 3 GDPR) with reference to the processing of personal data. Personal data according to Article 4 GDPR are data relating to a natural person. This may be an identifier like an national identification number or an email address, quasi-identifiers, which allow identification when combined with other information, like a date of birth, or sensitive information like a location linked to a natural person. Processing is any kind of operation done on personal data including collection, storage and transmission. Many businesses processes nowadays included some kind of data processing on personal data of their customers. In this case, the organization counts as data controller (or processor) in terms of the GDPR and the business process must comply with the regulation.

The most fundamental requirement is the determination of the lawfulness of data processing. Only in certain cases defined in Article 6 GDPR processing is lawfully allowed. The most common exception cases for businesses are *"data subject has given consent"* and *"necessary for the performance of a contract"*. But even in these cases the data protection is still restricted. The consent, for example, is only given to one or more specific purposes. For some types of data— called *special categories of personal data* and defined in Article 9 GDPR—the processing has even higher barriers. Here processing is only allowed under specific conditions, e.g. *"data subject has given explicit consent [...] for one or more specific purposes"*. Examples for these special categories of data are genetic data, health data or sexual orientation.

Further, the business process (and of course also its implementation) must fulfill a number of obligations. The most important ones are defined in Article 25 GDPR ("Data protection by design and by default"). Here appropriate organizational and technical data protections measures are requested. This includes means like data minimization or pseudonymization. Another obligation for processing of personal data is an appropriate level of security (Article 32 GDPR), i.e. ensuring (among others) integrity, confidentiality and availability of the processing system. This requirement is well known from other domains outside the data-protection scope like IT security management (e.g., [14]).

If a data processing system *"is likely to result in a high risk to the rights and freedoms of natural persons"* (Article 35(1) GDPR) the controller is obliged to perform a *Data Protection Impact Assessment (DPIA)*. This is a systematic analysis of the processing system with respect to the privacy risks and possible impacts on the data subject due to data protection flaws. However, the GDPR does not define specific DPIA methods, it only lists some minimum requirements for a DPIA (Article 35(7)). There are different DPIA specifications available, e.g., from the ISO/IEC [13] or from the French data protection authority Commission Nationale de l'Informatique et des Libertés (CNIL) [7]. The data controller must (in consultation with its local data protection authority) pick one DPIA method. Another issue is the assessment of the necessity of a DPIA. Article 35(3) GDPR lists some examples of cases where a DPIA is required, but no precise definition is given.

3   Colored BPMN

As described in Sect. 2.2, data processing is an issue in many business processes. To raise awareness for this, it can be helpful to represent data protection critical actions in process models. Personal data itself in BPMN is represented as data objects. The processing of the data is represented as activities. In Sect. 2.1, it is explained that coloring is a tool to raise awareness. Therefore, the coloring of activities and data objects is described in the following subsections.

3.1   Activities

In [3] Bartolini et al. conclude, that there should be special *"BPMN activities that represent[s] actions relevant for the protection of personal data"* [3, p. 423]. Additionally to their more technically focused approach, we think (a) that those activities should be visible at first sight and (b) that it needs a differentiation between different stages of data processing. For that we suggest the coloring of those activities in traffic light colors.

Like in traffic lights, green is most positive color. It means, that no personal data is processed in this activity or that personal data is processed by the data subject itself. In both cases, data protection doesn't need to be minded.

Activities, in which personal data is processed (by another person than the data subject), are colored yellow or red. If the lawfulness of data processing is based on Article 6(1)b–f GDPR (e.g., performance of a contract, vital interests of the data subject), then the activity is colored yellow. In all other cases, the GDPR requires consent of the data subject (Article 6(1)a GDPR). These activities that require consent are colored red. An overview of the rules for coloring activities can be seen in Table 1.

Table 1. Rules for coloring activities

Color	Type of activity
Red	Consent required
Yellow	Permitted data processing
Green	No relevant data processing

Activities can be atomic tasks or sub-processes. In case of a sub-process, it is advisable to color the sub-process red, if there are any red activities in the sub-process and yellow, if there are yellow activities, but no red ones. Green should only be used if all activities in the sub-process are also green. If the sub-process is not modeled yet, it might be filled clear (white). Also, in case the modeler is unsure, which color is right, activities may remain clear, too.

3.2 Data Objects

Beside the activities, also the data objects are relevant regarding data protection, because they can contain personal or non-personal data. Like above, we suggest a traffic light coloring with three stages:

A green data object contains non-personal data like product data. Yellow data objects contain personal data like names, addresses, birthdays etc. and red data objects contain special categories of personal data based on Article 9(1) GDPR or relating to criminal convictions and offenses referred to in Article 10 like described in Sect. 2.3. The coloring rules are summarized in Table 2.

Data Storages. Additional to data objects, BPMN also provides so called *data storages*, which basically represent databases. The problem with coloring those data storages is, that it is unclear, which data is stored there, because theoretically the data storage could be empty in the process instance, when it is, for example, the first instance of this process. In this case the data storage would be marked green. But in a future instance of the process, there could be

Table 2. Rules for coloring data objects

Color	Type of data
Red	Special categories of personal data
Yellow	Personal data
Green	Non-personal data

(special categories of) personal data and the data storage should not be green anymore.

Therefore, we suggest to think of the "worst case" when modeling the process. This means, if the data storage is intended to contain special categories of personal data, it should be colored red and if it is only intended to contain "normal" personal data, it should be colored yellow. Only if the data storage does not contain any personal data at all, then it should be colored green.

Like discussed in Sect. 3.1, if the modeler is unsure which color to use, data objects and data storages may remain clear.

3.3 Modeling

Usually business processes are modeled by people who are not very experienced with data protection. So the inclusion of this aspect must be easy and may not require to deep insight in GDPR. Our approach of coloring activities is relatively easy because it only uses a limited number of additional elements (the three colors), that furthermore are quite intuitive. Hence most process modelers should be able to do most of the coloring after a short training period.

Compared to the activities, the coloring of data objects is even easier, because the rules are very exact. Even someone, who does not have a lot of knowledge about data protection, should be able to differentiate between the three different categories.

To validate the coloring, it could be useful to let the data protection officer check the process model. Even though he is not a domain expert for most of his company's processes, he will likely be able to verify the coloring. Moreover the data protection officer could give hints for process optimization.

A further idea is the automation of the coloring. This would certainly be helpful, but is quite difficult. Starting points could be natural language processing (NLP) or the use of ontologies in combination with a set of coloring rules. But there are two problems: First of all, the specification of the rules is not trivial because there are a lot of special cases, where individual consideration is needed. Nevertheless, there are many "easy" cases, that could be defined and be a starting point for at least a partial automation. The other problem is the process model itself. Often things are not modeled explicitly but are taken for granted by the modeler. For example, a data object called *customer data* may include special categories or not. For the domain expert, this may be clear, but for a NLP-algorithm it is not.

Technically, the coloring of BPMN process models poses no problem since many popular modeling tools like Signavio and Camunda allow it. The example in Sect. 4 is modeled with the Camunda modeler[1] which supports the coloring of basically every BPMN-Object in five different colors.

4   Use Case

4.1   Example Process

As an example for our approach, we look at an abstracted process of a registration at a public transport company. The process model is shown in Fig. 2. For the paper, additionally to the coloring, the three stages of data processing are marked by numbers (1 = green, 2 = yellow, 3 = red).

The process model consists of two main participants: The transport company and the customer. The precondition of the depicted process is that the customer visited the transport company's website and clicked on a registration button.

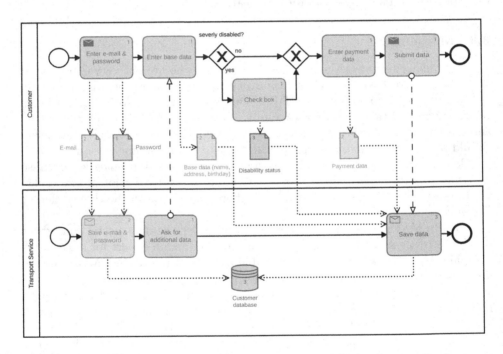

Fig. 2. Example process of a customer registration (Color figure online)

In the process model the customer basically just enters his data like username and password, some base data and possibly his disability status (to get a

---

[1] https://camunda.com/products/camunda-bpm/modeler/.

discount). All the activities are colored green, even if personal data is processed, because the data subject itself is processing the data and this is not relevant regarding data protection. However, the customer handles data objects of all the colors: Most of the data objects are yellow, as they contain personal data like the e-mail address, name, postal address, birthday and payment data. All those pieces of data are obvious personal data, but none of these is part of the special categories of personal data defined in (Article 9 GDPR). Nonetheless, in the customer pool is one green data object. It contains the password which is not considered as personal data. Moreover, the pool contains one red data object, which contains the disability status that is manifestly part of the special categories of personal data.

The pool of the transport service is also quite short. Basically the entered data is saved and it is asked for more data. The demand for additional data must obviously be green, because there is no data processing in this activity. The two saving activities on the other hand, are colored yellow respectively red, based on the data, that is processed: In the first activity, an e-mail address (and a password, which is irrelevant from a data protection viewpoint, because it is not personal data[2]) is processed. This processing is necessary, because the company needs a direct communication method for the performance of the contract, what is a reason for data processing according to Article 6(1)b GDPR. In the last activity on the other hand, additional data of a special category is processed, that is not legitimized in Article 9(2)b–j. Therefore consent of the data subject is necessary and the activity has to be colored red. Besides the activities, the company pool also contains a data storage, in which all customer data is saved. The data storage is red, because it contains personal data of a special category in form of the disability status.

Of course, this process model for presentation reasons is quite abstract and does not represent a real registration process.

4.2   Optimization

One of the aims described in Sect. 1 is the optimization of business processes regarding data protection. A first step for optimizing a process could be a look at red elements in the process models. Sometimes those elements can change so that they can be colored yellow afterwards. Of course the same is true for yellow elements that can be changed to green elements.

In the example above, a starting point is the data storage *Customer database*. This data storage is red, because it includes the disability status which is part of the special categories of personal data. This causes special security requirements for the data storage. According to Article 32(1) GDPR *"appropriate technical and organizational measures"* shall be implemented. Examples for such measures are encryption or pseudonymization. Further details on information security are not given by the regulation itself. Therefore, appropriate security management

---

[2] Nevertheless, the password must of course be stored in a secure manner.

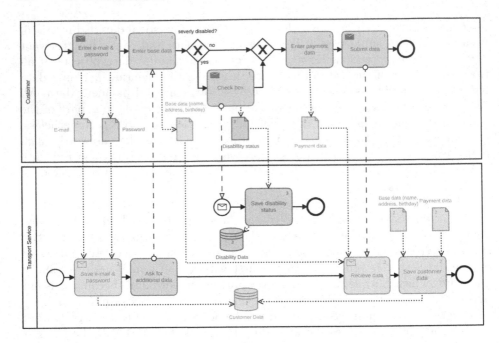

Fig. 3. Optimized process model

specification, like ISO 27000 [14], or specific recommendation for secure process-ing of personal data must be consulted, e.g., [9]. But in selecting appropriate measures, amongst other things the severity of the risk for the data subject has to be considered (Article 32(1) GDPR).

So in the presented use case it could make sense to split the data storage in two separate parts: One with the normal customer data like name and address and another one only with the disability status. Of course it would be neces-sary to link those two data storages with a key. This method would fulfill the requirement of pseudonymization for the disability status. Moreover it would be possible to store a part of the data in a public cloud and another part locally. Besides the data storage of course the task *Save data* could be split similarly.

The optimized process model is displayed in Fig. 3. Although the optimized process is more complex than the original one, it is still more sensible regarding data protection as explained above.

5   Related Work

The idea of representing data protection in process models is quite new. But a few publications can be found on this topic. Some design patterns for the BPMN modeling of data protection requirements are presented in [2]. In [5] the consent of a data subject is explicitly modeled in BPMN process models. This work could be combined with the approach presented in this paper. An ontology-based approach to achieve data protection compliance in process models is depicted in [3].

Additionally, there are some approaches that include security issues, which is a related field. Rodriguez et al. defined elements to extend BPMN with security requirements. Graphically they use padlocks with five different abbreviations in them that represent different security requirements like *"AttackHarmDetection"* or *"AccessControl"*. These requirements are also relevant with respect to data protection and they even have one notation element for *"Privacy"* [23]. A newer example for BPMN model extensions for expressing security concerns is [16]. Besides the markings in the process model in this approach, ontologies represent the security requirements [6]. In [24] a quite specialized approach for minding security concerns in the design of service oriented architectures is presented.

The general topic of extending BPMN is for example addressed in [21]. Paper [25] presents an overview over a multitude of different BPMN extensions which may serve as pattern for our model extension.

The usability of graphical models in general and business process models and means to optimize the effect are discussed in [11]. Virtual reality like VR-BPMN [18] may be used to express process models. In this case, an additional marking which expresses the risk of activities or data objects may be a further option. Furthermore, an improved 3D business process model may support the decision making [22]. This might also support eliminating privacy and data protection problems.

The use of traffic lights in the context of data protection is not a new idea. The commissioner for data protection of Berlin, Germany used this notation 2020 to rank video conference tools with respect to data protection [4].

6 Conclusion

In this paper, we presented a concept for representing data protection requirements in a business process model in an easy to use and understandable way. We have shown how business processes modeled using the BPMN notation can be annotated using an intuitive color scheme. Data objects are dyed according to their data protection critically, processing activities according to the lawfulness of processing (e.g., consent required). The goal of our approach is to allow a process modeler (with limited data protection knowledge) to identify critical parts of the business process. These findings can be used to change the business process (e.g., add activity for asking for consent), discuss the business process inside the organization (e.g., with the management or the data protection officer), or to apply the required privacy and data protection measures during the design phase.

In future work we are planning to implement a prototype and perform a user study to prove the usability as well as advantages and disadvantages of our approach. We will also research possibilities for automatic or semi-automatic coloring of business processes. This includes also investigating the dependencies between activities: activities may be uncritical alone, but pose a threat if combined. One possibility to automate the coloring could be a business rule engine like *Drools*[3]. Finally, we will research how our approach can be used in connection with a DPIA. The colored business model might be used to decide if a DPIA is required and also to create a data flow of the process, which is typically a part of a DPIA (e.g. in [13]).

References

1. Adam, S., Riegel, N., Jeswein, T., Koch, M., Imal, S.: Studie - BPM suites 2013. Technical report, Fraunhofer IESE, Kaiserslautern, Germany (2013). https://www.iese.fraunhofer.de/content/dam/iese/de/dokumente/oeffentliche_studien/Fraunhofer_IESE_Studie_BPM-Suites2013.pdf
2. Agostinelli, S., Maggi, F.M., Marrella, A., Sapio, F.: Achieving GDPR compliance of BPMN process models. In: Cappiello, C., Ruiz, M. (eds.) Achieving GDPR Compliance of BPMN Process Models. LNBIP, vol. 350, pp. 10–22. Springer, Cham (2019). https://doi.org/10.1007/978-3-030-21297-1_2
3. Bartolini, C., Calabró, A., Marchetti, E.: Enhancing business process modelling with data protection compliance: an ontology-based proposal. In: Proceedings of the 5th International Conference on Information Systems Security and Privacy, pp. 421–428. SCITEPRESS - Science and Technology Publications, Prague (2019)
4. Berliner Beauftragte für Datenschutz und Informationsfreiheit: Hinweise für Berliner Verantwortliche zu Anbietern von Videokonferenz-Diensten. Technical report, Berliner Beauftragte für Datenschutz und Informationsfreiheit (2020)
5. Besik, S., Freytag, J.C.: Managing consent in workflows under GDPR. In: ZEUS (2020)
6. Chergui, M.E.A., Benslimane, S.M.: A valid BPMN extension for supporting security requirements based on cyber security ontology. In: Abdelwahed, E.H., Bellatreche, L., Golfarelli, M., Méry, D., Ordonez, C. (eds.) MEDI 2018. LNCS, vol. 11163, pp. 219–232. Springer, Cham (2018). https://doi.org/10.1007/978-3-030-00856-7_14
7. Commission Nationale de l'Informatique et des Libertés: Privacy Impact assessment (PIA) (2019). https://www.cnil.fr/en/privacy-impact-assessment-pia
8. Elliot, A.J., Maier, M.A., Moller, A.C., Friedman, R., Meinhardt, J.: Color and psychological functioning: the effect of red on performance attainment. J. Exp. Psychol. Gen. **136**(1), 154–168 (2007)
9. ENISA: Handbook on Security of Personal Data Processing (2017). https://www.enisa.europa.eu/publications/handbook-on-security-of-personal-data-processing
10. European Parliament and Council: Regulation (EU) 2016/679 of the european parliament and of the council of 27 April 2016 on the protection of natural persons with regard to the processing of personal data and on the free movement of such data, and repealing directive 95/46/EC (general data protection regulation) (text with EEA relevance) (2016). http://data.europa.eu/eli/reg/2016/679/oj/eng
11. Ferreira, J.J., de Souza, C.S.: Communicating ideas in computer-supported modeling tasks: a case study with BPMN. In: Kurosu, M. (ed.) HCI 2013, Part I. LNCS, vol. 8004, pp. 320–329. Springer, Heidelberg (2013). https://doi.org/10.1007/978-3-642-39232-0_36
12. Goldstein, K.: Some experimental observations concerning the influence of colors on the function of the organism. Am. J. Phys. Med. Rehabil. **1**(1), 147–151 (1942)

---

[3] https://www.drools.org/.

13. International Organization for Standardization: ISO/IEC 29134:2017 information technology - security techniques - guidelines for privacy impact assessment (2016). http://www.iso.org/cms/render/live/en/sites/isoorg/contents/data/standard/06/22/62289.html
14. International Organization for Standardization: ISO/IEC 27000:2018 (2018). https://www.iso.org/cms/render/live/en/sites/isoorg/contents/data/standard/07/39/73906.html
15. Jacobs, K.W., Hustmyer, F.E.: Effects of four psychological primary colors on GSR, heart rate and respiration rate. Percept. Mot. Skills **38**(3), 763–766 (1974)
16. Maines, C.L., Llewellyn-Jones, D., Tang, S., Zhou, B.: A cyber security ontology for BPMN-Security extensions. In: Wu, Y., et al. (eds.) 15th IEEE International Conference on Computer and Information Technology, Ubiquitous Computing and Communications; Dependable, Autonomic and Secure Computing; Pervasive Intelligence and Computing, Liverpool, United Kingdom, pp. 1756–1763. IEEE (2015)
17. McShane, C.: The origins and globalization of traffic control signals. J. Urban Hist. **25**(3), 379–404 (1999)
18. Oberhauser, R., Pogolski, C., Matic, A.: VR-BPMN: visualizing bpmn models in virtual reality. In: Shishkov, B. (ed.) BMSD 2018. LNBIP, vol. 319, pp. 83–97. Springer, Cham (2018). https://doi.org/10.1007/978-3-319-94214-8_6
19. OMG: Business Process Model and Notation (BPMN), Version 2.0. Standard, Object Management Group (2011)
20. OMG: Business process model & notation (BPMN) (2021). https://www.omg.org/bpmn/
21. Ramos-Merino, M., Santos-Gago, J.M., Álvarez-Sabucedo, L.M., Rorís, V.M.A., Sanz-Valero, J.: BPMN-E2: a BPMN extension for an enhanced workflow description. Softw. Syst. Model. **18**(4), 2399–2419 (2019)
22. Rehring, K., Greulich, M., Bredenfeld, L., Ahlemann, F.: Let's get in touch - decision making about enterprise architecture using 3D visualization in augmented reality. In: Bui, T. (ed.) Proceedings of 52nd Hawaii International Conference on System Sciences, HICSS 2019, Grand Wailea, Maui, Hawaii, USA, pp. 1–10. ScholarSpace (2019)
23. Rodriguez, A., Fernández-Medina, E., Piattini, M.: A BPMN extension for the modeling of security requirements in business processes. IEICE Trans. Inf. Syst. **E90D**, 745–752 (2007)
24. Saleem, M.Q., Jaafar, J.B., Hassan, M.F.: A domain-specific language for modelling security objectives in a business process models of SOA applications. Int. J. Adv. Inf. Sci. Serv. Sci. **4**(1), 353–362 (2012)
25. Zarour, K., Benmerzoug, D., Guermouche, N., Drira, K.: A systematic literature review on BPMN extensions. Bus. Process. Manag. J. **26**(6), 1473–1503 (2020)

Trackers in Your Inbox: Criticizing Current Email Tracking Practices

Shirin Kalantari[✉], Andreas Put, and Bart De Decker

imec-DistriNet, KU Leuven, Leuven, Belgium
{shirin.kalantari,andreas.put,bart.dedecker}@kuleuven.be

Abstract. Email is among the cornerstones of our online lives. It has evolved from carrying text-only messages to delivering well-designed HTML contents. The uptake of web protocols into email, however, has facilitated the migration of web tracking techniques into email ecosystem. While recent privacy regulations have impacted the web tracking technologies, they have not directly influenced the email tracking techniques. In this short paper, we analyze a corpus of 5216 emails, give an overview of the identified tracking techniques, and argue that the existing email tracking methods do not comply with privacy regulations.

Keywords: Email tracking · Third party tracking · Privacy regulations

1 Introduction

Our email inboxes contain traces of most of our online interactions. Today, email delivers messages involving order confirmations, notifications and reminders, social media updates, password recovery links, marketing materials and newsletters, in addition to personal communications. With the persistence of trackers on web traffic, one would also expect the presence of trackers in users' inboxes. In fact it has been suggested that almost 16% of personal conversation emails and 99% of bulk email communications in users' inboxes contain some form of tracking mechanisms [26]. These findings are also confirmed by several academic studies regarding newsletter emails [3,4,22].

In simple terms, email tracking is accomplished by embedding remote resources in an HTML email while making the requests to retrieve these resources identifiable. This simple yet effective strategy is becoming increasingly pervasive to the extent that it has been proposed by several online tracking businesses as *"the solution for cookie-less tracking across devices"* [5,11,21].

Email tracking often involves third parties who receive fine grained, personal information about the recipients such as the newsletters they are subscribed to, online services they are using, their email reading habits, and potentially even IP addresses. This information might be valuable to spammers for *personalizing* their phishing and spamming attacks, as including personalized context in

© Springer Nature Switzerland AG 2021
N. Gruschka et al. (Eds.): APF 2021, LNCS 12703, pp. 156–167, 2021.
https://doi.org/10.1007/978-3-030-76663-4_9

phishing attacks amplifies their impacts. For example, the *Emotent* phishing campaigns, identified as one of the *"top malware threats affecting Europe"* [12], employed such techniques. Furthermore, there are businesses interested in sneaking into users' inboxes to gain business insights from their bulk emails. In 2017 *Unroll.me*, a free service that allows users to manage their newsletter subscriptions, sold parts of its users' data to Uber [16].

While recent studies suggest that many of the technologies employed in web tracking are impacted by new privacy regulations [7,20], there has been little academic activity concerned with investigating whether the existing email tracking techniques abide with these regulations. Therefore, our study aims to initiating a debate on the compliance of current bulk email communication tracking methods with existing privacy regulations. For this purpose we analyzed the newsletter emails of 142 websites and evaluated their email tracking techniques, answering the basic questions: which data is actually being collected, by whom, and for which purposes?

2   Background

This section contains an overview of the main entities in bulk email communications and background information on HTTP emails and HTTP requests. The term 'bulk email' refers to non-conversational emails that target a broad range of recipients such as newsletters, marketing campaigns and order confirmation.

2.1   Main Entities

The main entities that drive bulk email communications are:

Campaign owners: These are the businesses that employ email communication to reach their audience.

End users: The end users, or email recipients, either explicitly subscribe to newsletters or receive bulk emails as part of the services they are using (e.g., social media updates, online purchase confirmation, reminders, etc.). Users access their email through *Email Clients*, also called Mail User Agents (MUAs). MUAs can be categorized into two major types: web clients like Gmail, and local mail clients like Thunderbird and iOS Mail.

Third Party: The campaign owner might want to include a number of third parties into their campaign emails. For example they might integrate advertisement partners such as Facebook or Instagram Ads, email optimization services such as mailing list sanitation tool *ZeroBounce*[1] or subject line personalization service *phrasee*, and/or marketing platforms such as *Salesforce*[2] or *Google Analytics*[3].

---

[1] https://www.zerobounce.net/.
[2] https://www.salesforce.com/.
[3] https://analytics.withgoogle.com/.

Email Service Providers (ESPs): Campaign owners often outsource the actual email process to an ESP. This entity manages the mailing list, provides email templates, and most importantly sends out the campaign emails. Examples of well-known ESPs include Mailchimp, Selligent, and Campaign Monitor. In addition, an ESP provides integration tools, allowing marketers to seamlessly integrate third parties into their marketing platform.

Mailbox providers: Each email address is registered with a mailbox provider. It offers email hosting for users to send, receive and store their email messages. Gmail and Yahoo! are examples of widely used mailbox providers. Additionally, mailbox providers offer email security services such as spam filtering, malware detection, and transport layer encryption to protect users from malicious content.

2.2   HTML Emails

Despite supporting styling and rich text formatting, HTML emails have been criticized for their security and privacy issues since their inception [6,25,29,30]. First of all, certain HTML tags could be exploited in the context of email. For instance, including malicious code within a `<script>` tag in an HTML email could allow for wiretapping email communications [31]. Secondly, interacting with certain HTML elements embedded in the email can result in the execution of a series of HTTP requests that include detailed information about the recipient. These requests are made by the email client in order to load the remote resources included within HTML emails.

Partial countermeasures have been adapted to minimize the scope of these two issues of HTML emails. Some HTML tags are removed by the email clients before rendering the email. However, there is no standard that defines *safe* HTML tags. Therefore, it is left to email clients to decide which elements to remove from an HTML email. For example, some email clients even execute scripts within HTML emails [27].

An important advantage of HTML emails is the possibility to embed remote resources such as hyperlinks and images. Together, these two types account for 98% of all remote resources in newsletter emails [17]. However, HTML emails introduce new threats to the user's privacy, as it allows to embed identifiable information in the requests made by the email client. This problem can be quite severe as these requests are made as soon as the email client renders the HTML email.

As a countermeasure, email clients block remote resources either by default or through user settings. While this stops the HTTP-based tracking, it negatively impacts user experience and provides no protection once the user decides to load remote contents. Despite the shortcoming of current countermeasures in resolving privacy and security issues of HTML emails, they are still the de facto choice for receiving newsletter emails.

2.3 HTTP Requests

When clicking on a URL or loading a remote resource, the email client executes an HTTP request. This request can be represented as follows:

GET request-URL [request-header]*

In this representation *GET* identifies the type of request. GET requests are the most common type of HTTP requests, and are used to request data from a specified resource or webserver. Next, the *request-URL* represents the address of the remote resource. In newsletter emails, senders often embed personalized tracking tokens in the *request-URL* [9,15,17,22]. Such a tracking token could be any string that maps to the recipient email address, or identity, at the server side. Personalized URL tokens have been used in email for more than 20 years [29], and they are still pervasively used in newsletter emails [15,17,22]. From a technical perspective personalized URL tokens can be seen as cookies included in the URL instead of HTTP headers. This technique has recently gained traction in web as a form of cookie-less tracking [8]. Finally, the *request-header* consists out of one or more HTTP headers. These headers are attached by the email client to the request in order to help the webserver that serves the remote resource in providing a tailored response.

After a client executes an HTTP request, the webserver will return an *HTTP response* of the following form:

Status-code [response-header]*

Webservers use these status-codes to briefly convey information to clients about the status of their request. Two of the most well known status-codes are: 200 OK (the request was successful) and 404 Not Found (the server cannot find the requested resource). Other status-codes indicate that the client needs to execute further steps. For example, redirect responses (ranging from 300 to 308) indicate that the client needs to get the requested resource using another URL. Redirect chains have been used for tracking purposes by involving third parties before serving a resource [1,9,10]. The *response-header* consists out of one or more HTTP headers that allow the server to pass additional information about the response. For example, the response header *Set-Cookie* is used to set a cookie on the email client and *Cache-Control* header specifies the caching policy for the requested resource informing the email client how to deal with subsequent requests for the same resource; whether to load it from cache storage or whether to make a fresh HTTP request.

3 Related Work

In academic literature, email tracking has been viewed as the consequence of loading remote resources in HTML emails. Bender et al. [3] identified that senders do adapt their sending behavior according to the information conveyed though email tracking. For instance, they send fewer emails to less engaged inboxes and personalize the email content based on the device that the recipient uses for opening their emails (e.g. iPhone users receive more contents related to Apple products).

Based on the assumption that tracking and functional contents are separable, Fabian et al. [13] gathered a corpus of newsletter emails and identified a number of features for tracking images. The email corpus and the detection method were extended in [4] and [15]. These identification techniques aim to improve the content blocking, by allowing non-tracking and functional contents to load.

Englehardt et al. [9] found that loading remote contents in an email can leak the recipient's email address to third parties by analyzing a large scale corpus of commercial newsletters. Xu et al. [32] illustrated the feasibility of email tracking for launching a long-term surveillance attack against the recipients. They also conducted a user study and concluded that the majority of participants were unaware of the privacy risks of email tracking.

Maass et al. [22] developed PrivacyMail[4], an email transparency platform that reports a privacy score and an elaborate analysis of email tracking practices for each newsletter. In [17] the author discussed the privacy risks of email tracking for obtaining read receipts and discussed the shortcomings of existing countermeasures.

4   Methodology and Datasets

This section give an overview of the dataset that was used and the analysis performed on it.

Dataset: Two main approaches are used in literature to assemble a corpus of mailing-list/newsletter emails: manual and automated approaches. In the manual approach, applied by [3,15,22], a human searches a website for a newsletter subscription form and signs up email addresses. In the automated approach, as used in [9,17], an automated crawler will analyse web-pages in search for newsletter subscription forms. Next, the crawler attempts to sign up email addresses to the subscription without user interaction. While this offers obvious benefits, it has two important shortcomings for our use-case. Firstly, the automated approach needs adaptation for use in multi-language contexts, such as EU-based newsletters, in order to detect the subscription form. Secondly, its performance decreases when it is used for subscribing multiple identities to a newsletter, due to the non-deterministic nature of most crawlers. Thus, we decided for a corpus with manual subscription in which multiple identities are subscribed to each newsletter. In addition, we included the corpus collected by Maas et al. [22] in PrivacyMail.

---

[4] https://privacymail.info/.

Email Preprocessing: A preprocessing step was performed on each email object in the corpus. First, the HTML was extracted from the email body. From the HTML code, the URLs of hyperlinks and images were extracted. We also checked whether the HTML emails contain embedded images using Content-ID or data URI schemes [24]. Both the `List-Unsubscribe` header and the unsubscribe link within the HTML part were used to determine whether opt-out options are provided. To find the unsubscribe link, the method used in [17] was adapted with additional unsubscribe keywords in French, German and Dutch.

Identifying Third Parties: We define the first party as the domain name of the website to which the user was subscribed, its sub-domains and possibly a related but different top-level domain (e.g. we considered urbandccay.com a first party to urbandecay.co.uk). Consequently, third parties are any other domains different than the first party domains.

To find third parties included in an email we used a static and a dynamic search. In the static approach we performed a text search in the email body for the domain names used in the sender's email address (e.g. example.com in info@example.com) and the URLs of remote resources (i.e. links and images). In the dynamic search, we looked for third parties in the redirect chain of the HTTP request for loading remote images. However, the remote resources in older emails are often deactivated, causing the HTTP request to return an error code. Therefore, only emails sent at most one month prior to this study are considered, as the SPAM-ACT requires opt-out options to stay at least 30 days functional after an email is sent [14]. On the first attempt we loaded images in 5216 emails, from 142 senders between the period of 2020-03-23 to 2020-04-23.

Regarding the information that each third party could receive via emails, third parties that are included through the email address receive the email address of the recipients, other third parties that are included through the HTTP requests might set cookies on the user's device and receive the personalized tokens that are included in the request URL. Moreover, since HTTP depends on transport layer protocols, these third parties also receive metadata such as the IP address and the user agent of the recipient. For identifying personalized URL tokens, we used the differential method used in [3, 15, 17, 22], and compared the structure of request URL in emails sent to multiple users.

5   Result

While our analysis is ongoing, our initial results provide insights into privacy hazards of email tracking.

General Findings: All the 5216 emails in the analyzed corpus are HTML-enabled. This shows the uptake of HTML emails in recent years since Bender et al. [4] detected 72% of emails in their newsletter corpus as HTML in 2016. For the majority of emails we were able to find an opt-out option: 89% of emails included the *List-Unsubscribe* header and for approximately 93% of emails we were able to find an unsubscribe link. Our dataset confirms the popularity of remote images and links in email as 90% of emails included more than 8 remote images and 11 links. On the other hand embedded images are rarely used as only 3 senders used embedded images inside their emails. In one email the image was embedded using the data URI scheme and the rest used *Content-ID* scheme.

Third Parties in Email: In the analyzed corpus, 89% of the emails embed resources from at least one third party with a mean and median of two per email. Figure 1 indicates the number of third parties that senders include in their newsletter emails. In total, 12 senders use a third party domain in the email address that they used for sending their newsletter emails. The majority of third parties are included through HTTP requests. In 1619 emails (31% of the total emails) from 29 senders, new third parties are included through the redirect chain of HTTP requests for loading images. Regarding the information that third parties receive, 62 senders allow third parties cookies to be set on recipients' devices and the majority receive personalized URL tokens. Also note that every HTTP request leaks TCP/IP metadata such as IP address and time-zone. Table 1 summarizes the top third parties in our corpus and the type of information that they receive.

Table 1. The most common third parties by number of sender. *Aggregated result for different domains.

Third party	Information received	Number of senders
Mailchimp*	Metadata, URL token, cookie	26
Klaviyo*	Metadata, URL token	22
shopify.com	Metadata, URL token	15
amazonaws.com	Metadata, URL token	12
returnpath.net	Metadata, URL token	11
Google*	Metadata, URL token	10

Next, the caching policy of remote images in emails has been analyzed. Interestingly, we noticed that in emails of 90 senders (64% of all senders) either a no cache or a short cache policy of maximum 2 h is used for remote images. Thus, these senders and the third parties they include in their emails receive fresh HTTP requests potentially every time the recipients open these emails.

6   Discussion

Our results mainly confirm the findings of previous studies: email tracking is very common and it leaks information to third parties. However, the main goal of this study is to initiate a debate on the compliance of current email tracking practices with privacy regulations. We also want to call for collaboration between legal

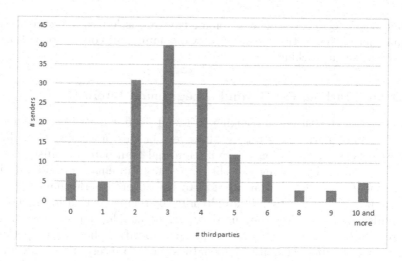

Fig. 1. Third party distribution per sender.

and technical communities since mitigating the privacy risks of email tracking requires a mutual effort.

An interdisciplinary effort is required to fully investigate the compliance of mass email communication. We illustrate the importance of this effort by indicating a shortcoming in the existing technical approaches. The third party analysis is performed in this paper and many of the previous related works only provide a partial view on the email tracking ecosystem. This analysis is based on the assumption that a third party service uses a different domain name than the sender. While trivial at first, this assumption does not always hold: a tracker can control a subdomain of the first party, through DNS CNAME setting. Dimova et al. [8] recently conducted a large-scale analysis of CNAME tracking in web, detecting it in almost 10% of top 10K websites. Although such large-scale analysis is missing for email datasets, CNAME trackers has been identified in newsletter emails. Kalantari [17] found an example of a CNAME tracker which uses the sender domain to serve advertisement in newsletter emails and bypass the privacy protection block lists. Similarly, we find two ESPs that perform tracking while hiding under the sender domain. The ESP Klaviyo[5], deploys CNAME tracking to control a subdomain of the sender [18]. The other ESP, Selligent[6], appears to track users by requiring their software to be installed on the first-party webserver. This software will then process HTTP requests with a specific URL structure. We find the URL structure of Selligent in 1159 emails (that is 22% of all emails) in our corpus.[7]

---

[5] https://www.klaviyo.com/.

[6] https://www.selligent.com.

[7] The URL structure was detected based on the answer provided in Stack-overflow at https://stackoverflow.com/questions/33002037/which-email-software-is-used-optiext-optiextension-dll-in-url.

While a full legal assessment of email tracking is left as a future work, in the remainder of this section we criticise two common misconceptions about the legitimacy of email tracking.

6.1 Email Tracking Far Beyond a Legitimate Interest

Senders may argue that email tracking is lawful since it measures the effectiveness of the email marketing strategy. However, for this processing to be lawful, a balance between information minimization and transparency must be maintained. First of all, by making the HTTP requests in email individually identifiable, senders can measure far more than the "overall performance" of their campaign. It enables them to individually identify recipients that interacted with their emails and the devices they used among other information. Furthermore, as our results illustrate the majority of senders specify a short cache period for remote resources in their email which enables them to receive these information *every time* the recipient interact with these emails.

Finally, email tracking could only be considered legitimate if senders fulfill their information obligation toward recipients. They might use email tracking to offer optimized or tailored services to their recipients. For example, many ESPs offer send time optimization services [19,23,28] to deliver emails according to the recipients email reading habits. Similarly, Bender et al. [3] noticed that the content of newsletter campaigns are adjusted based on the email client that the recipient uses for reading previous emails (i.e. iPhone users receive more contents related to Apple products). However, we believe that an explicit user consent should be obtained for service personalization and the subscribed users should be able to opt-out from personalized tracking while still receiving the non-personalized newsletters.

6.2 Email Tracking Far Beyond a Data Protection Interest

Some senders might argue that email tracking can be used to protect the privacy of recipients as they stop sending emails after a certain period of recipient inactivity (e.g. one year). In fact, when Bender et al. [3] exhibited different email reading behavior for email addresses subscribed to the same newsletters, they noticed a significant difference in the campaigns' sending rates: the less engaged inbox started receiving emails at a lower frequency.

However, adapting sending rates mostly serves the interest of sender: it prevents frustrated users from unsubscribing from their mailing-list or reporting their emails as spam, which jeopardizes their reputation and delivery rate. It should be noted that for users the consequences of unsubscribing from a newsletter is different than receiving fewer emails. Unsubscribing from email communications often entails legal obligations that protects the recipient for example by mandating the erasure of user's data.

7   Conclusion

Although email tracking is performed by hackneyed techniques and despite the awareness of academic community about its consequences, there has been little interest in evaluating email tracking from the eyes of privacy regulations. However, it should be noted that *"Many perverse aspects of information security that had been long known to practitioners but just dismissed as 'bad weather' have turned out to be quite explicable in terms of the incentives facing individuals and organisations"* [2].

Email privacy guidelines have not been adapted as the email ecosystem has evolved and they do not protect users against the current methods of email tracking. Email technologies on the other hand are advancing at a rapid pace. Gmail recently enabled Accelerated Mobile Pages (AMP) for newsletter emails, which allow recipients to directly make transactions from their emails[8]. To overcome the risks of email tracking a collaboration between legal experts and technical scholars is needed to formalize technically sound guidelines based on existing privacy regulations.

Acknowledgments. We would like to thank Pierre Dewitte for his insightful comments during the early stages of this research, as well as Max Maass and PrivacyMail (https://privacymail.info/) for their willingness to share data related to this study.

References

1. Acar, G., Eubank, C., Englehardt, S., Juarez, M., Narayanan, A., Diaz, C.: The web never forgets: persistent tracking mechanisms in the wild. In: Proceedings of the 2014 ACM SIGSAC Conference on Computer and Communications Security, CCS 2014, pp. 674–689. ACM (2014). https://doi.org/10.1145/2660267.2660347
2. Anderson, R., Moore, T.: The economics of information security. Science **314**, 610 (2006). https://doi.org/10.1126/science.1130992
3. Bender, B., Fabian, B., Haupt, J., Lessmann, S., Neumann, T., Thim, C.: Track and treat - usage of e-mail tracking for newsletter individualization. In: Twenty-Sixth European Conference on Information Systems (ECIS2018), Portsmouth, UK, June 2018
4. Bender, B., Fabian, B., Lessmann, S., Haupt, J.: E-mail tracking: status quo and novel countermeasures. In: Proceedings of the thirty-seventh international conference on information systems (ICIS), Dublin, Ireland, December 2016
5. Conversant: Five building blocks of identity management. https://www.conversant media.com/hubfs/US%20Conversant/IMAGE%20ILLUSTRATIONS%20and%20 VIDEOs/Resource-center-assets/PDFs/Five_Keys_to_Identity_Resolution_24Apr 2019.pdf. Accessed 15 Dec 2020
6. Coursen, S.: Solving the problem of html mail (2002). https://www.securityfocus. com/columnists/58. Accessed 02 Feb 2021
7. Dabrowski, A., Merzdovnik, G., Ullrich, J., Sendera, G., Weippl, E.: Measuring cookies and web privacy in a post-GDPR world. In: Choffnes, D., Barcellos, M. (eds.) PAM 2019. LNCS, vol. 11419, pp. 258–270. Springer, Cham (2019). https:// doi.org/10.1007/978-3-030-15986-3_17

---

[8] https://amp.dev/about/email/.

8. Dimova, Y., Acar, G., Olejnik, L., Joosen, W., Van Goethem, T.: The cname of the game: Large-scale analysis of dns-based tracking evasion. In: Proceedings on Privacy Enhancing Technologies (2021). https://arxiv.org/pdf/2102.09301

9. Englehardt, S., Han, J., Narayanan, A.: I never signed up for this! Privacy implications of email tracking. Proc. Priv. Enhanci. Technol. **2018**(1), 109–126 (2018)

10. Englehardt, S., Narayanan, A.: Online tracking: a 1-million-site measurement and analysis. In: Proceedings of the 2016 ACM SIGSAC Conference on Computer and Communications Security, CCS 2016, pp. 1388–1401 (2016). https://doi.org/10.1145/2976749.2978313

11. Epsilon: The way the cookie data crumbles: People-based profiles vs. cookie-based solutions (2019). https://www.epsilon.com/hubfs/Cookie%20Crumbles.pdf. Accessed 15 Dec 2020

12. Europol: Internet Organised Crime Threat Assessment (IOCTA) 2020. European Union Agencyfor Law Enforcement Cooperation (Europol) (2020)

13. Fabian, B., Bender, B., Weimann, L.: E-mail tracking in online marketing - methods, detection, and usage. In: 12th International Conference on Wirtschaftsinformatik, March 2015

14. FTC.gov: Can-spam act: a compliance guide for business. https://www.ftc.gov/tips-advice/business-center/guidance/can-spam-act-compliance-guide-business. Accessed 17 Feb 2021

15. Haupt, J., Bender, B., Fabian, B., Lessmann, S.: Robust identification of email tracking: a machine learning approach. Eur. J. Oper. Res. **271**(1), 341–356 (2018). https://doi.org/10.1016/j.ejor.2018.05.018

16. Isaac, M., Lohr, S.: Unroll.me service faces backlash over a widespread practice: selling user data (2017). https://nyti.ms/2pYH0Eb. Accessed 15 Dec 2020

17. Kalantari, S.: Open about open rate? In: IFIP International Summer School on Privacy and Identity Management. Springer, Cham (2021, to appear)

18. Klaviyo Help Center: How to set up dedicated click tracking. https://help.klaviyo.com/hc/en-us/articles/360001550572-Setting-Up-Dedicated-Click-Tracking. Accessed 20 Feb 2021

19. Klaviyo Help Center: Smart send time in klaviyo (2021). https://help.klaviyo.com/hc/en-us/articles/360029794371-Smart-Send-Time-in-Klaviyo. Accessed 21 Feb 2021

20. Lefrere, V., Warberg, L., Cheyre, C., Marotta, V., Acquisti, A.: The impact of the GDPR on content providers. In: The 2020 Workshop on the Economics of Information Security (2020). https://weis2020.econinfosec.org/wp-content/uploads/sites/8/2020/06/weis20-final43.pdf

21. LiveIntent: Overview of custom audiences (2020). https://support.liveintent.com/hc/en-us/articles/204889644-Overview-of-Custom-Audiences. Accessed 15 Dec 2020

22. Maass, M., Schwär, S., Hollick, M.: Towards transparency in email tracking. In: Naldi, M., Italiano, G.F., Rannenberg, K., Medina, M., Bourka, A. (eds.) APF 2019. LNCS, vol. 11498, pp. 18–27. Springer, Cham (2019). https://doi.org/10.1007/978-3-030-21752-5_2

23. MailChimp: Insights from mailchimp's send time optimization system (2014). https://mailchimp.com/resources/insights-from-mailchimps-send-time-optimization-system/. Accessed 20 Feb 2021

24. Masinter, L.: The "data" URL scheme. Internet Requests for Comments, August 1998. https://tools.ietf.org/html/rfc2397

25. Müller, J., Brinkmann, M., Poddebniak, D., Schinzel, S., Schwenk, J.: What's up Johnny? - covert content attacks on email end-to-end encryption. In: 17th International Conference on Applied Cryptography and Network Security (ACNS 2019), pp. 1–18 (2019)

26. One More Company: State of email with 1.5 billion emails processed (2017). https://evercontact.com/special/email-tracking.html

27. Poddebniak, D., et al.: Efail: breaking S/MIME and openPGP email encryption using exfiltration channels. In: 27th USENIX Security Symposium (USENIX Security 18), pp. 549–566. USENIX Association, Baltimore, August 2018. https://www.usenix.org/conference/usenixsecurity18/presentation/poddebniak

28. Roberts, C.: Announcing send time optimization (2017). https://www.campaignmonitor.com/blog/new-features/2017/05/announcing-send-time-optimization/. Accessed 20 Feb 2021

29. Storm, D.: The hidden privacy hazards of HTML email (2000). https://strom.com/awards/192.html. Accessed 01 Feb 2021

30. The Tor Project: Towards a tor-safe mozilla thunderbird reducing application-level privacy leaks in thunderbird, July 2011. https://web.archive.org/web/20200618193439/trac.torproject.org/projects/tor/raw-attachment/wiki/doc/Torify HOWTO/EMail/Thunderbird/Thunderbird\%2BTor.pdf. Accessed 02 Feb 2020

31. Voth, C.: Reaper exploit. http://web.archive.org/web/20011005083819/www.geocities.com/ResearchTriangle/Facility/8332/reaper-exploit-release.html. Accessed 15 Dec 2020

32. Xu, H., Hao, S., Sari, A., Wang, H.: Privacy risk assessment on email tracking. In: IEEE INFOCOM 2018 - IEEE Conference on Computer Communications, pp. 2519–2527, April 2018. https://doi.org/10.1109/INFOCOM.2018.8486432

Author Index

Aouad, Lamine   106

Bielova, Nataliia   47
Bouvry, Pascal   123

De Decker, Bart   156

Fischer, Michael   23

Garcia, Kimberly   3
Gruschka, Nils   143

Kalantari, Shirin   156
Kermezis, Georgios   89
Kolokotronis, Nicholas   89
Kuppa, Aditya   106

Le-Khac, Nhien-An   106
Limniotis, Konstantinos   89
Lo Iacono, Luigi   23

Mayer, Simon   3

Nouwens, Midas   47

Paseri, Ludovica   123
Put, Andreas   156

Railean, Alexandr   70
Reinhardt, Delphine   70
Roca, Vincent   47

Santos, Cristiana   47
Speck, Andreas   143

Tamò-Larrieux, Aurelia   3
Tolsdorf, Jan   23
Toth, Michael   47

Varrette, Sébastien   123

Windrich, Melanie   143

Zihlmann, Zaira   3

Printed in the United States
by Baker & Taylor Publisher Services